INTERFACES AND US

INTERFACES AND US

User-Experience Design and the Making of the Computable Subject

Zachary Kaiser

BLOOMSBURY VISUAL ARTS
LONDON • NEW YORK • OXFORD • NEW DELHI • SYDNEY

BLOOMSBURY VISUAL ARTS
Bloomsbury Publishing Plc
50 Bedford Square, London, WC1B 3DP, UK
1385 Broadway, New York, NY 10018, USA
29 Earlsfort Terrace, Dublin 2, Ireland

BLOOMSBURY, BLOOMSBURY VISUAL ARTS and the Diana logo
are trademarks of Bloomsbury Publishing Plc

First published in Great Britain 2023

Cover design by Daniel Benneworth-Gray

Bloomsbury Publishing Plc does not have any control over, or responsibility for,
any third-party websites referred to or in this book. All internet addresses given in
this book were correct at the time of going to press. The author and publisher regret
any inconvenience caused if addresses have changed or sites have ceased to exist,
but can accept no responsibility for any such changes.

A catalogue record for this book is available from the British Library.

A catalog record for this book is available from the Library of Congress.

ISBN: HB: 978-1-3502-4525-9
        PB: 978-1-3502-4524-2
        ePDF: 978-1-3502-4527-3
        eBook: 978-1-3502-4526-6

Typeset by Integra Software Services Pvt. Ltd.
Printed and bound in India

To find out more about our authors and books visit www.bloomsbury.com
and sign up for our newsletters.

CONTENTS

LIST OF FIGURES

ACKNOWLEDGMENTS

I owe both the pleasure and challenge of writing this book to the people who have cultivated my two strongest personality traits: intellectual curiosity and a sense of social responsibility. In this book, as in my personal and professional life, I have sought to synthesize these qualities. Doing so is not always easy, but I have benefitted immensely from the support of many people, including those who I mention below.

I want to first thank my mother, Aviva Kaiser, whose influence on my intellect and my moral compass is impossible to overstate. Her complete and total support for my pursuit of any interest no matter how seemingly bizarre or frivolous is the likely origin of my passion for interdisciplinary research. My father, Robert J. Kaiser, Jr., is a passionate advocate for justice, and he instilled in me that same passion along with a willingness to argue for what I believe is right. My grandfather, Dr. Robert J. Kaiser Sr., who, along with my grandmother, MaryAnn Kaiser (of blessed memory), taught me how rewarding it is to be a teacher. My wife, Rabbi Lisa Stella, with whom our daughter Lillian and I share our warm and loving home, has been a partner in a lifelong journey of learning and inquiry. In 2016, after seeing one of my talks, she told me that my work was about helping people see each other, deeply and compassionately, as humans. This observation laid the foundation for this book, and Lisa's unyielding support is partly responsible for this book actually existing somewhere besides my own mind. I also want to thank my friend—my brother, really, if not by blood then by ideology, politics, and neurotic predisposition—my partner and collaborator in practically everything, Dr. Gabi Schaffzin. He has always championed my ideas and my work. Our children are less than two months apart, and he has been a partner both in my intellectual journey and in my journey as a parent. Gabi and I have collaborated frequently with another friend, Sofie Hodara, whose creativity, enthusiasm, and craftsmanship were central in producing *The Dr. Pawel Norway Dream Machine*, a project featured prominently in this book. There are many others without whose help that project wouldn't have happened, including Trish Stone at UC San Diego's Calit2 and Timothy Belknap and Ryan McCartney at Icebox Projects in Philadelphia.

The content of this book is the result of more than ten years of teaching, research, artistic practice, and professional design practice. It is difficult, therefore, to thank all the folks who have made contributions along the way, but there are a number of people who have had a tremendous influence on my work or shaped it in a significant way, and I want to mention them here. First, Dr. Kathleen Fitzpatrick, who, amidst her incredibly busy schedule as the Director of Digital Humanities at Michigan State University, took the time to read my first draft manuscript in its entirety and offer her feedback. She truly lives out the generosity of scholarship about which she writes so eloquently. Meanwhile, even before I started writing this book, my friend and colleague, Dr. Marisa Brandt, had begun introducing me to many of the texts featured here. She is a brilliant scholar whose reading recommendations are unparalleled. Throughout my time at MSU, Dr. Karin Zitzewitz has been a wonderful friend and mentor along my professional academic journey. She has truly been an inspiration for me as both a scholar and leader. Two other individuals in my home department at Michigan State—the Department of Art, Art History, and Design—are crucial to mention here: Rebecca Tegtmeyer and Ben Van Dyke. Rebecca and Ben have been my go-to support system at work throughout our time together as colleagues, and I owe a significant portion of my career to Rebecca, who helped hired me as a junior colleague back in 2014. I would also be remiss if I did not thank Christopher Long, Dean of the College of Arts and Letters here at Michigan State. I would not feel emboldened to pursue my various and often wide-ranging interests if it weren't for his support and mentorship over the years. I also want to acknowledge the work of the many students I have had over the past eight years of teaching at MSU: they have taught me as much, if not more, than I have taught them, and I am indebted to the enthusiastic participation of many of them, including some whose work is featured in this book.

Michigan State has been my intellectual home since 2014, but this book has its origins, at least in part, in a classroom at St. John's Manhattan Campus, where I participated in the Design Incubation Writing Fellowship in 2017. I am grateful to the organizers of that fellowship for their warm reception of my work and their encouragement to pursue a project that went beyond the article I workshopped there. I spent some time during this fellowship with Dr. Elizabeth Guffey, whose work with Dr. Carma Gorman on the journal *Design and Culture*, has been an inspiration and offered me an intellectual orientation within "design" that appreciates its interrelationships with other fields. Carma, meanwhile, I must thank, for her tireless work advancing our field and in part because she shepherded my very first academic article to publication. Around the time I attended the Design Incubation Fellowship, I met with someone whose work makes an appearance a number of times throughout this text—John Cheney-Lippold. John was one of the first people to tell me that I was onto something with this book idea, and he read and offered feedback on the very first version of the proposal for the book, way back in 2017.

Last, I would like to offer my gratitude to my commissioning editor, Louise Baird-Smith, who took a chance on this project and helped the book become the text that I was hoping it could be.

It has been difficult to produce this work during a global pandemic that has laid bare the massive inequities on which capitalism both thrives and preys. And it is doubly difficult to proceed with confidence that the work contained in this book will remain, or be, relevant as the changes wrought by climate change and a crumbling neoliberalism continue to accelerate. I hope for better days ahead, and that hope is, to a great degree, the result of my interactions with the individuals who I have mentioned here.

December 2021

ABOUT THE AUTHOR

Zachary Kaiser is Associate Professor of Graphic Design and Experience Architecture at Michigan State University, USA. His research and creative practice examine the politics of technology and the role of design in shaping the parameters of individual, social, and political possibility. His work has been featured in national and international exhibitions, and his writing, on topics ranging from the future of the arts in higher education to dream-reading technologies, appears in both scholarly and popular publications.

INTRODUCTION

Laws of Love

In the fall of 2015, in a beautifully shot and designed television advertisement, IBM claimed that they could find and create "algorithms for love."[1] A computer screen flashes a new line of code and a woman, walking through a European city at dusk, smiles, pushing away her hair. IBM's commercial reads like a triumphal decree of power over any potential disaster or malady. "What does the world know today," the commercial begins, not with narration, but with white type, set in Helvetica, over an aerial shot of a power plant, "that we didn't know yesterday?" The music—"This Time Tomorrow," by the Kinks—increases in volume. Primarily acoustic, building steam as it increases in volume and tempo, uplifting, energetic, but not too fast. It's perfect.

> "We know," the commercial continues, as the typography emerges tastefully from behind a train set against a picturesque sunset, "how to listen to data …"
> CUT to another view of the same train—"… to prevent a derailment."
> CUT to the image of an eye blinking. "We know …"
> CUT to an image of a brain scan—"… how to transform healthcare with data."
> CUT to a close-up of a pill—"We know …"
> CUT to a medication being bottled—"… how to identify a counterfeit …"
> CUT to a young woman walking into a lecture hall—"… and spot a potential dropout …"—CUT to her sitting in her seat—"… in time to help."
> Rapid cuts build along with the energy of the music: the drums, vocals, and instrumentation begin to crescendo. "We know how to track epidemics with phones."
> CUT. "Hear the origins of the universe."
> CUT. "Write algorithms for love."
> CUT. "We know."
> CUT. "how to help predict a crime."
> CUT. "traffic jam."
> CUT. "blackout."

CUT. "breakdown."
CUT. "trend."
CUT. "harvest."
Faster cuts. "Wind."
CUT. "Cyberattack."
Extremely fast cuts. "Injury."
"Delay."
"Smog."
"Clog."
"Leak."
"Wildfire."
"Drought."
"Storm."
"Pattern."
"Swarm."
"Strike."
"Surge."
And finally … "In time to act."
The shot holds on an emergency worker in the rain.
CUT to a small child with a laptop in what is presumably a "developing nation."
From the right edge of the frame, the text, still in white, still in Helvetica, enters the frame.
"Once we know, we can't unknow."

***

Back in 1862, however—before big data, before IBM's Watson, before The Kinks, and before Helvetica—Wilhelm Wundt seemed to have beaten IBM to the punch. Wundt, the founder of experimental psychology, declared that "statisticians had demonstrated that there are laws of love just as for all other human phenomena."[2] Wundt was the man who helped psychology depart from philosophy. He advocated for psychology to take on an experimental, empirical, and epistemological approach that mimicked the natural sciences. Wundt thought that "at least in humans experimentation could reveal law-like regularities of inner (psychological) reality."[3] He developed a "physiological psychology" that sought to, in a laboratory setting, control the physical conditions of experiments in order to repeatedly elicit, and where possible, measure the *internal* psychological phenomena of a subject. But Wundt thought of this "physiological psychology" as a kind of subset of a broader discipline of psychology that was inclusive of concepts such as culture, history, and morality. In part because of the limited scope of translations and limited access to his texts, his ideas about physiological psychology—experimental psychology— reached prominence and were interpreted as an articulation of the discipline of psychology itself and not as part of an expansive idea of psychology.[4]

One of Wundt's innovations was the idea of the unfortunately named "psychophysical parallelism." Basically, he argued, all psychological phenomena had corresponding physical phenomena, and the two were irreducible. The idea was that psychologists studied the psychological aspect of consciousness, while others, such as neurophysiologists, studied the physiological aspect, but they were really studying the same subject, just from different perspectives. "[E]xperience dealt with in the natural sciences and in psychology are nothing but components of one experience regarded from different points of view: in the natural sciences as an interconnection of objective phenomena and, in consequence of the abstraction from the knowing subject, as mediate experience; in psychology as immediate and underived experience."[5]

By the 1890s, however, Wundt felt forced to argue that psychology itself was *not* a natural science, meaning that it was irreducible to biology or the nervous system of a subject. It was, instead, the study of the apprehension of experience, which was *partly* physiological but not wholly. At the same time, he argued, psychology employed the *methods* of the natural sciences: experimentation and observation. Wundt claimed that "physical measurement deals with quantitative values" while "[p]sychical measurement on the other hand, deals in the last instance in every case with qualitative values."[6] Yet, throughout his work, he continually refers to psychological "facts." This indicates what Wundt saw as the ultimate purpose of psychology: the discovery (through empirical practice and experimentation) of generalizable laws that "govern mental life."[7] Furthermore, Wundt sought laws that would be, to a great degree, universal and apply even to the mental life of animals.

Wundt's inspiration to find generalizable laws that would determine "the logical form of all mental phenomena" emerged from his immersion in an intellectual milieu that was dominated by the early days of statistics. His early work suggested that "statistics could offer to psychology, through the apprehension of a large number of facts, rich material for analysis that would bring, rather than vague assumptions, conclusions of mathematical certainty." Drawing on the work of the founder of statistics as a discipline, Adolphe Quetelet, via Thomas Buckle, Wundt felt able to declare: "Everywhere, where the material for the observations is sufficient, the law of large numbers imposes itself—i.e., isolated deviations, which we ascribe to chance or individual will, cancel each other out, and the historical and natural law finds its clear and complete expression."[8] The kind of psychology best suited to the use of statistics he called "social psychology," meaning the psychology not of individuals, but of large groups of people. At the same time, however, Wundt saw statistics as inherently limited. While able to reveal some kind of universal laws about human behavior, they functioned to demonstrate "causes" and not "motives." In other words, statistics were explanatory, not predictive.

What changed between Wundt's declaration in 1862 that there are *laws of love*, just as there are for all other human phenomena, and IBM's claim that it can write *algorithms for love*? And what actually is the difference between these two claims? And what, you might legitimately ask here, is the point of talking about this in a book about design?

I would like to begin by answering the last question first. What exactly do Wilhelm Wundt and IBM's self-aggrandizing claims about its technologies have to do with a book that is about user-experience design? The answer lies in how seriously we take IBM's claim to knowledge. I am inclined to look at IBM's claim that "once we know, we can't unknow" from a slightly different perspective. What I want to find out is *how* do we know? If we take this truism at face value, that "once we know, we can't unknow," I think it is important to figure out how that knowing takes place to begin with. And I think the moment of "once we know" happens at the *interface*.

All of IBM's technologies have interfaces that go along with them—ranging from their suites of big data analytics for businesses[9] to their various adaptations of the Watson platform for healthcare.[10] It is only at the moment of interaction with the interface that users are made to believe the claims that IBM makes in their commercials. In other words, it is only when the interface shows predictions from a predictive model making their way into reality, when their appearance is scientific, and when the inputs displayed on the screen appear to be "data."

Central to this book is the idea that we encounter, *at the interface,* the *knowing* to which the IBM commercial refers. Again, however, more questions might arise from such an assertion. For example, where do the claims made by IBM (or other companies that work in predictive analytics, such as Google or Facebook), which its interfaces subsequently confirm, originate? And, furthermore, what are the implications of accepting that which we gather from the interface as the kind of *knowing* that IBM claims it is? And what happens when what we know is wrong but we can't unknow it?

The interface is more than an object or a thing. It is a *moment in time* where the histories, ideas, and assumptions underlying a particular technology meet the user's ideas about themselves and about others. In doing so, the interface helps produce new ideas about people, and therefore also has certain implications for how they conduct themselves in the world, how they imagine society, and how they treat each other. The way individuals treat each other, and the way they feel they are supposed to or able to treat each other—far from being about some sort of "across the aisle" political discourse or the nuances of appropriate emoji selection—indicates and has implications for how people embody the world they want to (or don't want to) live in. It is, in many ways, the source of an ethical imagination that shapes everyday life in ways that are barely perceptible. To a great degree, the design of digital products establishes the contours of one's understanding of oneself and, therefore, of others. Perhaps you woke up in the morning, glanced at your Amazon Halo or Ōura ring interface to see "how well" you slept or whether you are "ready" for the day, or examined "insights" about your collaborative projects with the help of Microsoft's Viva or MyAnalytics. This is one of the concerns at the core of this book: that the interface is the meeting point between a user and a version of the user which is produced not only through technology but through a collection of histories, ideas, and assumptions—all of which are barely perceptible to the user. To think through this concern in some more detail, we will follow the line of questioning about Wundt and IBM that I began earlier, and, along the way, we will encounter the other concerns at the heart of this book.

What is the difference between Wundt's claim there are laws of love just as for all other human phenomena, and IBM's claim that it can write algorithms for love? To begin with, Wundt saw a difference between what he called *social psychology* and *individual psychology*. Social psychology was about the psychology of large populations and included things like divorce or suicide rates across a society. To be able to understand some general "laws" about love that explained certain social phenomena within society, such as divorce rates, seems to be within the bounds of Wundt's *social psychology*. This is precisely the kind of situation in which he argued statistics could be useful for augmenting the psychologist's toolbox of observational techniques. But IBM, at least given the combination of imagery and text within the context of the commercial, seems to suggest that in writing algorithms for love, it can *predict* love not only for society but for *individuals*. IBM's claim might be based on the difference between the statistics of Wundt's time and its data-driven analytics. Contributing to IBM's claim might also be the ability to dynamically categorize individuals to create unique profiles that can be situated in comparison with other individuals and categories of individuals, in real time.

To be able to predict something based on a model, however, no matter how granular the model, requires that the behavior of the individuals being modeled and predicted adhere to the model. The better they adhere to the model, the more accurate the predictions. *The interface* is what makes users believe the utility of the model and makes the predictions convincing. It produces, legitimizes, and circulates an idea about the self that people then come to adopt. This idea about the self is what this book seeks to examine, and is what I call the *computable subjectivity*: when an individual believes they are both computing—meaning they operate according to computational processes—and computable—meaning they can be entirely understood by computers, and no part of them escapes this.

Interfaces and Us, then, seeks to describe the computable subjectivity, examine its history and consequences, and detail the role of user-experience design in its adoption and reproduction. The computable subjectivity, I will argue, has three key characteristics that underpin its development and proliferation, and it is these characteristics and the role of UX in their propagation that form the three chapters in the middle of this book: (1) the ideological commitment to the equivalence of "data" and "world"; (2) the aspiration to be both legible to, and predictable by, computers—an aspiration which soothes the feeling of fragmentation that accompanies an adherence to the belief that data and world are one in the same; and, (3) the adoption of a morality that is based on becoming normal through computational self-optimization.

Before we consider how users meet this idea about themselves at the interface however, the first question I posed above must be addressed. What changed between Wundt's declaration in 1862 that there are *laws of love*, just as there are for all other human phenomena, and IBM's claim that it can write *algorithms for* love, that, implicitly at least, those algorithms work for any number of individuals, that the algorithms are predictive, and that they can help people *find* love? And in some ways, that's where the first chapter of the book begins.

The Historical and Conceptual Underpinnings of the Computable Subjectivity

The first chapter of the book seeks to build a foundation for understanding the characteristics of the computable subjectivity, their consequences, and the role of UX in their propagation. It links together four historical and conceptual threads: biopolitics, the "value of convenience," computing as a "freeing" countercultural idea, and the rise of Cybernetics. Together, these ideas support a form of governance based on the "free" market as a system of information exchange. This chapter tries to show how these ideas, taken together, paint a picture of people who are always trying to, more or less selfishly, optimize themselves and their surroundings.

Although this is not a book about history per se, the boundary drawn around the kinds of histories that are pertinent to designers is often too limiting. For example, the history of Graphic Design (e.g., Meggs[11]) has often been taken to be a history of forms, such as posters, books, prints, typefaces, etc.[12] It has not been a history of technology, much less a history of ideas and political-economic structures that shaped those technologies. Despite the necessity of some parameters, the epistemic bounds of "design" (regardless of the type of design someone does) do not allow for the kind of interconnection that defines the character of historical events.

This chapter seeks to situate the design of interfaces today within a particular historical context. This context is defined by a strange kind of individualism wherein people fetishize convenience-enhancing technologies because they see their bodies as limits to be overcome. Such technologies utilize principles from Cybernetics, a science of systems originally developed for military use during the Second World War.[13] The theories of Cybernetics, which assumed everything—soldiers, weapons, and nation-states alike[14]—to be information processing systems, became generalizable, and, when combined with ideas from politics and economics, created a powerful way to think about people, markets, and societies. Anything could be seen as an information processor, made from smaller information processing units, which, when given the right information at the right time in the right form, could make decisions in their own self-interest that would also be beneficial to the optimization of the systems of which they were a part. Such information would need to be legible to the information processors—whether people or machines, essence did not matter—that were part of a given system. Thus, the impetus for capturing data about anything and everything is catalyzed.

Are We and Our World Nothing but Data?

The second chapter of the book examines the first of the three core characteristics of the computable subjectivity: the ideological commitment to the equivalence between "data" and "world." This chapter describes the history and consequences of this ideological commitment as well as the role of UX in its propagation and acceptance. Beginning with an individual's dreams, something that once appeared impossible to quantify, the chapter presents one history of the way meaning and measurement come to be confused. It describes the perception, originating in physics in the early twentieth century, that the tools by which experimental and empirical investigations were carried out were effectively mechanisms that served to translate the "world" being observed into "data." If gathered correctly, the data could be used to make generalizations about the world, while the original mechanism of translation could disappear. I show that this concept would have strange reverberations throughout society, culminating in a confusion of measurement with meaning and reinforcing ideas about systems and the commensurability of people and computers. Things that may have previously seemed silly or unnecessary to quantify—mood or meditative state, for example—become not only quantifiable but seem to be impossible to understand without becoming quantified. In order for individuals to succumb to the belief that "data" and "world" are one and the same, however, this ideology must be made to seem natural. This chapter describes several important ways in which the naturalization of the equivalence between "data" and "world" occurs, focusing in particular on the interface and the cultivation of habit.

Fragmentation, Prediction, and Identity

For data about every aspect of everyday life to be captured, life itself must be fragmented. Instead of contiguous, in relationship with every other part of life, individual aspects of life are defined, separated, and quantified, and the "smooth" space of everyday life becomes "striated." In his famous "Postscript on the Societies of Control," philosopher Gilles Deleuze wrote that "[t]he numerical language of control is made of codes that mark access to information, or reject it. We no longer find ourselves dealing with the mass/individual pair. Individuals have become '*dividuals*,' and masses, samples, data, markets, or '*banks*' … The operation of markets is now the instrument of social control and forms the impudent breed of our masters."[15]

The third chapter of the book looks at the history and consequences of the second of the core characteristics of the computable subjectivity: the aspiration to be legible to, and predictable by, computers, which soothes the feelings of fragmentation that emerge once everything must become data in order to be understood. The chapter also demonstrates how UX positions this computational legibility as the answer to the problem it itself poses. Beginning with theorists of modernity, who, following Marx, were concerned about the fragmentation and alienation that arises under industrial capitalism, this chapter examines how individuals in society are "alienated" from their labor and lives alike when life must be fragmented into quantifiable bits in order to become "knowable." This produces an "ontological insecurity."[16] Such intense alienation yields a desire to become whole again. Computation, ironically, offers that possibility by demonstrating that individuals can be truly "knowable," if only all the "data" about them can be captured. Devices that algorithmically anticipate individuals' activities, ranging from FitBits to Microsoft's productivity tools, and the interfaces through which people experience them, present a coherent version of the self that provides a new ontological security.

New Normals and New Morals

If everything from individuals to societies and from smart watches to smart cities is composed of "data," and if those information processing systems (whether people or nation-states) can optimize themselves by becoming completely legible to, and predictable by, computing, then a new kind of moral imperative emerges. If an individual can live a "healthier" life according to the software that analyzes their body fat composition and heart rate, for example, through adopting additional computational tools, then they may feel morally obligated to do so. Or perhaps the promotional materials for a new startup suggest that it's possible to cure certain mental illnesses just through its app, and will thus save employers and insurers money—this company is expressing a kind of morality of individualist computational self-optimization. This is the third characteristic of the computable subjectivity: the moral imperative to normality through computational self-optimization. The fourth chapter examines the history and dire consequences of this new morality, as well as the role of UX in its penetration into society. The chapter begins with a specific example: professors, whose ideas about what it means to teach and do research, are radically reshaped by the computable subjectivity. Under this new regime of morality, they come to see their value through the metrics by which their return-on-investment is judged. This example, along with several others, is woven throughout the chapter, which suggests that when morality comes to be supplanted by technique, interpersonal interaction is instrumentalized in the service of meeting a metric, and nothing more.

Is the Computable Subjectivity Actually the Problem? If So, What Do We Do?

The fifth chapter of the book explicitly articulates a potential counterargument to the analysis that the book presents, namely: is the computable subjectivity a function of capitalism, and, as such, is it capitalism that is actually the problem? Could it be that understanding oneself as computing and computable would not have any of the deleterious effects the book examines if it were to be experienced under a different political-economic order? In this chapter, I argue that the current manifestation of the computable subjectivity is unique to capitalism and the role of design within it, but that its existence, however different, would be equally dangerous under an ostensibly more "just" political economic order. Therefore, there is some reason to believe in the pursuit of a society that eschews the computable subjectivity regardless of political economy. Under a neoliberal political-economic regime, I suggest that one space from which the computable subjectivity might experience some productive resistance is from design education. This chapter then articulates one approach to fighting the computable subjectivity through the education of UX designers, the individuals designing the interfaces where the computable subjectivity and its characteristics are legitimized and circulated in society. The interventions described in this chapter are what I call a "reformist" approach to change, meaning that they make incremental changes and work within existing institutional and structural arrangements. I offer some examples from my own practice as an educator in order to demonstrate what this might look like.

Concluding by Way of Beginning

The concluding chapter of the book returns to the question of political economy and presents an alternative analysis that also suggests the computable subjectivity would be a dangerous force under a different political-economic system, including aspirational ones such as "fully-automated luxury communism." This analysis of the relationship between the computable subjectivity and political economy leads to the heart of the concluding chapter, which is to say, the heart of what I hope is very much not a conclusion, but a beginning. The majority of the concluding chapter is devoted to the "revolutionary" approach to reimagining design education, particularly in order to rectify the pernicious effects of the computable subjectivity on individuals and society. Indeed, the existence of a "reformist" approach as I described in Chapter 5 implied the existence of a "revolutionary" approach, and it is this, admittedly speculative, project that I explore in the conclusion to the book. Drawing on the work of individuals and communities engaged with ideas of conviviality, degrowth, and communal autonomy—ranging from theorists and designers to communities and movements from across the globe—this chapter seeks to produce a sketch of a fundamentally new kind of relationship between design and society.

The Co-Constitutive Nature of Design, Design Scholarship, and Design Education

Throughout this book, I reflect on my own work as a designer, artist, and educator as an entry point for discussing the concepts within each chapter. Reflecting on, and writing about, my practice—in any of these capacities—is not intended to be self-aggrandizing. Rather, it is core to the research, scholarship, and teaching in which I am engaged: my projects inform my teaching and my scholarship, my teaching and my scholarship inform my projects, and my projects and my scholarship inform my teaching. I see it as impossible to untangle any of these elements of my work from the others. As such, *this book itself is an act of education*, a pedagogical project. This co-constitutive nature of creative practice, scholarship, and pedagogy also shapes how I conceive of the audience for this book—a heterogeneous group of scholars and practitioners as well as the students they teach, including: (1) design academics who teach primarily in practice-based programs, such as those teaching UX, Interaction Design, Graphic Design, and Human-Computer Interaction (HCI); (2) academics who teach more on the "theory" side, especially those identifying with Design Studies and Science and Technology Studies (STS); and, (3) advanced undergraduates and graduate students who study under groups (1) and (2). Additionally, I hope this book may be of use to design practitioners working in the tech sector and who are interested in the implications of their work.

Much of this book addresses ideas that might, at first glance, seem tangential to UX. This is, in part, because of the epistemic closure required to make UX a legitimate "discipline" in the first place. Paul Dourish writes eloquently about this conundrum, which he calls the *legitimacy trap*, in which a claim to legitimacy produces an "obstacle toward progress or redefinition." Indeed, Dourish writes, the legitimacy trap of UX centers on the way UX staked its claim to legitimacy in its early days and its disciplinary aspirations through "usability" and "efficiency."[17] Graphic Design, the field from which I began my journey to UX, has experienced a similar legitimacy trap. Like other disciplines, advances in technology and methodology in the "hard" sciences have caused Graphic Design to grapple with its nature as a field of knowledge production. Graphic Design has sought to legitimate itself through method and through specialized discourses that result in a kind of epistemic closure. It could not be a discipline without disciplinary boundaries, nor could it establish a notion of expertise without delineating specifically what that expertise is in.[18] A constant striving for academic legitimacy through epistemic closure and the shift from craft to pre-professional academia have resulted in a lack of awareness about the interconnections between "Graphic Design" and the fields that study the things graphic designers help create.

Legitimacy traps in UX and Graphic Design have led to an epistemic closure that precludes the questioning of what these fields are really *for* and what their *effects* really are. This has led to a lack of literature that takes seriously the role of the interface—and specifically the role of User-Experience Design (UX), Interaction Design, and Graphic Design—in the politics of today's consumer technologies. The existing literature, coming from a wide array of disciplines, often privileges either the visual experience or the functionality of the technology itself. Rarely, however does it do justice to the dynamic interplay between meaning and function. Even more rarely does it address the consequences of this interplay for the user and society. This gap in the literature is often reflected in the lack of interaction between Science and Technology Studies (STS) programs and the explicitly pre-professional UX and/ or Graphic Design programs at institutions where both are housed. Literature that does link UX, Interaction Design, or Graphic Design with STS is not well-known by designers nor is it produced by those *doing the designing*. Furthermore, this literature rarely addresses the broader social and political-economic consequences of its object of study. It is worth noting that my analysis is also shaped by my position in a research institution in the United States, and other, perhaps qualitatively different analyses would emerge from other institutional positions and geographic locations.

In a situation in which the legitimacy of UX or Graphic Design is predicated on a limitation of scope, discussions of effects and implications—such as those that appear in this book—might seem "esoteric." But design is connected deeply to our own subjective perceptions of ourselves, so we must engage the "esoteric" of psychology and philosophy. These perceptions emerge as the result of interactions with technology and have *material effects* that support particular ways of seeing the world that are embedded in the technologies themselves, reinforcing the very ideas on which those technologies were built. So we must engage Science and Technology Studies and Political-Economy as well. For designers to *understand* and interrogate these "esoteric" qualities of design, their relationships to people and society are to empower designers to change society and to undo some of the damage that they've done precisely because they've been mired in a tunnel-vision of the "practical" (e.g., usability, frictionless interactions, convenience-enhancement, etc.). In some sense, this is an effort to think less about how interfaces work, and more about how they *work on us*. To say that users or designers cannot be concerned with the topics this book addresses is to willfully ignore that everyday life is mediated by technologies that become naturalized, that the ideas underlying those technologies become legitimate precisely because the interfaces to those technologies make them easy to use and better align users and designers with expectations of daily life today, expectations reified by interfaces. It is my hope that this book contributes to an exploding of the epistemic boundaries of UX and perhaps subverts its legitimacy in order to reconfigure what its purpose is in the first place.

***

Let us return now to Wilhelm Wundt, who, 150 years before IBM, suggested that there were statistical laws that governed everything, including love. While they seem similar, there is a fundamental difference between the proclamations of Wundt and those of IBM: it is the difference between explanation and prediction. When computational models are used to predict the outcomes of particular phenomena, it becomes necessary for the subjects of those predictions to behave according to the laws or models being used. And when political-economic systems rely on the accuracy of these predictions, the utility of predictive analytics like IBM's "algorithms for love," becomes evident. Design both legitimates the explanation and makes the model an aspiration. In doing so, it changes people's ideas about who they are and who they can be. These ideas are then reinscribed into other new technologies in a cycle that circulates and amplifies the dangers of the computable subjectivity. This book is one small effort to break this cycle. I thank you for beginning that project with me.

Notes

1   IBM UK & Ireland. "IBM: Making the World Smarter Every Day." YouTube video, 01:01. Posted [August 2015]. https://www.youtube.com/watch?v=ESx-RNGRhUE

2   Ian Hacking, "How Should We Do a History of Statistics?" in *The Foucault Effect: Studies in Governmentality*, eds. Graham Burchell, Colin Gordon, and Peter Miller (Chicago: University of Chicago Press, 1991), 182.

3   Alan Kim, "Wilhelm Maximilian Wundt," in *The Stanford Encyclopedia of Philosophy*, ed. Edward N. Zalta, Fall 2016 (Metaphysics Research Lab, Stanford University, 2016), https://plato.stanford.edu/archives/fall2016/entries/wilhelm-wundt/.

4   Robert H. Wozniak, "Classics in Psychology, 1855-1914: Historical Essays," ed. Christopher D. Greene (Bristol, UK; Tokyo: Thoemmes Press; Maruzen, 1999), https://psychclassics.yorku.ca/Wundt/Physio/wozniak.htm.

5   Wilhelm Wundt, *Outlines of Psychology*, trans. Charles Hubbard Judd (New York: Wilhelm Engleman, 1897), https://ia800207.us.archive.org/1/items/cu31924014474534/cu31924014474534.pdf: 314.

6   Wundt, *Outlines of Psychology*, 323.

7   Saulo de Freitas Araujo and Annette Mülberger, *Wundt and the Philosophical Foundations of Psychology: A Reappraisal* (New York: Springer, 2016): 26.

8   Wundt, cited in Araujo and Mülberger, 33.

9   E.g., https://www.ibm.com/analytics/spss-statistics-software.

10   E.g., https://www.ibm.com/us-en/marketplace/watson-care-manager.

11   Philip B. Meggs and Alston W. Purvis, *Meggs' History of Graphic Design*, 6th ed. (Hoboken, NJ: Wiley, 2016).

12   Tibor Kalman, Abbot Miller, and Karrie Jacobs, "Retro-Spectives: Two Views of Deisgn-Er-Appropriation: Good History Bad History," *Print* 45, no. 2 (1991): 114–23.

13   See: Norbert Wiener, *Cybernetics or Control and Communication in the Animal and the Machine*, 2nd ed., 14. print (Cambridge, MA: MIT Press, 2007).

14 Peter Galison, "The Ontology of the Enemy: Norbert Wiener and the Cybernetic Vision," *Critical Inquiry* 21, no. 1 (1994): 228–66.

15 Gilles Deleuze, "Postscript on the Societies of Control," *October* 59 (1992): 3–7.

16 Horning, "Sick of Myself," *Real Life*, accessed November 9, 2018, https://reallifemag.com/sick-of-myself/.

17 Paul Dourish, "User Experience as Legitimacy Trap," *Interactions* 26, no. 6 (October 30, 2019): 46–9. https://doi.org/10.1145/3358908.

18 See, for example: Anna Vallye, "Design and the Politics of Knowledge in America, 1937–1967: Walter Gropius, Gyorgy Kepes." Doctoral Dissertation, Columbia University, 2011.

1 HISTORICAL AND CONCEPTUAL ROOTS OF THE COMPUTABLE SUBJECTIVITY

Introduction: Disrupting the Insurance Industry—"Convenience" and "Freedom"

This chapter will connect disparate histories and ideas to show—at least in part—the origins of the *computable subjectivity*: the idea of the self as computable, able to be understood by computers, and computing, operating according to computational processes. These histories also demonstrate how this conception of the self becomes useful to corporations and governmental entities, and the way it emerges as an aspirational ideal in society. By synthesizing these different historical and conceptual threads, I will also introduce some terminology and historical references that will be important components of the subsequent analyses presented in the book. Moreover, because subsequent chapters, which examine different characteristics of the computable subjectivity and its consequences, will rely on the ideas and histories presented here, I hope to demonstrate that UX design and its role in society are not ahistorical but instead deeply linked with a number of developments in science, technology, and political economy. Thus, I implicitly make the case that understanding, studying, and doing UX requires an interdisciplinary and historically situated approach. Before we begin, however, I would like to tell you a story about a project that sought to "disrupt" the insurance industry. It's a story that we'll come back to throughout the chapter because it demonstrates in a concrete way the syntheses of the historical and conceptual threads that I will present.

***

During our final year of graduate school at the Massachusetts College of Art and Design, three of my colleagues and I started a design consultancy. We envisioned our company as a way to blend the work we had been doing in graduate school with our past experiences in industry. In doing so, we hoped to find a happy medium for ourselves—earning a living doing the work for which our training prepared us, while at the same time "owning" our labor, taking control of our lives and careers. It was idealistic, but the encouragement of successful projects, as well as kind words from graduate advisors and industry contacts, seemed to confirm its potential. We soon realized, as many startups do, that all is not as it seems at first. We took on projects with which we were not particularly comfortable so that we could fund the work about which we were excited. Such tradeoffs are unsurprising for anyone running their own design studio.

Sometime in the fall of 2013, we were contacted by an insurance executive about a project on which their company's "technology team" was working. They were creating a digital platform that was intended to "disrupt" the traditional insurance industry model by creating an efficient way to pair users with specific insurance policies from a variety of providers. The platform would link data about an individual from their Facebook and Google profiles with their answers to a short series of questions. Through the user's answers to these questions, additional inferences about them were made relative to other individuals who had used the service, as well as to databases of statistics about various populations. This allowed the insurance company to match the user with specific insurance policies extremely quickly, without the user having to do much, thereby "freeing" the user to spend time on other things. This system relied on several algorithms to infer a number of data points about the user that were incorporated into the matching system. It proposed to make the insurance purchasing experience more convenient, efficient, and hyper-personalized, streamlining the use of insurance agents and reducing the time for purchasers to make decisions. Furthermore, it was unique in that it was housed at an actual insurance company.

Our role as user-experience (UX) designers on the project originated from a much simpler request from the client about branding the visual experience of the platform itself. When we suggested that it was not in the client's best interest to separate the structure of the product and the "visual design," the client began to involve us in discussions about the overall UX. However, as a result of our initial role in the process and the development team's hesitance to share the functioning of their algorithms with us, our access to information about the back end of the system was limited. Our interactions with the development and tech team were limited to two brief meetings, after which very little information about the functioning of the platform was shared in a concrete manner. We inferred many of the functional aspects of the platform from these brief conversations as well as through our interactions with the project lead on the client side. Such a limited understanding of the technical capabilities of the platform hampered the design of the user experience and, actually, contributed to my interest in learning more about systems of algorithmic inference and recommendation, and how these shape everyday life.

In the course of the project, we developed a number of user scenarios, a typical task for a UX team. One such scenario focused on an individual who is not actively shopping for insurance but had purchased their current policy a number of years ago. This particular user happens to be reading through her Facebook feed and comes across a post from a friend who has just used this innovative insurance platform. The friend's post might say something like, "finally switched my car insurance—can't believe it took me so long to find out about this!" This particular post is not a "sponsored post" or inline advertisement, but rather just a quickly tapped out status update from a friend, who includes a link to the platform's website, where she found her new insurance policy. This behavior might seem odd (at least it did to me), but, in 2010, 20 percent of people who purchased insurance shared about the purchase or the purchase process online.[1, 2]

Curious about her friend's experience, our user clicks the link in the post. She is greeted by a bright and friendly interface with text that refers to, surprisingly, her curiosity about learning more about insurance (but does not necessarily refer to her as being interested in *purchasing* insurance). Because the user might just be interested in insurance, we did not want to scare her away by talking about *buying* insurance. This was a key element of the system of interactions we were designing. We needed the system to be contextual in the sense that it could identify platforms from which users were directed to the site, and potentially the text or links that had brought the person to the site (e.g., the actual content of a search query or a post).

The user begins by answering a few questions about herself and what she values (e.g., "Michael Kors vs. Macchu Picchu" as a way to indicate whether the user is more interested in using her money for retail or travel). She is intrigued, and starts considering that it's possible her current insurance doesn't really reflect her priorities. As this initial set of questions—which are fun and not overtly "insurance-related"—ends, our user decides to continue by answering a number of more insurance-specific questions, including the types of insurance she has and the types of insurance she might not have but in which she's interested. The interface tells her that the process that she's just gone through, as well as the additional questions she is about to answer, will help the platform match her with insurance policies that are the best fit for her. During this secondary series of interactions, the user is also introduced to her "insurance friend," a person who is available to answer any questions the user might have about the insurance matching process. We doubted that the user would reach out to her "insurance friend," but we thought that it would create an even greater sense of personalization. After a detailed, but not burdensome, series of questions that pertained to the specific kinds of insurance in which our user was interested, she is matched with the top three insurance policies from a variety of providers for her, as well as short explanations about why these policies were best. The explanatory text would be tailored to the user and reflect what we had learned about her based on her interactions with the insurance-matching interface as well as the website from which she had arrived, a post on which had originally piqued her interest. The user could then, if she chose, move forward with purchasing the insurance. At any time during the process the user could pause her progress and create a login for the site, as well as share her experience on her preferred social networks.

This story is one of a number of narrative scenarios that my team and I developed during the design process. Each story related to how a user accessed the insurance platform, the website from which they arrived, and the different predispositions of the personas we developed. As might be pretty clear by now, there are a number of data points being gathered about the user along the way, from the website and type of post on that site (as well as the specific language in that post) that brought the user to the insurance platform in the first place, all the way through the experience. The insurance platform also compared the user's responses to the questions during the matching process to other users who had been determined, in some way, to be "similar." Not unlike Amazon's "customers who bought this item also bought" or Netflix film recommendations, the algorithms developed by the tech team were able to produce and analyze a database of users and their interactions with the insurance platform in order to compare users with one another, categorize them, and recommend courses of action to specific users who exhibited traits that aligned with a particular category. Additionally, the system could make other inferences about the user based on things like the type of browser being used and the operating system on which that browser is working. For example, users on a newer MacOS might be subjected to different insurance rates than someone on an old Android OS. Later in this book, I will discuss some of the implications of this dynamic categorization—what John Cheney-Lippold has termed the "measurable type"—and the "modulation" that can be exerted as a result of such profiling.[3]

Insurance, however, is still a relatively simple endeavor: it is something people need and it is based on a limited number of factors that are primarily financial and therefore quantifiable. So why would more sophisticated algorithms and a better user experience or a more attractive interface, for that matter, make a difference in shopping for insurance? Why would users want to use it and why would companies want to be matched with users through it?

While we did not learn all the secrets of the company's algorithms, we did learn in a meeting with their lead technologist that they had over 100 data points that they utilized to match users with specific insurance policies from the companies that had signed up to use their service. What would the company need this for? Wouldn't they just need to know certain things about my car? But would my social media tell them more? What if I logged in with Facebook? Would they know how frequently I drank? What about my credit card data? Would they know I was sometimes a frivolous spender? Would these things cause my homeowners' insurance premiums to go up? What personal habits, medical conditions, or family situations might make me less "insurable" and, therefore, result in a higher premium?

This insurance platform typifies many of today's most widely used digital services, ranging from Amazon and Netflix to travel websites such as Orbitz and Kayak. Throughout this chapter, I will use this story about the "disruptive" insurance platform to help demonstrate the importance of the four historical and conceptual threads that lay the groundwork for the following chapters: biopolitics, convenience, the countercultural idea of "freedom" associated with computing, and the rise of Cybernetics.

Platforms like the insurance platform we worked on are rife with paradoxes—they are designed and built to make their owners or developers money, but also to make our lives easier and more pleasurable. Designers, like my students and me, focus on making things within these systems *easy* for the *user*. We are praised when we make products intuitive, demanding the least cognitive effort on the part of the user in the hopes that the user will be more likely to continue using the product or service. Indeed, when we learn about UX design in school, it is primarily in service of producing the user experience with the least friction, something that is, in the end, "easy" to use. However, such systems and the intuitive design thereof have both intended and unintended consequences that cater to incisive biopolitical control, which remains, at the time of this writing, the perfect partner for a smoothly functioning neoliberal capitalism.

Each of the four topics that this chapter will address has received a great deal of scholarly attention over the last several decades, and this book doesn't seek to compete with this rich body of literature. *This book is, however, intended to better illuminate the moral and ethical implications of designers' roles in a seemingly rational endeavor.* Consequently, I have been selective in my readings of these histories, picking out specific moments and theorists that best illustrate the connections this chapter attempts to make. These connections are, one might say, pillars on which the computable subjectivity rests, and so it's important to begin here, before moving on to considering the characteristics of the computable subjectivity, how UX participates in legitimizing and propagating it, and the consequences thereof.

Producing and Looping, or, Biopolitics and Biopower

The concepts of *biopolitics* and *biopower*, which come from the work of Michel Foucault, are central to this book. Like other terms Foucault invented or employed, they are sometimes difficult to get accustomed to, but they are, nonetheless, precise. Foucault argues that one of the key transitions that (Western) society underwent was a shift in the type of power that is exerted on the people living within a given nation-state. In this transition, power changes from being disciplinary and emerging from past events—such as incarceration or rehabilitation—to a productive force. This productive power sees the individual body and the social body as objects of government and therefore of political and scientific problems, training its focus on the processes that enable and sustain life. It is, in other words, a "power to make live," *biopower*. This should not be confused with a benevolent power, but should instead be understood as a different means of governing populations. *Biopolitics*, maybe most succinctly summarized by Rachel Adams, is then a politics of society, as opposed to a politics of sovereignty.[4] The history of statistics[5] is a testament to the emergence of biopolitics: it is about regulation and prediction of those things that influence the biological processes of the living population.

For example, designers have long obsessed over ergonomics, because poor ergonomic design not only makes people less comfortable, but it makes them less *productive*, less able to do the jobs that they *should* be doing within society. Biopower not only counts and quantifies, but out of those calculations it produces categorizations and norms. Consider the famous and recently re-released *Humanscale* manual by Niels Diffrient (and reissued by IA Collaborative in 2017).[6] Ergonomics are driven by statistics about the human body, and, in particular the "average" or "normal" human body. Biopower is therefore exerted, in this sense, through the normative force of particular design decisions that cater to some bodies but not others.[7] Another, more recent and disturbing example of incisive and forceful regulatory biopower is an app that "reminds you to smile more," by utilizing the Affectiva SDK and its facial expression recognition technology.[8]

Ian Hacking's histories of statistics show how the quantification and categorization at the heart of biopolitics enable new modes of control. When an insurance provider, for example, determines a user to belong to a particular category (income, net worth, spending habits, etc.), that user is then guided toward different decisions, which might impact their life chances in general, but also reflect the ideas about people that are embedded in the insurance company's software. This is an example also of Hacking's interest in "how names interact with the named."[9] His "looping effect" shows how classifications of people are not static. Instead, he argues, classifications of people:

> are moving targets because our investigations interact with them, and change them. And since they are changed, they are not quite the same kind of people as before. The target has moved. I call this the "looping effect". Sometimes, our sciences create kinds of people that in a certain sense did not exist before.[10]

Hacking calls this, "making up people." Scientific categorizations produce "effects on the kinds of people to whom they are applied."[11] When the "measurable types" of algorithmic categorization are applied to you, you are classified and placed in relationship with others who, within the confines of the kinds of data being measured, are "similar." You are then treated like those people and they are treated like you, perhaps recommended similar products and services. Individuals therefore act in different ways depending on how they have been categorized by the systems with which they interact. With ever-increasing reliance on computational systems that utilize algorithmic inference and recommendation in order to make things easier and more efficient, like shopping for insurance, the productive aspects of everyday life come to be dominated by Hacking's "looping effect." Similar to Hacking's "looping effect" is John Cheney-Lippold's "modulation." It is the connection between dynamic categorization and the modulation it enables as partially constitutive of the productive nature of biopower.

Biopolitics and biopower are at their core about the *productive* prediction and regulation of the things that enable and sustain human living and functioning. They are not necessarily about the regulation of populations by traditional disciplinary methods of control like laws enacted by elected representatives, which, when broken, may lead to incarceration. Furthermore, biopolitics and biopower are not necessarily centralized and are not monolithic in nature. They operate subtly and often without any knowledge on the part of those who are complicit in their workings.

Instead of disciplinary power, biopower thus regulates mortality by directing basic life processes.[12] It also, as in the quite different cases of both mid-century ergonomics and more recent computational insurance recommendation systems, enables the productive and reproductive activity of individuals in society. That one's productive and reproductive activity—the maintenance of economic productivity and physical health—is enhanced through biopolitical means, perhaps might conjure up an image of FitBit's interface. FitBit and similar products not only claim to help a user understand their activities through quantification, but they give a user simple and easy-to-understand feedback about those activities, theoretically "freeing" a user from worrying about whether they are *really* getting enough exercise. Indeed, biopower produces certain kinds of freedom that allow individuals both to be productive (and reproductive) *and* regulated. And what could be more *freeing*, more (re)productivity enabling, than the convenience of computing that does nearly everything for you? If people are completely quantifiable and computable, new modes of biopolitical control can be exerted.

But what does all this have to do with UX design? This is a question that my students ask and will be a refrain repeated throughout this book. This question has answers that operate at two levels of UX design education. The first level we might consider to be the form of the interface itself. The interface is the site at which users receive feedback about the actions they take when engaging with a digital product or service. The interface is also what prompts a user to take a particular action. It does not punish the user but rather enables them to be productive. The interface is the space of the exertion of a productive power that itself is the very thing through which the looping effect emerges in life of the user. Systems of algorithmic inference and recommendation shape users' lives by "tailoring the conditions of possibility."[13] This tailoring is defined by a seizing of agency in which certain courses of action are prioritized, while other courses of action, which might be equally possible, disappear—a shifting and narrowed conception of "freedom," one that is then legitimized and presented back to the user through the interface. The interfaces to algorithmic systems of inference and recommendation—insurance apps and Netflix alike—are the constricting, movement-limiting garments, sometimes even straight-jackets, that emerge from that tailoring process.

Shopping for insurance, and subsequently purchasing it, is a productive activity that is socially necessary. It is obviously not a form of disciplinary power being exerted on the user. Instead, the user shopping for insurance has a number of choices that she can make about her purchase. She is "free" to choose, or not, and can do so with increasing efficiency and convenience, giving her more "free time." But the choices we as the designers presented to the user shape her sense of possibility without revealing to her the workings of the system from which those choices emerged. Much of this book is dedicated to unpacking the "workings of the system," ranging from the historical and material conditions from which a particular kind of reliance on computing emerges, to the function of inference and recommendation algorithms themselves, keeping in mind the relationships between these ideas and the interface itself. This is the second of the two levels of UX design education to which I referred in the previous paragraph: an appreciation of the historical conditions out of which emerge the technologies that we design. Biopower and biopolitics are key aspects of the histories from which the technologies that powered our "innovative" insurance platform were built. Not only do biopower and biopolitics make the technology possible, they are embedded in the platform itself, becoming real for the user only at the moment of interaction.

The Value of Convenience

Computing that enhances convenience, like that innovative insurance platform, is seen as both possible and desirable when people come to view themselves as able to be understood by computers. And our insurance platform was *very* convenient. It helped insurance shoppers "save time," allowing them, in theory, to do the things that really "mattered," without needing to get bogged down in any sort of technical or financial jargon. They didn't have to leave their houses to meet with an insurance agent and were assured a certain level of personalization despite this. Convenience is a key reason for which people adopt various technologies, and the high value placed on convenience has a long history that connects it to capital accumulation, debt, and the Protestant work ethic.[14] The value of convenience is also closely connected to the biopolitical control that certain forms of freedom entail, such as the time-saving capabilities of digital products and services, which shape the conditions of possibility for those who use them.

Contemporary convenience-enhancing technologies range from digital tools like Google Maps to technoscientific inventions such as Soylent—which claimed to "free" its consumers from thinking about food—to products that combine the digital and the physical, like Nest Thermostats. Each of these products is heralded for its ability to make certain tasks more convenient for their users, thereby saving time, allowing users to do things they really *want*. The importance of the ability for technologies to make things more convenient and therefore save time should not be underestimated. In his book, *The Value of Convenience: A Genealogy of Technical Culture*, Thomas Tierney argues that the characteristic trait of modernity is the shift from seeing the body as something that "makes demands to be satisfied" to something that has "limits" to be overcome.[15] He writes, "far from sanctifying the body and the life processes, modernity is distinguished by the ability of the masses to free themselves from the limits of the body through the ravenous consumption of technology."[16] Think about how many advertising campaigns use this idea of transcending corporeal limitations to advertise their convenience-enhancing technological products and services. One example—which is instructive of the lengths to which techno-utopians might go—was Laundroid, "the world's first laundry folding bot," by a Japanese studio called Seven Dreamers.[17] In 2017, shortly before the project was shut down, the machine took 5–10 minutes to fold a single t-shirt. The attempt to produce such a device, nonetheless, and the amount of capital invested, clearly demonstrates the "value" placed on convenience.

Less absurd examples of convenience-enhancing technologies abound. The copywriting from a 2015 Blue Apron commercial is a nice illustration:

> *Inside everyone is an incredible cook—someone who can cook an amazing meal any night of the week. Farm fresh ingredients. Step by step recipes. Delivered to your door for $9.99 a meal.*[18]

Blue Apron's technology makes grocery shopping unnecessary—it's an incredible time-saver. And while its "technology" is not necessarily apparent to someone receiving a Blue Apron meal kit, their key technological innovation is supply chain logistics. For example, "Blue Apron collects data on its customers that allows for predictive modeling of demand."[19] To be so convenient, Blue Apron must construe its customers as data.

Meanwhile, the Internet of Things seemed to herald an era of ultra-convenience. Constantly capturing data about a user's everyday activities, "smart objects," things like refrigerators and washing machines embedded with internet-connected computing, could anticipate a user's needs. Such systems "reduce cognitive load"[20] on users, making decisions for them. Doesn't get much more convenient than that, right? Products shipped to your house before you need them, movies queued up to watch before you even decide you want to watch one.

But how did such a high value come to be placed on "convenience" and technologies that produce it? Part of Tierney's analysis examines the role of Puritanism's rise in the uniquely American obsession with convenience and its attendant technological fetishism. In an interesting twist that at first appears incongruous with conspicuous consumption and planned obsolescence, Tierney argues that the American obsession with convenience and saving time by fetishizing technologies that claim to do as much, is actually a form of modern "asceticism" that descends from the Puritans, a branch of Protestantism that sought to further reform the Church of England during the sixteenth and seventeenth centuries.

The Puritans have in common with contemporary technophiles a revulsion of the body and its earthly limitations as well as an obsession with saving time. Like the Puritans, Americans "save time" in order to engage in their "calling," which, today is defined by their role in the economy. Perhaps one might think here of Silicon Valley entrepreneurs, guzzling Soylent[21] so that they don't have to make decisions about what food to eat, saving precious time for their "disruptive" innovations. Or one might think of enhancing the convenience of shopping for insurance. It is important to note here that one's "role" in the economy is not limited necessarily to a job, but rather, to one's participation in the circulation of capital. Indeed, the more time someone saves, both at work and on tasks like feeding themselves or their families, the more they can spend on this "calling." An efficient person, like an efficient society, is productive. There is therefore a moral dimension to fetishizing technologies that make life more convenient. We will return to this new concept of morality in Chapter 4.

Freedom and Countercultural Technocracy

Seeing oneself as computing and computable is what allows the technologies of convenience to "work," to free individuals to engage in their "calling." This view of the self has, strangely, also become central to aspirations of self-actualization and "authenticity." To be free to engage in one's calling might also be understood as the freedom to be one's true self. The possibility of authentic self-realization through "freedom" is a hallmark of the countercultural movement that sprang up during the 1960s. Paradoxically, the rhetoric of freedom used by this movement to resist the mechanization of the nascent computer age and its military roots reappeared in the 1990s as a way to describe the "revolutionary" potential of the internet, built with those very same military-backed technologies. This, as Fred Turner demonstrates, is no coincidence.[22]

Turner's history of the shift from "counterculture" to "cyberculture" chronicles the links between the counterculture movements in the San Francisco Bay Area and the entrepreneurial endeavors of its neighbor to the south, Silicon Valley. Turner suggests that the cultural meaning of information technologies shifted from being an instrument of power and control within the military-academic-industrial complex in the 1960s to a symbol of freedom and individual self-actualization in the 1990s. This kind of freedom was precisely the ideal originally used by the counterculture to resist the military-industrial management of life in the 1960s.

The seeds of the pursuit of the improvement of the self as a way to achieve a more just or equitable society, as opposed to the more traditional mechanism of political action toward social change, had been sown in the 1960s and 1970s by the counterculture movement after their break from the New Left. These ideas were cultivated by Stuart Brand's *Whole Earth Catalog*. Embodying ideas of systems and information theory, the *Whole Earth Catalog* helped the back-to-the-land generation not only try to become self-sufficient, but produce new forms of social organization that resisted the hierarchies they were trying to escape. The *Catalog* presented an incredible array of products and tools, books and resources, situating the reflections of "rural hippies" alongside the writings of the foremost computer scientists of the time. In their encounters with early Cybernetics and systems theory through the *Whole Earth Catalog*, the counterculture movement's members began to turn toward technology and mind—and *not* collective action and politics—as the foundations of a new, more egalitarian society. Some, such as Richard Brautigan in his poem "All watched over by machines of loving grace," adopted computing as a vision of egalitarianism.

Like the Puritans, the techno-utopians of the *Whole Earth* era as well as present-day Silicon Valley soothsayers have seen the body as presenting limits to be overcome on a quest toward true authenticity and self-actualization. John Perry Barlow's 1996 "Declaration of the Independence of Cyberspace" offers a canonical and comically naïve[23] example:

> Your legal concepts of property, expression, identity, movement, and context do not apply to us. They are all based on matter, and there is no matter here. Our identities have no bodies, so, unlike you, we cannot obtain order by physical coercion. We believe that from ethics, enlightened self-interest, and the commonweal, our governance will emerge.[24]

The convenience of the computational products and services that began to proliferate in the 1990s seemed to allow individuals to pursue their "callings" and gave them the freedom to develop their authentic selves even as they eschewed corporeal limits. This transcending of limitation requires a commensurability between people and computers, and Cybernetics provided such a commensurability.

The Selfish System: Cybernetics and Rational Choice Theory

Those who participated in the transition from counterculture to cyberculture, who believed the idea that technology, *not* politics, would produce a better society, were convinced that *systems*—whether an individual person, a family, or a nation-state—when understood as information processors, could achieve stability and freedom. This idea underpinned even the seemingly simple insurance platform I helped design. It would make shopping for and purchasing insurance more efficient, freeing the user to spend more time pursuing their "calling."

When I was working on the insurance platform project, I could not help but think of "smart city" rhetoric emerging from companies like IBM at the time.[25] The vision they presented was one of perfect prediction and control given the right technologies capturing the right information at the right times. And they made it seem like it was *possible*. What we were doing in designing this insurance platform was oddly exciting because it was like a small-scale version, implementing some of the same ideas. We needed to get the right information at the right time in order to get the outcome we were looking for. The idea of a system operating perfectly as a result of having the right information at the right time is the basic underpinning of Cybernetics.

Cybernetics originated in the 1940s and has a long and complex history. Instead of making an inevitably futile attempt at a short history of an immense field of study, I will focus on a few salient aspects of the history of Cybernetics in order to demonstrate its foundational importance to the idea that people can be understood as computing and computable, and to link it to the historical concepts chronicled in this chapter. Cybernetics is central to the history *and* future of UX design and it is one of the key elements of the technoscientific milieu from which major innovations in computing emerged. It is these very innovations that have become the backbone of the digital products and services for which I and my students now create interfaces.

Cybernetics, a term coined by Norbert Wiener in 1948, can be simply described as "the circulation of information in response to an external stimulus."[26] While Wiener defined it as "the study of control and communication in the animal and machine," Orit Halpern suggests that it might be better defined as "a science of control or prediction of future events and actions."[27] Indeed, "Wiener's innovation was to express the problem of uncertainty as an information problem."[28] This significance should not be understated: if all uncertainty is effectively an information problem, then complete prediction and control is possible given the right systems of information transfer and exchange. In Wiener's 1948 book, *Cybernetics; or, Control and Communication in the Animal and the Machine*, he also defines Cybernetics as a field for "the study of messages as a means of controlling machinery and society."[29] Wiener's theory was fundamentally a probabilistic worldview, and as such, things in themselves did not matter. What mattered instead was the relationship to everything else.[30] The question of essence became irrelevant.

One of the basic principles of early Cybernetics was the idea of *homeostasis*, which was demonstrated most directly by W. Ross Ashby's homeostat:

> The homeostat was an electrical device constructed with transducers and variable resistors. When it received an input changing its state, it searched for the configuration of variables that would return it to its initial condition. Ashby explained that the homeostat was meant to model an organism which must keep essential variables within preset limits to survive.[31]

Ashby also used as an example an engineer at the controls of a ship. Keeping the ship from crashing preserved its homeostasis. The engineer and the ship functioned as a cybernetic system.

Originally, the ideas of homeostasis and feedback were developed through Wiener's work with Julian Bigelow on an anti-aircraft apparatus during the Second World War.[32] Both "pilot and the anti-aircraft gunner observed patterns of error in their attempts to attack and escape and regulated their behavior accordingly." This was a response to "negative feedback."[33] Wiener postulated that all things could be treated as systems, whether the aircraft or the pilot, the gun or the gunner, whether society or any of its constituent parts. In their research, Wiener and Bigelow suggested that humans were, to some extent, no different than machines and could therefore be modeled as such. In his subsequent text, *The Human Use of Human Beings: Cybernetics and Society*, he argued that "society could be seen as a system seeking self-regulation through the processing of messages."[34] This idea opens the conceptual floodgates to the notion that, given enough information, anything and everything can be modeled. That the essence of the thing is irrelevant, whether it's a person or a machine or an insurance plan, is core to the way we design computational products today. Those products are predicated on interoperability between people and objects, so those things must become commensurable, and that can only happen by seeing them in a particular way.

The spread of early Cybernetics as a universal science of systems was a key factor in the shift of the cultural connotations of information technology from controlling to liberating.[35] And further, this science originated from Wiener's optimism that society as an informational system could become egalitarian and democratic. Cybernetics was and has been applied to anything and everything—biology, neurology, sociology, and, of course, warfare.[36]

While Cybernetics has a much more complicated history than the introductory words which I've devoted to it here,[37] one of its most important and long-lasting effects is that it resulted in a new approach to understanding human beings, who would henceforth be seen "primarily as information-processing entities."[38] This influence is undeniable, shaping today's most ambitious technological projects, for which UX designers create the interfaces. Take, for example, Sidewalk Labs and the failed 2017 partnership between Alphabet (Google) and the city of Toronto to redevelop the Quayside neighborhood as a model for the Smart City.[39] The proposal by Sidewalk Labs, a subsidiary of Alphabet (Google), was a thinly veiled attempt by Google to privatize Toronto's municipal services under the auspices of efficiency, convenience, and the liberating potential of new technology.[40] "Welcome to Quayside," the proposal boasted, "the world's first neighbourhood built from the internet up."[41] Sidewalk Labs describes previous urban "innovations" such as Rome's aqueducts and Manhattan's street grid as "platforms."[42]

While the idea of computation as a metaphor will be discussed extensively throughout this book, Alphabet's proposal is a tour-de-force of computational metaphor creating a legitimacy not only for privatization but for the idea that anything and everything, including people, operate according to computational processes.

"In Quayside," the proposal goes on, "the physical and the digital will converge into a platform for urban innovation, accelerating the pace of solutions."[43] The "platform" innovations of major metropolises were, they suggest, innovative and transformative, improving life for all in those places. Sidewalk Labs' proposed platform comprises "physical, digital, and standards layers,"[44] which would produce a sophisticated, networked urban environment including modular construction, ubiquitous sensors, self-driving vehicles, and municipal-service robotics, all connected via proprietary software. Sidewalk Labs aligns its platform with the historical urban innovations of generations past, such as the Roman aqueducts and the street grid of Manhattan.[45] Yet the proposal fails to mention that the aqueducts were not built by a private corporation accountable only to its shareholders or capable of including some and excluding others through proprietary, black-boxed techniques.[46] Its platform would, they say, create a "close-knit community that uses data to improve city services." In discussing the "digital layer," of the platform, the proposal describes the falling cost of ubiquitous sensor technology which would allow it to capture enormous amounts of data about the city and accurately model it. The following paragraph reads as though it might have been written during the Cold War by Wiener or one of his colleagues:

> Once fine-grained data are available, it will be increasingly possible to develop a digital model of the performance of the neighbourhood, and use that model to evaluate the effect of various decisions. The ability to predict the consequences of possible interventions, and to refine the model based on measurement of actual outcomes, is an accelerant to improving the livability of the neighbourhood ... [A]s Sidewalk experiments with various weather mitigation strategies, it will get real-time *feedback* on temperature and wind speed from a high-density mesh of sensors. That will enable the real-time evaluation of different interventions. (emphasis mine)[47]

Sidewalk Labs claimed that the enhancement of convenience and productivity in the "smart city" could be achieved through the treatment of every problem as an information problem, and *everything* as an information processor. Given the right information at the right time in an understandable form, systems should be able to self-regulate through their constituent parts pursuing their own optimal states. These ideas resonate deeply with those of early Cybernetics.

The failure of the Sidewalk-Quayside project merits some comment here. Through the dedicated work of activists, many focused on the concept of digital privacy and concerned about the surveillance required to achieve Sidewalk Labs' cybernetic dream, Sidewalk Labs pulled out of their engagement with the city of Toronto.[48] The dissolution of the project and the uncertainty about the future of the "smart city" in Toronto, however, has not deterred Sidewalk Labs—which still features the proposal on their website—nor has it deterred techno-utopians in Silicon Valley and beyond who are committed to the broader project of making everything "smart."[49]

Game Theory and Rational Choice Theory: Selfish Information Processors and Social Equilibrium

At the beginning of the Cold War, the RAND Corporation, the most important military think tank of the twentieth century, resuscitated from academic obscurity a concept called Game Theory.[50] Game Theory and Cybernetics shared their origins as systems-theoretical approaches to understanding the dynamics of armed conflict. While Cybernetics grew out of Wiener's research on man-machine communication in anti-aircraft systems, interest in Game Theory at RAND emerged out of the need to model and predict the moves adversaries would make in the zero-sum game of nuclear conflict.

The most well-known example of Game Theory is the Prisoner's Dilemma. There are a number of variations of the scenario, but the basic idea remains the same. Suppose you have stolen a valuable gemstone. You are contacted by an individual expressing interest and the means by which to purchase the stone from you. You agree to a plan: you will hide the gemstone in one predetermined location while the purchaser will hide the money in another predetermined location. At a certain time, you will both go to pick up what the other has left. You realize, of course, that you could cheat your buyer by holding onto the gemstone *and* going to pick up the money. And, it's possible that your buyer realizes the exact same thing. So what do you do? The *rational* move, suggests Game Theory, is always to betray your partner, because at least you will end up with the gemstone, and you might even get the money, too.

Game Theory was introduced in 1944 by John Von Neumann and Oskar Morgenstern in their *Theory of Games and Economic Behavior*.[51] The work was a "study of interactions between strategic actors by mathematically defining what it means to be 'rational' in all conceivable decision contexts involving payoffs against the actions of other similar actors."[52] While ignored by the economics community, Von Neumann and his research found a home at the RAND Corporation. There, the appendix on "expected utility theory," which "set forth axioms for rational decision-making in risky and uncertain circumstances,"[53] would be put to use in making tactical and strategic nuclear decisions in the Cold War.

Game Theory would have an immense influence on a variety of disciplines, the luminaries of which coalesce around Rational Choice Theory (RCT). The impact of RCT, a framework for analyzing and predicting human interaction at micro and macro scales, can very much still be felt today. Its most prominent tool of prediction and analysis was Game Theory, but it included other decision theories as well. RCT emerged during the cold war, and "[i]t is no exaggeration to say that virtually all the roads to rational choice theory lead from RAND."[54] RAND's analytical and predictive frameworks constituted a "regime of knowledge production," in which "the formation of these tools and concepts led to a far-reaching and comprehensive system for defining appropriate beliefs and actions."[55] This knowledge regime produced groundbreaking research on decision-making that relied exclusively on probabilistic outcome modeling, which turned RCT into a "science" that could address any possible situation of rational decision-making.[56]

James Buchanan's Public Choice Theory—a more explicitly political variation of RCT—laid out clearly the role for politics under neoliberalism. Buchanan had spent the summer of 1954 at RAND,[57] so, in the 1970s, as he became increasingly concerned with the threat of "social anarchy," Buchanan turned toward the Prisoner's Dilemma and Hobbes's *Leviathan*. Buchanan concluded that "no one ever really consents to a social contract, and that status quo property rights cannot be metaphysically or historically justified. Hobbes' idea of submitting to the sovereign, regardless of the actual terms for each individual, on a voluntary basis invites the additional assumption that any specific terms will only be agreeable if backed by sufficient coercive power."[58]

Game Theory, RCT, and Cybernetics provided the intellectual foundations for most of the technological products and services we use today, ranging from smart watches to smart cities. These theories became universalizing approaches to complex problems that enfolded both humans and non-humans alike, including climate change.[59] Despite their origins in military strategy research, these theories offered the possibilities for a world in which disaster could be averted and human potential fulfilled. In Cybernetics, this would come through systems of prediction and control enabled by frictionless information transfer in a society infused with ubiquitous computation. In Game Theory, rational individuals in pursuit of their own self-interest could produce a socially beneficial equilibrium— or homeostasis—without compromise or the interference of disingenuous politicians.

By modeling everything—from people to nation-states—as information-processing machines, Cybernetics and Game Theory become a way to legitimize "enlightened self-interest" for social stability. It echoes the dynamic equilibrium of the homeostat. A flattened, hierarchy-free world in which everyone could be themselves and seek their own true authenticity was a world in which people did not need to compromise in the service of broader political goals or the collective good. The collective good would be an emergent property of the system itself. Not only should the body be approached as presenting limits to be overcome in the service of self-actualization but the body politic could not possibly have any value in this new networked society, if it could even be called a "society." The preceding statement may evoke the aspirations of projects such as the insurance platform I helped design as well as Sidewalk Toronto. Both are predicated on the enhancement of convenience through frictionless information exchange, thus allowing users to pursue their own self-interested goals while at the same time producing a homeostasis or equilibrium through constant adjustments facilitated by the cybernetic circulation of data through the system, whether that is electricity use or insurance premiums.

Markets as Information Processors: Cybernetics and Economics

The political-economic system at the heart of Western societies since the 1970s is predicated on seeing people and markets as information processors. This came about because of developments such as Cybernetics and Rational Choice, as well as because of the work of Friedrich Hayek. Writing in the 1940s, Hayek believed that individual freedom was the cornerstone of democracy, and that individual freedom was only commensurable with *laissez-faire* economics; therefore, the only valid form of economy that could preserve democracy was free-market capitalism.[60] Hayek argued that all social planning is by definition coercive because a society composed of individuals would never be able to agree completely on shared goals and common ends. Individualism was, in his view, forever pitted against collectivism. Cybernetics and RCT seemed to resolve this conundrum. People can be individuals, but in seeking their own enlightened self-interests, society will arrive at a homeostasis—an equilibrium that is acceptable for all. Hayek foreshadowed this technological resolution. He posited that within an unregulated market that had a free flow not only of capital but also of information and given access to the right information at the right time, humans would make rational self-interested decisions and these decisions would result in an equilibrium that benefitted everyone. "Hayek had proposed that 'the market' be conceptualized as a gigantic distributed information conveyance device."[61] He wrote:

> It is more than a metaphor to describe the price system as a kind of machinery for registering change, or a system of telecommunications which enables individual producers to watch merely the movement of a few pointers, as an engineer might the hands of a few dials.[62]

Understanding the market as the ultimate information processor positions Cybernetics as a perfect tool to manage the world under neoliberalism. The cybernetic ideal, just like the Hayekian market ideal, is a frictionless system of information exchange that is able to deliver instantaneous feedback to an individual in response to their decisions. The insurance platform I helped design invokes this cybernetic dream because the system is self-regulating. The user's risks are calculated in real-time based on data about an individual that uses demographic information, her Facebook profile, and an analysis of the user's answers to a short series of questions which infers characteristics about her based on the answers of others whom the system has determined to be "like" her.

If the market is an information processor, and Cybernetics construes everything as an information processing machine, then it follows that one could conceive of *everything* in terms of the market. This is how "the market" was able to rise to power as the predominant problem-solution framework for governance in society: this is the "neoliberal governmentality."

The Neoliberal Governmentality

Neoliberalism has achieved a certain cultural currency, becoming a shorthand pejorative, especially on Twitter, for things people hate about capitalism. But it's not *just* capitalism.

It represents an important break with traditional liberalism that emerges precisely because of the histories we've examined in this chapter. Neoliberalism can be difficult to describe because of its ubiquitous use, but Lambert Strether's pithy, though crude, definition might be helpful: (1) "because, markets!"; (2) "go die!"[63] Point (1) addresses the idea that anything and everything should be explainable in terms of the market, and point (2) addresses the ideas about biopower and biopolitics that are described above—not that you will be killed per se, but that life itself, and, therefore, mortality are regulated via market-based mechanisms. It also alludes to the callous treatment of individuals when they are seen through the lens of neoliberal governance. It sounds inhumane because neoliberalism is.

Neoliberalism is, however, not always as it seems. For example, despite the rhetoric of the "free market" determining the success or failure of a product or person, major corporations and the elite managerial class who oversee their operations are routinely rescued by mechanisms that operate outside the rules of the market. Neoliberalism is selective in its application of its own ideology. Because of the historical anti-political roots of neoliberalism in RCT, today's financial elite operate neither "inside nor outside of the law, neither applying rules nor breaking them."[64] Will Davies explains:

> When liberal disciplines, methodologies, laws and regulations are abandoned in favour of cybernetic systems of digits, machines and prices (including those of markets), what remains is a type of elite power which interprets what is on the screen, explains what it means, converts it into narrative, but possess no authorship or authority over it.[65]

Elite power is the cybernetic automaton, and neoliberalism is an "attempt to imagine and design a new form of elite power, which lacks the aspiration to act on behalf of the public."[66]

> The ideal neoliberal agent is a type of cyborg who is able to mediate constantly between capital at its fingertips and the quantitative data relayed by the market, without stopping to reflect consciously on what it is doing.[67]

When both the market and people are seen as information processors, the market becomes the lens through which all issues are seen. And because it is quantitative, this lens can be programmed into everything people use—the "smart" objects with which they live their lives.

Michel Foucault coined the term "governmentality" as a neologism combining "governmental" and "rationality." Governmentality is not about the specifics of a particular form of political economy, but about the way in which problems and solutions are framed and how "market," "population," and "state" are defined relative to those problem-solution frameworks.[68] In neoliberal governmentality, the dominant problem-solution framework is the market, which becomes the "common rationality." In neoliberalism, "freedom" is supposedly produced by turning everything into a "market," such as performance goals that supplanted bureaucratic structures in healthcare or public service. Ironically, this "freedom" produces new sorts of controls that reinforce the common rationality of the market and of the rational method itself. This irony is present in Buchanan's Public Choice Theory:

> To neoliberals like Buchanan, in any exchange transaction, each party has the incentive to cheat the other. Because individuals are incapable of forming binding agreements by consent, trade itself must be encased within a system of government-enforced sanctions to ensure that no one opts to cheat the other. This leads to a great irony: if we are to have a minimal state in which the unfettered market thrives, then that state needs to be able to broadly monitor and enforce that market … Solving the Prisoner's Dilemmas abounding throughout society requires pervasive inspections of individuals' activities.[69]

This echoes the ironies of the "smart city," which can only be "smart" through pervasive surveillance and data capture, undermining the "freedom" it supposedly confers on its inhabitants.

When the market functions as the "common rationality," individuals must become *entrepreneurs of themselves*. Built on the theory of humans as self-interested rational actors, neoliberalism infuses the process of framing problems and developing solutions to those problems. Solutions to both personal and social problems become about self-improvement that equates "efficiency" or "productivity" with morality. Any time such a problem-solution framing seems inadequate, more quantification and surveillance seems to be the solution: metrics that don't do a good job of incentivizing people to become more efficient beget more metrics. This irony is the result of a commitment to a particular problem-solution framework and a particular "rational" method. Instead of a society built on mutual support and aid, self-interest and the entrepreneurship of the self invariably produce better outcomes for society—or so we are told. The way we are told, however, is subtle. There are not Ayn Rand quotes on billboards, or wheat-pasted on every street corner like Soviet propaganda. Instead, the "common rationality," our neoliberal governmentality, is embedded within the products and services we use every day—exactly those products and services that purport to be convenience-enhancing, making us more productive or efficient, helping us save time. Neoliberal ideology as well as a whole history of ideas about people that originated with modeling nation-states on the brink of nuclear war is now embedded within consumer products and services for which we, UX designers, create the interfaces.

Even prior to the Coronavirus pandemic, the West had entered a political-economic era in which the question of whether or not it is still "in" neoliberalism or even capitalism is a legitimate one to pose, as McKenzie Wark has done.[70] It is my goal in this text not only to look at neoliberalism but to look in some ways beyond it. However, even if the United States or "the west" has entered a theocratic *cyberlibertarianism*[71] or something else entirely, vestiges of liberal political economy persist, and different populations in society are subjected to different rules and different market relations. What is clear, and what I hope this chapter has laid the groundwork to understand, is that UX design manifests governmentality by being constructed within specific problem-solution frameworks. Behind these frameworks are certain political-economic ideas about how "market," "population," and "state" should be defined and how they should interact.[72]

Conclusion: Foundations and Ramifications

This chapter has sought to weave together the historical and conceptual threads that gave rise to the idea that people can—and should—see themselves as computing and computable. This is the backdrop against which the adoption of this computable subjectivity, and all that it entails, should be seen. All of this background lays the groundwork for the descriptions of the core characteristics of the computable subject, its effects on people and society, and the role of UX in its adoption and propagation. As I will attempt to elucidate in the remainder of this book, *an understanding of what is actually relatively recent history is essential in seeing the broader trajectory of the ideological project in which today's UX/UI designers are implicated.* This ideological project is built on a particular kind of rationalism that has its roots in the science of Cybernetics and in RCT. Today's computational products and services and the interfaces we design for them come from a particular technoscientific milieu that comprises certain historical circumstances and material conditions. And we, user experience designers, are the inheritors of that legacy, producing apps and digital products and services that are built on particular assumptions about the human condition as well as a particular valuation of "convenience." We, as designers, are part of a project of instrumental rationality that seeks to equate method with morals, productivity or efficiency as "good." As I will examine in subsequent chapters, the apps and services that we design produce feedback loops that shape human behavior, reconfiguring everyday life, and creating the boundaries of possibility for everyone in society.

Notes

1. "The Zero Moment of Truth for Insurance Study," *Think with Google*, April 2011, https://www.thinkwithgoogle.com/consumer-insights/consumer-trends/zmot-insurance-study/.

    Customer loyalty in insurance is relatively low. In a 2010 Accenture survey, 43 percent of respondents planned to purchase their insurance online, possibly without interacting with a broker or agent at all. Interestingly, "35% percent of consumers say they are willing to pay more for insurance in return for personal advice." This statistic, combined with the increase of online insurance purchases creates an atmosphere in which emerging technologies, and specifically, algorithmic inference and recommendation, become attractive ways to create efficient systems of "personalization" without the high cost and possible inefficiencies of interpersonal interaction.

2. Accenture Research and Serge Callet, "Channeling Growth: Accenture 2010 Global Survey on Multi-Channel Insurance Distribution," 2010, https://insuranceblog.accenture.com/wp-content/uploads/2013/07/Channeling_Growth-Accenture_2010_Global_Survey_on_Multichannel_Insurance_Distribution.pdf.

3. John Cheney-Lippold, *We Are Data: Algorithms and the Making of Our Digital Selves* (New York: New York University Press, 2017).

4. Rachel Adams, "Michel Foucault: Biopolitics and Biopower," *Critical Legal Thinking*, May 10, 2017, https://criticallegalthinking.com/2017/05/10/michel-foucault-biopolitics-biopower/.

5. Ian Hacking, *The Taming of Chance* (Cambridge [England]; New York: Cambridge University Press, 1990).

6. See: https://humanscalemanual.com/store (available for purchase since 2018).

7. Gabriel Schaffzin, "Graphic Pain: A History if the Tools Mediating Pain Quantification," Doctoral Dissertation, University of California San Diego, 2020, https://escholarship.org/uc/item/4hj021v8.

8. Affectiva, "SDK on the Spot: Emotion-Enabled App Hopes to Make People Happier—One Smile at a Time," August 3, 2017, https://blog.affectiva.com/sdk-on-the-spot-emotion-enabled-app-promotes-more-smiling. And, George Moore, Leo Galway, and Mark Donnelly, "Remember to Smile: Design of a Mobile Affective Technology to Help Promote Individual Happiness through Smiling," in *Proceedings of the 11th EAI International Conference on Pervasive Computing Technologies for Healthcare* (PervasiveHealth '17: 11th EAI International Conference on Pervasive Computing Technologies for Healthcare, Barcelona Spain: ACM, 2017), 348–54, doi:10.1145/3154862.3154936.

9. Ian Hacking, "Making Up People," *London Review of Books* 28, no. 16 (August 17, 2006): 23–6.

10. Hacking, "Making Up People."

11. Hacking, "Making Up People."

12. Michel Foucault, *The History of Sexuality*, ed. Vintage Books (New York: Vintage Books, 1990).

13 John Cheney-Lippold, "A New Algorithmic Identity: Soft Biopolitics and the Modulation of Control," *Theory, Culture & Society* 28, no. 6 (November 2011): 164–81, doi:10.1177/0263276411424420.

14 Thomas F. Tierney, *The Value of Convenience: A Genealogy of Technical Culture*, SUNY Series in Science, Technology, and Society (Albany: State University of New York Press, 1993).

15 Tierney, *The Value of Convenience*.

16 Tierney, *The Value of Convenience*, 42.

17 Seven Dreamers, "Laundroid the World's 1st Laundry Folding Bot," accessed April 5, 2017, https://web.archive.org/web/20170302174929/https://laundroid.sevendreamers.com/en/.

18 *Blue Apron TV Commercial*, "A Better Way to Cook," 2015, http://www.ispot.tv/ad/7F05/blue-apron-a-better-way-to-cook.

19 SRT, "Blue Apron: Fixing the Food Delivery Supply Chain," *Harvard MBA Student Perspectives, Technology and Operations Management*, December 9, 2015, https://digital.hbs.edu/platform-rctom/submission/blue-apron-fixing-the-food-delivery-supply-chain/.

20 Joël van Bodegraven, "How Anticipatory Design Will Challenge Our Relationship with Technology," Technical Report (Association for the Advancement of Artificial Intelligence, April 2017), https://www.aaai.org/ocs/index.php/SSS/SSS17/paper/viewFile/15352/14582.

21 See: https://soylent.com/, which, as of 2021, bore the headline: "Let us take a few things off your plate," and "When there is no time, grab a Soylent and have a nutritious meal that is as easy as it is delicious!"

22 Fred Turner, *From Counterculture to Cyberculture: Stewart Brand, the Whole Earth Network, and the Rise of Digital Utopianism* (Chicago, IL: University of Chicago Press, 2008).

23 Barlow's assertion that there is no matter in cyberspace is echoed in the absurd rhetoric of the "cloud" today. Neither takes into account the very material nature of the internet—the super-cooled server rooms that use more energy than the towns in which they are located; the bauxite which is mined and then refined into aluminum out of which components for these servers are constructed; or the Coltan mined and refined, which is turned into capacitors that are used in nearly every stage of the production of the web.

24 John Perry Barlow, "A Declaration of the Independence of Cyberspace," *Electronic Frontier Foundation*, 1996 (January 20, 2016), https://www.eff.org/cyberspace-independence.

25 IBM, *IBM TV Commercial*, "Making the World Smarter Every Day," 2015, https://www.ispot.tv/ad/7mGT/ibm-making-the-world-smarter-every-day.

26 Matteo Pasquinelli, "Abnormal Encephalization in the Age of Machine Learning," *E-Flux Journal* 75 (September 2016), https://www.e-flux.com/journal/75/67133/abnormal-encephalization-in-the-age-of-machine-learning/.

27 Orit Halpern, *Beautiful Data: A History of Vision and Reason since 1945*, Experimental Futures (Durham: Duke University Press, 2014): 25.

28 Tiqqun, *The Cybernetic Hypothesis*, 2001, https://theanarchistlibrary.org/library/tiqqun-the-cybernetic-hypothesis.

29 Norbert Wiener, *Cybernetics or Control and Communication in the Animal and the Machine*, 2nd ed. (Cambridge, MA: MIT Press, 2007).

30 N. Katherine Hayles, *How We Became Posthuman: Virtual Bodies in Cybernetics, Literature, and Informatics* (Chicago, IL: University of Chicago Press, 1999).

31 Hayles, *How We Became Posthuman*, 65.

32 Peter Galison, "The Ontology of the Enemy: Norbert Wiener and the Cybernetic Vision," *Critical Inquiry* 21, no. 1 (1994): 228–66.

33 Fred Turner, *From Counterculture to Cyberculture: Stewart Brand, the Whole Earth Network, and the Rise of Digital Utopianism*, 1. paperback ed. (Chicago, IL: University of Chicago Press, 2008), 21.

34 Turner, *From Counterculture to Cyberculture*, 22.

35 Turner, *From Counterculture to Cyberculture*.

36 Hayles, *How We Became Posthuman*.

37 Paul N. Edwards, *The Closed World: Computers and the Politics of Discourse in Cold War America*, Inside Technology (Cambridge, MA: MIT, 1997).

38 Hayles, *How We Became Posthuman*, 7.

39 Sidewalk Labs, "Sidewalk Labs Vision Section of RFP Submission," 2017, https://storage.googleapis.com/sidewalk-labs-com-assets/Sidewalk_Labs_Vision_Sections_of_RFP_Submission_7ad06759b5/Sidewalk_Labs_Vision_Sections_of_RFP_Submission_7ad06759b5.pdf.

40 Evgeny Morozov, "Google's Plan to Revolutionise Cities Is a Takeover in All but Name," *The Observer*, October 21, 2017, sec. Technology, http://www.theguardian.com/technology/2017/oct/21/google-urban-cities-planning-data.

41 Sidewalk Labs, "Sidewalk Labs Vision Section of RFP Submission," 15.

42 Sidewalk Labs, "Sidewalk Labs Vision Section of RFP Submission," 17.

43 Sidewalk Labs, "Sidewalk Labs Vision Section of RFP Submission," 15.

44 Sidewalk Labs, "Sidewalk Labs Vision Section of RFP Submission," 17.

45 Sidewalk Labs, "Sidewalk Labs Vision Section of RFP Submission," 17.

46 Evgeny Morozov, "Google's Plan to Revolutionise Cities Is a Takeover in All but Name," *The Observer*, October 21, 2017, sec. Technology, http://www.theguardian.com/technology/2017/oct/21/google-urban-cities-planning-data.

47 Sidewalk Labs, "Sidewalk Labs Vision Section of RFP Submission," 72.

48 Brian J. Barth, "How a Band of Activists—and One Tech Billionaire—Beat Alphabet's 'Smart City,'" *OneZero*, August 13, 2020, https://onezero.medium.com/how-a-band-of-activists-and-one-tech-billionaire-beat-alphabets-smart-city-de19afb5d69e.

49 See, for example: Google's patent application that aspires to make literally everything you own connected to the internet. Mike Murphy, "Google Wants to Connect Everything You Own to the Internet," *Protocol—The People, Power and Politics of Tech*, February 7, 2021, https://www.protocol.com/google-patents-internet-everything.

50 S. M. Amadae, *Rationalizing Capitalist Democracy: The Cold War Origins of Rational Choice Liberalism* (Chicago: University of Chicago Press, 2003).

51 John Von Neumann and Oskar Morgenstern, *Theory of Games and Economic Behavior*, 60th anniversary ed, Princeton Classic Editions (Princeton, NJ; Woodstock: Princeton University Press, 2007).

52 Amadae, *Rationalizing Capitalist Democracy*, 6–7.

53 Amadae, *Rationalizing Capitalist Democracy*, 7.

54 Amadae, *Rationalizing Capitalist Democracy*, 11.

55 Amadae, *Rationalizing Capitalist Democracy*, 28.

56 Amadae, *Rationalizing Capitalist Democracy*.

57 Amadae, *Rationalizing Capitalist Democracy*, 78.

58 S. M. Amadae, *Prisoners of Reason: Game Theory and Neoliberal Political Economy* (New York, NY: Cambridge University Press, 2016): 178–9.

59 See the highly influential and cybernetic-methodological book about ecological collapse, *The Limits to Growth*: Donella H. Meadows and Club of Rome, eds., *The Limits to Growth: A Report for the Club of Rome's Project on the Predicament of Mankind* (New York: Universe Books, 1972). See also the important political-economic critique of the book, articulated most clearly in Johan Galtung, "'The Limits to Growth' and Class Politics," *Journal of Peace Research* 10, nos. 1–2 (1973): 101–14.

60 Amadae, *Rationalizing Capitalist Democracy*, 18.

61 Philip Mirowski, *Machine Dreams: Economics Becomes a Cyborg Science* (Cambridge; New York: Cambridge University Press, 2002), 371.

62 FA Hayek, "The Use of Knowledge in Society," *The American Economic Review* 35, no. 4 (1945): 527, cited in William Davies, "Elite Power under Advanced Neoliberalism," *Theory, Culture & Society* 34, nos. 5–6 (September 2017) 227–50, doi:10.1177/0263276417715072.

63 Lambert Strether, "Neo-Liberalism Expressed as Simple Rules," *Naked Capitalism*, March 17, 2014, https://www.nakedcapitalism.com/2014/03/neo-liberalism-expressed-simple-rules.html.

64 Davies, "Elite Power under Advanced Neoliberalism," 227–50, doi:10.1177/0263276417715072.

65 Davies, "Elite Power under Advanced Neoliberalism."

66 Davies, "Elite Power under Advanced Neoliberalism," 236.

67 Davies, "Elite Power under Advanced Neoliberalism," 238.

68 Majia Holmer Nadesan, *Governmentality, Biopower, and Everyday Life*, Routledge Studies in Social and Political Thought 57 (New York: Routledge, 2008), 1.

69 Amadae, *Prisoners of Reason,* 180.

70 McKenzie Wark, "The Sublime Language of My Century," *Public Seminar*, May 14, 2016, http://publicseminar.org.dream.website/2016/05/the-sublime-language-of-my-century/.

71 David Golumbia, "Cyberlibertarianism: The Extremist Foundations of 'Digital Freedom.'" Clemson University, September 5, 2013, http://www.uncomputing.org/wp-content/uploads/2014/02/cyberlibertarianism-extremist-foundations-sep2013.pdf.

72 Nadesan, *Governmentality, Biopower, and Everyday Life*.

2 DATA=WORLD

Introduction: Can You "See" Your Dream Data?

In mid-nineteenth-century London, a visionary (if misguided) doctor named Pawel Norway began a series of experiments intended to prove that, given the right physiological data, he could visualize the dreams of his patients. Dr. Norway's brief 1841 treatise, *Computable Transformation of Human Qualities to Those of a Visible Dream Memory*, (Figures 2.1 and 2.2) is an obscure but intriguing thesis on the possibility of inferring dream content from the behavior of a subject after he or she has awakened.

Developed over 100 years before the discovery of REM sleep, *Computable Transformation* argues that human bodies produce residual energy—a type of corpuscular molecule—that emits all day. He believed that this energy, including its velocity coming off the body and temperature, could be collected and measured. From this information, it would be possible to reconstruct prior dreams.

My colleagues, Dr. Gabi Schaffzin and Sofie Elana Hodara, and I came across Dr. Norway's *Computable Transformation* at an old book shop in Mangalia, Romania. We immediately saw a link between Dr. Norway's work and the contemporary Quantified Self movement, which both seek to infer certain macro-level understandings of the body and mind from micro-level data. Although Dr. Norway never fully implemented his theories, he produced a number of etchings, which sought to translate collected data points into visualizations.

Given ubiquitous access to sophisticated sensor technologies and the computing power to analyze the data gathered by those technologies, Gabi, Sofie, and I believed that we might be able to recreate Dr. Norway's experiments, producing an algorithmic exploration of the content of someone's dreams. In our first hybrid performance-exhibition (2016), entitled *The Dr. Pawel Norway Dream Machine*, we exhibited Dr. Norway's book and reproductions of the plates from the book, alongside a contemporary reimagining of his experimental process, utilizing a range of quantified-self (QS) technologies, including EEG monitors,

FIGURE 2.1 Dr. Pawel Norway's treatise: *Computable Transformations of Human Qualities to Those of a Visible Dream Memory*. Courtesy the Author.

FIGURE 2.2 An enlargement of one of the plates from Dr. Norway's book. Courtesy the author.

FitBits, temperature sensors, and muscle sensors. Attaching the sensors to volunteers from our audience, we engaged in "dream readings" that input the data captured by the various devices into an algorithmic system we developed to both visualize and sonify[1] this data. The output of our proprietary algorithmic system borrows from the quasi-representational nature of Dr. Norway's drawings, incorporating imagery and visuals produced and shared by the large swath of humanity living its lives on social-media outlets, resulting in an algorithmically generated multimedia tapestry (Figure 2.3 and 2.4).

The story of Dr. Pawel Norway and his book is—perhaps obviously, perhaps not—a fiction, an absurdist fable. This fable, when combined with the *Dream Machine* performance, which uses "real" data from the various technologies implemented therein (EEG data, FitBit data, etc.), underscores the connection between Dr. Norway's obvious pseudoscience and today's QS products and services. In both cases, inferences are made about an individual based on a translation of human experience into mathematical symbolization. Then, a secondary translation is executed, that which establishes visual (and, in our performance, sonic) equivalencies for the mathematical symbols gathered.

In both the first performance as well as in subsequent editions in Philadelphia in 2017, some audience members were incensed by what they saw as the audacity of quantifying and visualizing something so intimate as one's dream. Meanwhile, other audience members were frustrated that the dream reading hardware and software weren't more accurate. Both these quite visceral reactions suggest,

FIGURE 2.3 A subject viewing their algorithmically generated dream visualization. Courtesy the author.

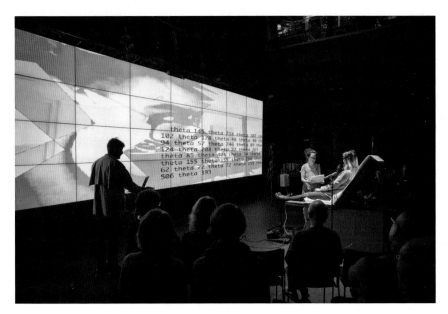

FIGURE 2.4 A subject viewing their algorithmically generated dream visualization. Courtesy the author.

in different ways, the manner in which an equivalence between "data" and the "world" has become an unquestioned ideology in society.

To suggest that Dr. Norway's data set was somehow imperfect, or that even today's most sophisticated consumer-grade biosensing technologies are not quite able to gather the exact data needed in order to understand the content of someone's dreams, is to miss the point. The belief that "if only our data were good enough" or "if only we had the perfect data set" is itself faulty. It is not about the data but about the belief that the data itself possesses an inherent equivalency to the world.

∗∗∗

At a conference for design educators, I witnessed evidence of the role of design in propagating the ideological commitment to the equivalence between "data" and "world." There, I attended a presentation by a designer about Actor-Network Theory and Deleuzian Assemblage theory.[2] Both of these theories are about how different things—whether people, computers, animals, the electrical grid, or potato chips[3]—all have agency in the occurrence of any given event. The presenter described how these theories can have empirical[4] significance attached to them because of the ability of sensor technologies to capture all of the data about a given event, arguing that data has "always been there." In other words, "data" and "world" are one in the same, and data itself precedes any kind of language to describe the world. These claims were supported with a variety of data visualizations which appeared scientific and sought to naturalize what should be a contentious proposition—that "data" equals "world."

This chapter is devoted to exploring the first of the three key characteristics of the computable subjectivity: the ideological commitment to the equivalence between "data" and "world," and the role of UX in the deep penetration of this idea into every aspect of society. It will describe some of the origins of this commitment as well as its consequences, and link these to the practice of UX design. In showing how the equivalence between "data" and "world" has become a pervasive feature of everyday life, I will demonstrate that the metaphors supporting this equivalence shape design practice, and, in doing so, they shape individual users' experiences of digital products and services.

Individuals who believe themselves and each other to be computable and computing must first come to accept, uncritically, that "data" and "world" are one and the same. But "data=world" is, first and foremost, predicated on a translation from the material, qualitative "world" to "data." Once this translation is complete, the findings from the "data" can be generalized back onto the "world." And, if executed properly, the thing doing the translating need no longer be considered part of the process. It is thus that the title of this chapter is also the fundamental translation and assumption that underpins all efforts to develop the various "smart" technologies, for which designers like me or my students create interfaces, user flows, and information architectures. We design the moments when users meet themselves, where they find, for example, their "SleepIQ score" to find out, purportedly, how "well" they are sleeping.[5]

In the cybernetic view, as we discussed in Chapter 1, everything from humans to anti-aircraft guns to societies can be viewed as a system. These systems are information processors that achieve equilibrium or stability, an *optimal* state, when the right information reaches the right part of the system at the right time in a form that can be understood by that part of the system. But through what mechanisms can such systems receive the "right" information at the "right" time? And what does this information *look* like, both for the computers embedded within these systems and for the people using them? These are questions of interaction and user-experience design. They are questions of graphic design, typography, symbolism, and iconography. But they are also questions of politics, economics, technology, science, and history.

If "data" and "world" are indeed equivalent, and if humans have some kind of sense experience of the world, then we, humans, must not only be *made of* data, or be computable, but be capable of *processing* that data, turning it into information, in other words, computing it. But, as in cybernetics, for data to move smoothly between different parts of a system, be they people, weapons, or thermostats, the data needs to become legible to all the parts of the system. The first step in this process is to figure out how to capture all this data. And in a world increasingly full of sophisticated sensor technology, it seems more and more likely that all of human and natural life will become datafied and captured. Only then can optimal information-exchange systems of the utmost efficiency be created. The promise of the capture and circulation of data about anything and everything is, for many corporations and organizations, a promise to make people "healthy" and cities "smart."[6] In the process, however, this promise will change the way people understand the world and themselves, it will shape how individuals believe what they believe, and it will change how they engage with one another.

There are many ways in which "data" has come to be equivalent to "world" and many ways in which this equivalence continues to be reinforced. In order to understand how individuals come to see themselves and each other as computable and computing, we must understand first how the equivalence between "data" and "world" is established and maintained. It is, however, not the goal of this chapter to give the reader a complete historical account of all the ways in which "data=world" has come to be an accepted proposition. This is impossible because such an assumption has its roots in a vast array of scientific and philosophical discourses over the last five centuries. Instead, this chapter is an attempt to trace the phenomenon of the adoption of "data=world" through a variety of discourses. It also hopes to demonstrate how user-experience design both assumes and helps construct this equivalence. When the equivalence between "data" and "world" is assumed and embedded in society, it allows for the computable subjectivity to take root.

As in the last chapter, I will try to highlight certain historical tendencies and features, and point the reader toward important primary and secondary literature such that, if the reader is so compelled to dig deeper, they have some places to start. In introducing connections and relationships across various fields, I hope to paint a new picture of how the kinds of things designers create are situated within historical, technical, scientific, and philosophical spaces. Decisions about where to draw the boundaries of what design is or isn't are even more arbitrary than we might imagine. This serves to introduce design into different discourses that might elicit a deeper understanding of its impact on individuals and society, particularly with regard to the design of interfaces.

Before moving on, however, it is important to recall another element of the histories we examined in the first chapter. A view that came to dominate economics and politics during the Cold War was that the "market" itself is a cybernetic system of information exchange, and, furthermore, that as a "cognitive" mechanism,[7] people and the market are not all that different. Since the price system can function as a universal equivalence, the market has assumed dominance as the framework within which solutions to all manner of problems must be conceived in order to be taken seriously. It is thus that the market is the dominant problem-solution framework of our era. As such, the relationship between "data" and "world" is also intimately connected to the way the "market" is the frame through which solutions to all manner of social and political problems are seen. It is important then, to understand that this ideological commitment to "data" equaling "world" serves to support the neoliberal governmentality and cannot be separated from it.

Data and World: An Origin Story

One important way that the idea of "data" equaling "world" came to permeate all aspects of society is through the influence of an idea called "operationalism" in psychology and the social sciences. In 1927, PW Bridgman published *The Logic of Modern Physics*, which introduced the term "operationalize" in order to describe and legitimate the translatability from "world" to "data" and back.[8] Bridgman writes, "we mean by any concept nothing more than a set of operations; the concept is synonymous with the corresponding set of operations."[9] This is the core of "operationalism," which "is based on the intuition that we do not know the meaning of a concept unless we have a method of measurement for it."[10] Operationalism is simultaneously a dogmatic commitment method as well as to measurement. The combination of these commitments might sound familiar: it is built into today's popular data-infused parlance as "metrics" or "analytics." Aronowitz and Ausch explain Bridgman's work in the context of the social sciences:

> Are "data" and a "world" the same thing? … One of the central claims of positivism is that the translation of the world, and all the complexity and empirical richness that implies, into data is a valid operation. PW Bridgman's *Logic of Modern Physics* (1927) introduced the term "operationalize" to the social sciences to describe this process. This translation permits the data to be regarded as "representing" the world so that a researcher's findings can then be easily "generalized" back to the world. Sometimes a researcher can ruin this translation, which is why criteria for "validity" become imperative. When properly accomplished, however, this translation need no longer be considered part of the process.[11]

The significance of Bridgman's work is twofold: (1) that anything meaningful must also be measurable; and, (2) that the relationship between the thing being measured and the measurement, when properly executed, was to be understood as one of total and complete equivalence. The influence of this simple idea was massive. George Rosenwald, Professor Emeritus of Psychology at the University of Michigan, emphasized Bridgman's role in the history of science, specifically in the field of psychology: "Bridgman's operationalist philosophy could hardly have shaped the course of psychological research more thoroughly or enduringly."[12]

Strangely, however, Bridgman's idea of operationalism actually emerges from the *nuances* of measurement in modern science. In fact, *The Logic of Modern Physics* was, in many ways, a response to and reexamining of physics in light of Einstein's special relativity.[13] He suggests that Einstein's work "compels a critique of much more than the concepts of space and time is made increasingly evident by all the new facts being discovered in the quantum realm."[14] In Bridgman's theory, a "concept" is something that can be defined by a series of operations which result in definite quantities. However, in Bridgman's view, concepts were not intended to be generalizable and did not extend beyond the situations in which they were originally defined.[15] Basically, Bridgman's contention was that different contexts required different kinds of measurements and different assumptions or conditions for those measurements. Each of these sets of operations then corresponds with a different concept, not units of measurement but literally ideas such as "length" or "distance" itself. Bridgman uses the idea of "length" as one primary case study.

"The space of astronomy is not a physical space of meter sticks, but is a space of light waves."[16] Indeed, measuring the distance between planets or between planets and their moons requires an inference about the time it takes light to go a given distance and return to its point of origin—an idea itself which is predicated on the notion that the beam of light would come back in the first place. Thus, Bridgman wrote: "In principle the operations by which length is measured should be uniquely specified. If we have more than one set of operations, we have more than one concept, and strictly there should be a separate name to correspond to each different set of operations."[17] Different kinds of measurements require different kinds of inferences and assumptions to be made, which are, often times, based on other measurements.

Despite his assertion that operations are contextual and different sets of operations correspond with fundamentally different concepts, such as different terms to describe "length." Bridgman showed a tendency to equate measurement operations with meaning. This implies that, for him, meaning was produced numerically. "If a specific question has meaning, it must be possible to find operations by which an answer may be given to it."[18]

Aronowitz and Ausch suggest, if only by association,[19] that Bridgman's work belongs within the history of the influential movement known as Logical Positivism or Logical Empiricism. Although some from the Logical Positivist movement briefly took up the banner of what they perceived as Bridgman's *operationalism,* the two are not synonymous. Bridgman was actually concerned with the way his ideas came to be known as a much broader philosophy of "operationalism." It had become something quite other than what he intended. At a conference, he once said:

> As I listened to the papers I felt that I have only a historical connection with this thing called "operationalism" … I have created a Frankenstein, which has certainly got away from me. I abhor the word operationalism … which seems to imply a dogma, or at least a thesis of some kind. This thing I have envisaged is too simple to be dignified by so pretentious a name; rather, it is an attitude or point of view generated by continued practice of operational analysis.[20]

Bridgman was also an individualist and believed that science was meant to be performed by the scientist, who should not rely on others' measurements or operations. Empiricism was truly a matter of one's *own* observation, and not that of others.[21] And yet, the influence of the "operation" and operationalism is long-lasting—and surprisingly so, especially in the human sciences and social sciences. Rosenwald's "Why Operationalism Doesn't Go Away" is most instructive for those of us who design or study consumer-grade computational products and services that aim to predict and control the vagaries of everyday life.

Specifically within the context of psychological research on cognitive dissonance, Rosenwald writes, "[T]he central questions which launched this research programme and which remain largely unanswered were concerned with the dynamics of cognition, and not with the sorts of variables which have inadvertently arisen in the evaluation of experimental designs."[22] Instead, to draw their conclusions, social psychologists have relied on a body of pre-theoretical knowledge, but this knowledge is not acceptable in what has attempted to become a laboratory science. In other words, Rosenwald argues, ironically, the result of a commitment to operationalism in the social sciences is an increase in technical knowledge without any increase in understanding of real life. "In brief, *because we wish urgently to gain mastery over pressing human perplexity, we are untiring in the pursuit of adequate operationalizations, and because we are relatively sophisticated about these perplexities, we tend to reject most of the attempted solutions as inadequate*" (emphasis his).[23] This is why there's never enough data, and why the answer to inaccuracy always seems to be the capture of additional data.

Computational Instrumentation: Templates and Translations

Through the distortion of Bridgman's ideas, the act of measurement became predominant, but operationalism's influence could not have been so massive without the technological developments which accompanied it. The permeating of everyday life by the ideas behind "operationalism"—namely that meaning and measurement are one and the same—is enabled by two important developments: (1) that everything becomes measurable; and, (2) that which does the measuring disappears. These developments have their origins in the sciences, in which computation has been used to help scientists observe processes that cannot be seen with the naked eye. This extension of empirical observation is called "instrumentation," and computational instruments have fundamentally changed what it means to "observe" the world. In his 2004 book, *Extending Ourselves*, Paul Humphreys argues that computational "instruments"—pieces of equipment that use computers to allow scientists to observe what would not be observable to the naked eye—occupy a strange space between "theoretical" and "empirical" science. These instruments change what might be considered observable and unobservable phenomena.[24]

In scientific instrumentation, Humphreys writes, the majority of computation is used for calculation. Calculation operates by the use of what he calls "templates," by which he means *mathematical equations that participate in the development of models.* These models then help scientists learn about the world. Templates are not necessarily mathematical expressions of scientific theories (though they *can* be, e.g., *F=mA*). Instead, templates are typically not limited to use within a given scientific field. These generalized templates frequently build on one another in order to produce a (computational) instrument itself, which might then be utilized within a particular scientific field. It is important to be clear that Humphreys is specifically addressing scientific practice, especially in research settings. And yet, the rhetoric of QS consumer products and services like FitBit is one of scientism. And it is through this rhetoric that we see ourselves in QS products and services. It is a rhetoric that suggests the measurements they take are not only accurate and neutral, but *scientific.*

Humphreys details the way computational instruments bridge rationalism and empiricism, and it is this bridging that enables the notion that "data=world" to permeate every aspect of society. For those readers who, like me, are designers and unfamiliar with the history of scientific epistemological debates, I think the *Stanford Encyclopedia of Philosophy* does a good job of introducing the difference between the two: "The dispute between rationalism and empiricism concerns the extent to which we are dependent upon sense experience in our effort to gain knowledge. Rationalists claim that there are significant ways in which our concepts and knowledge are gained independently of sense experience. Empiricists claim that sense experience is the ultimate source of all our concepts and knowledge."[25] This conversation around the nature of knowledge is not new, and the history of computing, while connected in different ways to both empiricism and rationalism, bears the indelible marks of a particular brand of rationalism that emerges from Descartes and Leibniz.[26] Indeed, the computer, as some have argued, was "Leibniz's Dream,"[27] a system that would eliminate ambiguity and subject everything to precise calculation. All the way back in 1704, Leibniz, the rationalist, seems to predict the issues that P.W. Bridgman, the individualist empiricist, was to encounter:

> The senses, although they are necessary for all our actual knowledge, are not sufficient to give us the whole of it, since the senses never give anything but instances, that is to say particular or individual truths. Now all the instances which confirm a general truth, however numerous they may be, are not sufficient to establish the universal necessity of this same truth, for it does not follow that what happened before will happen in the same way again. … From which it appears that necessary truths, such as we find in pure mathematics, and particularly in arithmetic and geometry, must have principles whose proof does not depend on instances, nor consequently on the testimony of the senses, although without the senses it would never have occurred to us to think of them.[28]

What is even more amazing, for those of us who are designers, is that the modern computer's history is very much a history of *two* of Leibniz's ideas: "a *lingua characteristica* (a perfect symbolism expressing truths) as well as his idea of *a calculus ratiocinator* (a mechanical means of dealing with the symbolism, by which truth could be decided or deduced)."[29] If you happen to be a designer, please read this quote again.

Leibniz was a *designer*. And his dream was a completely computable objective truth.

Computational Instruments: The MEMS-3 Accelerometer and the FitBit

Because empiricism and rationalism are bridged through computation, the rationalist tendencies of computation, namely its basis in abstractions of advanced mathematics, shape the kind of things people think they can observe. This is true for scientific instruments, but it is also true of consumer technologies. Unlike the sciences however, users are not domain experts in the kinds of things they are attempting to observe through consumer-grade computational instruments. These users are, in some ways, merely subject to the models built by those who might be, but are not even necessarily, domain experts in physiology or psychology.

The bridging of rationalism and empiricism requires computational instruments to produce a series of what I will call "translations" that mediate between the abstractions of rationalism and the observable world of empiricism. Illustrative of these translations, which produce an equivalence between "data" and "world," is the MEMS-3 accelerometer, a computational instrument to make movement "observable." It is this kind of technology, along with other similar technologies, with which UX designers often work without even knowing it.

The MEMS-3 accelerometer was one of the sensors inside early models of the FitBit activity monitor, a wearable device that tracked steps and heart rate. The accelerometer was used to measure the acceleration, in all three directions (horizontal, vertical, and depth), of a user's arm. Used in both scientific applications *and* consumer-grade applications, it comes in a variety of tolerances designed for different uses, such as cars, buildings, and medical devices. In 2017, FitBit's website told visitors that the Fitbit Alta HR contained a MEMS-3 accelerometer, which, FitBit said, "tracks motion patterns."[30] In a "help" article on the FitBit website was a section, entitled "How does my FitBit device count steps?" This is a good place to begin a simple analysis of the relationship between "data" and "world," even when "world" might be considered to be quantitative.

Fitbit devices use a 3-axis accelerometer to understand your motions. An accelerometer is a device that turns movement (acceleration) into digital measurements (data) when attached to the body. By analyzing acceleration data, our devices provide detailed information about frequency, duration, intensity, and patterns of movement to determine your steps taken, distance traveled, calories burned, and sleep quality. The 3-axis implementation allows the accelerometer to measure your motion in any way that you move, making its activity measurements more precise than older, single-axis pedometers.

Fitbit devices have a finely tuned algorithm for step counting. The algorithm is designed to look for motion patterns that are most indicative of people walking. The algorithm determines whether a motion's size is large enough by setting a threshold. If the motion and its subsequent acceleration measurement meet the threshold, the motion will be counted as a step. If the threshold is not met, the motion won't be counted as a step.

Other factors can create enough acceleration to meet our threshold and cause some over counting of steps, such as riding on a bumpy road. Our engineers have worked diligently on your tracker's algorithms to make sure that it does not pick up false steps or activity recordings while in a car. Unless you are driving in a car with a stiff transmission or on back country roads, your tracker should not give you credit for any work that you don't do.[31]

At the time this "help" article was posted, FitBit used, to the best of my knowledge, a combination of two "femto" MEMS-3 accelerometers.[32] The "femto" refers to the "femtometer," which is a very tiny unit of length. The accelerometer used the femtometer as a measure of the movement of a small mass inside the accelerometer. This mass is called the "proof mass." An "optomechanical" accelerometer, such as early "femto" accelerometers (ca. 2012),[33] works by sending a laser through an "optical cavity" between two tiny rails, one of which is attached to the "proof mass." As the proof mass moves, the size of the gap between the rails changes. This causes tiny deformations in the reflection of the laser, which in turn changes the intensity of the laser as it bounces back and forth. These changes are detected by the sensor as vibrations, which are likely measured in kHz. Using a *template*—in the parlance of Humphreys—the vibration measurements are converted into voltage. The voltage is converted into binary, using another template, and it is then sent out of the accelerometer as digital signals using either the SPI or I2C protocols. In both protocols, particular patterns of ones and zeros signify particular measurements or commands to the microcontroller to which the accelerometer is connected.

The FitBit microcontroller then converted the digital output from the accelerometer, using another template, into the kinds of measurements sent by its application programming interface (API). These measurements, at least for developers of applications for things like the FitBit watch OS, included numerical data in meters per second squared.[34] These measurements of acceleration and vibration were then put through yet another template or series of templates. It is difficult to tell, because in this case, those templates are FitBit's proprietary "finely-turned" algorithm in order to, at long last, output the counting of steps. The likelihood is that FitBit's algorithm compared the input data to sample input data based on a model of how "normal" people, on average, take steps. In other words, at least four different templates are combined to take something as simple as a "step" and allow the FitBit device itself to "count" it as a step. Even then, it may not count as a step depending on how the input data matches up to the model being used.

FitBit's translation from "world" to "data" is still one of, generally speaking, counting. Counting steps is quantitative, and we are not yet discussing the translation of qualitative phenomena into quantitative measures. So even though there are a number of translations needed to take one kind of counting—the number of steps you take—and turn it into an accurate digital output that is expressed through an interface in a variety of formats, it is a quantity-to-quantity relationship.

Such processes become even more abstracted when we consider something like the Sleep Number smart mattress' SleepIQ number or the personalized evaluative metrics produced by Eight, another smart mattress company. The "advanced biometric sensors" in the Sleep Number smart mattress as well as in the Eight mattress are "proprietary," or so the companies claim. It is likely that there are some variations of piezoelectric sensors and/or accelerometers, which themselves can be piezoelectric instead of optomechanical, to detect vibrations from breathing and tossing/turning (which are different types of vibrations, one being a number of orders of magnitude larger than the other). The Sleep Number smart mattress has used "ballistocardiography," which measures the vibration of the body in response to the ejection of blood into the large vessels of the heart with each heartbeat.[35]

Translations of data through various *templates*—similar to those of the accelerometer and microcontroller of a FitBit—are only part of the process of developing a "model" of "good" sleep, which allows companies to give a user a "sleep score." Computational models, whether those are models of how humans walk or how they sleep, have assumptions about people embedded within them. These assumptions are often founded on averages and standard deviations, so in order to give a user a sleep "score," a numerical definition of "good" sleep is needed, which is predicated on assumptions about how humans sleep. In this example, "data" only becomes to equal "world" not merely when filtered through an incredible number of templates and transformations, but also when it is situated within an array of assumptions about the relationship between people, the vibrational data they produce when sleeping, and the substantive quality of their individual sleep itself.

Now let us return to the idea of the relationship between "data" and "world." My suggestion that this relationship has emerged as an equivalence and not a mediated translation is not, at least right now, a normative judgment. The translation from "world" to "data" that then enables one to make assertions about the world and the *templates* that help produce the models that make this translation have led to innumerable scientific discoveries and technical innovations. These discoveries and innovations have changed the character of everyday life, mostly for the better. However, the mechanisms of translation—the templates that construct the models, the assumptions that underpin the technologies, and the technological innovations themselves, such as the "femto"-class MEMS-3 accelerometer—are made to disappear, particularly through the interface, and this disappearance has profound consequences.

How Computational Instruments Disappear

The disappearance of computational instruments such as the MEMS-3 accelerometer suggests that no translation between "world" and "data" has ever taken place at all, and indeed, that data *is* the world. This has enormous consequences for the way people understand computation itself (the very thing *doing* the translating). Designers create interfaces for the technologies that capture data,[36] so, in a strange way the translation from "world" to "data" must be visible. Yet the mechanism of capturing data also must disappear so that the user may interact with the interface as easily and conveniently as possible and, at the same time, make it seem as though data and world are equivalent once the data is captured. *This is the paradoxical situation into which all UX designers are placed today.* How does the mechanism of translation disappear if it must be used? When it does, how does this work, and what does it mean? How do the various mechanisms— from the hardware to the algorithms embedded within something like a FitBit, which translate "world" (someone's steps) into the "data" that gets displayed in an interface (the accounting of those steps, the calories burned through the taking of those steps, etc.)—disappear, such that "data" and "world" are perceived as one and the same? This disappearance happens through two primary means: (1) through a combination of "gray media" and "black boxes"; and, (2) through a naturalization produced by the interface itself.

Grey Media and Black Boxes: Obscuring the Disappearance

Matthew Fuller and Andrew Goffey's "grey media" includes enterprise-level group work software, company intranet platforms, database systems, and other managerial and organizational tools. Grey media possess, they say, a "sleek affectation to affectlessness."[37] Grey media *recede into the background of existence*, and this is how they do their work. They don't call attention to themselves. This greyness is central to their *design*. Even the idea of greyness itself denotes a color and by proxy a color *decision*, or maybe more appropriately, *indecision*.

The designers of the interfaces for these tools, whether they themselves identify as "interface designers" or not, in some way or another made it so. The designers made them grey. Like a moderately well-fitting—not tight, but not enormously baggy—grey suit, grey media invite us to take them seriously, or even more dangerously, they go unnoticed. The representations of people and various forms of qualitative and quantitative information are "facts," represented using approaches dictated by the experts who have taught us about "envisioning information" or the "visual display of quantitative information."[38] Indeed, the approach to information design championed by Edward Tufte and his acolytes is intentionally *grey*, and as designers, we are often told that this is the "correct" approach to information design, such that we communicate with as little editorial influence as possible. In their greyness, their mundane and functional appearance, grey media connote an authoritative neutrality.

Fuller and Goffey use the term "grey" to connote both this boring, matter-of-factness as well as a blending of "black box" and "transparent." In their grayness, gray media are neither black boxes in the sense that users are not kept from seeing them or some of their functionality, nor are they fully knowable or transparent. They are developed by corporations with intellectual property considerations and not subject to any kind of mandatory disclosure, but they often operate as a "middleman" between data input and end user functionality.

The FitBit interface, with its bright colors and fun animations, would not necessarily be considered "grey media." But, the FitBit's MEMS-3 Accelerometer itself and the various interpretive algorithms and mechanisms through which it translates "world" into "data" might be. Through its technical documentation, which indeed possesses that "sleek affectation to affectlessness," the ST Microelectronics MEMS-3 "femto" Accelerometer is, indeed, very gray.[39] Replete with numerous dry, black-and-white diagrams, the documentation is nearly inscrutable to the layperson, including designers who might even be competent programmers but not electrical engineers.

The ST Microelectronics MEMS-3 "femto" Accelerometer and its incorporation into the hardware and software of the FitBit create yet another layer of opacity that obfuscates its multi-step translation of "world" into "data." Recall that "Fitbit devices have a finely-tuned algorithm for step counting." FitBit doesn't tell its users what this algorithm is. Its patent applications merely explain some general functionality but have no specifics regarding the code, algorithms, or equations themselves. This "finely-tuned" algorithm, along with the process of fine-tuning, is part of FitBit's intellectual property and it is what gave the company a competitive advantage within the marketplace. It is a secret protected by law. Such systems are classified by Frank Pasquale as "black boxes," which possess, in his conception, a dual character: they are at once recording devices *and* systems whose inner workings are mysterious, with our understandings of them limited to observable inputs and outputs. Pasquale's book, *The Black Box Society*, addresses the dissonance between the legal protections afforded commercial entities which seek to keep certain parts of their businesses secret, and the decreasing spaces of protected privacy for persons in everyday life.[40]

The motivation for the construction and maintenance of black boxes like FitBit's algorithms is, not surprisingly, the market. As Nick Srnicek shows in his book

Platform Capitalism, "in the twenty-first century advanced capitalism came to be centered upon extracting and using a particular kind of raw material: data."[41] It's not relevant in this situation whether the data is "correct" or "accurate"—the data must only exist as such relative to the system in which the data are being recorded. It does not matter, for example, whether a user *is actually the same* as the version of that user that exists in Amazon's database as long as they continue to purchase the products that Amazon recommends to them. In some sense, the competition within today's platform capitalism is a competition over how much data can be captured and how that data can be used. Thus, the protections for maintaining trade secrets like algorithms become exceedingly important to platform capitalist firms such as Amazon or Uber, but also to other kinds of firms such as FitBit (as of January 2021, owned by Google[42]) or Sleep Number.

This is not to say that the code of something like FitBit's "finely-tuned" algorithms should be completely available for scrutiny. No layperson could understand it. It is instead to say that its nature as both gray media and black box produces a disappearance of the mechanisms that translate "world" into "data." This disappearance—*enacted at the interface*—is what enables the ideological commitment of "data" being equal to "world" to take hold.

Naturalization of a False Equivalence

The French philosopher and cultural theorist Roland Barthes[43] wrote that ideologies are naturalized when meanings are seen as denotative, instead of socially constructed based on a dominant cultural framework that has at its core a hegemonic ideology in which the particular meaning for an image or word emerges. In practice, this means that in every society there are dominant (hegemonic) ideas that represent a commitment to a specific way of thinking or being in the world. These ideas influence how words and images acquire their meaning, such that even the direct meaning of something—the *denotative* meaning, as opposed to the *connotative* meaning—is shaped by those dominant ideas. *Myth* is the system by which ideologies come to shape the things we accept as natural or normal. One of the most profound insights of Barthes's work is that *myth transforms history (something contentious and contingent) into nature (fact).*

The equivalence between "data" and "world" is *naturalized through UX*, in products and services such as FitBit, the Sleep Number Smart Mattress, Nest Thermostat, etc. These products and services establish an equivalence between "data" and "world" by design that signifies, in some way or another, a scientific legitimacy. Indeed, it is hard to argue with statements like Edward Tufte's dictum that "evidence is evidence," and when design is predicated on such absurdities, it naturalizes the formation of the evidence it presents. "Data=World" is naturalized when the paradox of computing being both the mode of data capture and the mechanism of translation between data and world is resolved—*by the UX designer.*

The most intuitive examples of such naturalization are the charts and graphs on every interface for "smart" products and services, such as smart mattresses, thermostats, and washers and dryers. But particularly fascinating here are sleep tracking applications and services, which produce and visualize a variety of metrics by which you can track your sleep patterns. Also of interest are emotion tracking wearables and meditation apps. These types of tools make multiple translations that equate "data" with "world." They suggest to a user that qualitative phenomena are themselves actually quantitative in nature, and, furthermore, that their behaviors or mental states can be "explained via computational processes" or are themselves computational. They do this, in part, through the interface.

In 2003, Jessica Helfand and William Drenttel critiqued the obsession of graphic design with science, writing: "It is as if science offers a kind of credibility that design itself lacks," and the authority conferred upon something via information design is "a false authority, particularly because we buy into the form so unquestioningly."[44] It is, they write, "modernism run amok."[45] Things that look like science become a way to show that "data" and "world" are equal. By designing things that *look* scientific, appealing to a prevailing notion of the hard sciences as ideologically neutral, designers make the mechanism of translation between "data" and "world" disappear, while at the same time offering users a way to input data and quickly and easily see the results.

FIGURE 2.5 An image of the mobile interface for the Feel® app. © 2022 Feel Therapeutics Inc., all rights reserved.

The *Feel* bracelet and its companion app offer an interesting example of this very phenomenon. Made by Sentio Solutions (now Feel Therapeutics), a company founded in 2015, Feel was launched for preorder sometime during 2017, at which time the company's website claimed that *Feel* was the "World's First Emotion Sensor & Mental Health Advisor." A 2018 version of the company's website claimed that *Feel* "recognizes and tracks your emotions, while providing real-time coaching to help you achieve your mental well-being goals." The website went on to promote the product's "Continuous Monitoring & Real-time Coaching and Intervention." It stated: "Feel wristband monitors a variety of physiological signals throughout the day to recognize changes in your emotions."[46]

The copy on the website continued: "*Feel* recognizes your emotions throughout the day," enabling users to "discover key emotional patterns."[47] The app (Figures 2.5 and 2.6) also included: "Real-time coaching and suggestions based on Cognitive Behavioral Therapy (CBT)"[48] and "Smartphone notifications provide a gentle push in the right direction and keep you on track towards meeting emotional well-being goals."

At the time of its launch for pre-order, *Feel*'s visuals were dominated by today's ubiquitous, friendly, quasi-minimalism and flat user interface design. These design decisions connoted a comfortable utility—not austere but not gaudy or unnecessary. Indeed, for an optimized life, Feel considered itself *essential*. Over the course of a year, however, *Feel*'s website, and interface, changed. What we can infer, regardless, is that early adopters would have seen some kind of display of changes in emotion over time, as a fever-chart and/or a series of facial expressions reminiscent of the famous Wong-Baker scale. Since then, its interfaces have turned more toward what might be perceived as "qualitative" data. And yet, by 2021, its website claimed to be "decoding mental health," as if mental health is a computational process that is full of data, both categorical and quantitative—sets of emotional categories and ranges of intensities for those categories (0–10).

In 2018, Upmood,[49] a Hong-Kong-based startup, entered the mood-sensing wearables market at a much lower price point than its competitors. Its interface design when it launched was more fun and childlike, with characters and "stickers" incorporated into the app that pairs with the device. "Upmood," its promotional collateral claimed, "gives an insight on your heart rate, stress level, vitality levels, and emotion to recognize oneself, characters, and feelings to properly manage your emotions." What does "vitality levels" even mean? In addition to the lower price point, Upmood tried to differentiate itself through its built-in social functionality. "Upmood pushes the limits of communication by taking advantage of genuine emotion to reconnect lost connections and spark real conversations by seeing others in their perspective." Upmood's app still utilized the semiotic tactic of data visualization in order to help users see patterns in their moods, but the primary visual experience was driven by cute illustrations, engagement with other users' profiles, and simple line-drawings of facial expressions that indicate various moods.

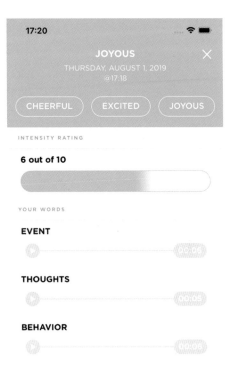

FIGURE 2.6 An image of the mobile interface for the Feel® app. © 2022 Feel Therapeutics Inc., all rights reserved.

The visual experience of the various mood-tracking products and apps varies quite a bit. There are two key tendencies in their visual and promotional rhetoric that I think tie them together:

1 Because, science!
2 Friendly health-care provisioning for the neoliberal self.

Certain aspects of both *Feel* and *Upmood* suggest that they are scientific in nature, even though their interfaces are not necessarily dominated by complex data visualizations. Their appeals to "science" come in various forms, sometimes overtly through copywriting or design, and sometimes more subtly. In 2018, Feel's website had a section called "science." When a user clicked it, they were taken to a page at the top of which a headline read "*Feel* the science." Meanwhile, Upmood, somewhat hilariously, claimed: "Through the PPG Sensor, we can collect biodata from your heart rate and contractions using only one wrist for an unprecedented level of accuracy."[50]

We can also *feel* the science through the interface, even without sophisticated charts and graphs. The sans-serif typography and flat UI are indeed "modernism run amok," echoing the era of high modernism in design that was full of hope for technological progress and universal design solutions. The simplicity, friendliness, even playfulness of the interfaces operates a level of meaning above the basic ideology that underpins it. History and assumptions are purified by the interface. The signifiers of numerical representation, in kHz, voltage, and types of quantities, and what they signify, vibrations or accelerations, are wiped away, becoming fact. They become the *form* of "steps" or "heart rate" which signify the *concepts* of "fitness" or "mood" which, together, produce the *signification* that in order to become a healthy, happy, productive, *optimized* human being, you must accept the equivalence between "data" and "world."

This needs to be naturalized in order for the totalizing cybernetic project of neoliberal governmentality to function properly. Recall that complete prediction and control is predicated on frictionless information exchange and the assumptions about motivations and behaviors of people as self-interested automatons. As Paul Edwards suggests: "Cognitive theories, like computer technology, were first created to assist in mechanizing military tasks previously performed by human beings ... Effective human-machine integration required that people and machines be comprehended in similar terms, so that human-machine systems could be engineered to maximize the performance of both kinds of components."[51]

In order for individuals to believe that they *need* to capture their entire lives as "data," they must believe that "data" is "real." This enables users to *aspire* to the model of themselves on which various technologies are based: they will *want* to *become* the black boxes, only defined by behaviors, self-interested, and non-cooperative except for when it benefits them. And even if users recognize that computation is somehow biased, they must believe that eventually, with the right data, the bias will be eradicated and the perfectly frictionless systems of cybernetic information transfer will be realized. Once that happens, the market as the dominant problem-solution framework will be the only rational system for solving societal and personal problems. All of this hinges on the naturalization of the equivalence between "data" and "world."

Naturalization through Habit

The formation of habits with computational products is another way in which the ideological commitment to the equivalence between "data" and "world" is naturalized. In everyday discourse, habit tends to be seen merely as the automation of behavior, which leads to a lack of freedom and awareness.[52] Habits, however, are complex and possess an intrinsically dual character. Habits enable us to be creative beings. Elizabeth Grosz writes:

> The alarm summons up a chain of actions: opening our eyes, turning off the alarm, getting out of bed, putting on slippers, and beginning the day. It is only because we undertake these activities in a state of half-consciousness that we have the energy and interest to undertake less routinized actions, to elaborate relatively free acts.[53]

Clare Carlisle, meanwhile, suggests that understanding the body itself as a habit is to see that its function is not predicated on it being the "object of attention."[54] Carlisle pairs this with the assertion that the body—as a habit—contains "traces of previous actions," sort of like muscle memory. Habits produce specific types of subjectivity that enable someone to focus on other acts,[55] but the subjectivity that becomes embedded within habit is not immune to influence—it does not spontaneously arise.

Through habitual interaction with computational products and services that naturalize, via the interface, the equivalence between "data" and "world," this ideological commitment to makes its way into users' habits, and their very bodies, such that they do not even consider it. Indeed, everyday discourse and, thus, everyday habits are penetrated by the vocabularies of those who *design* the products, services, architectures, and infrastructures of everyday life—the tools with which people unite in order to act.[56] It is important for those of us who are designers to remember that *we* cause the disappearance of the mechanisms that translate "world" to "data" and then equate that "data" with "world." We are responsible for the resulting habits that users form with the devices that have been built with this ideological commitment at its core.

Conclusion: The Great Inversion, or, Operationalism's Legacy

While the story of the wacky nineteenth-century physician, Dr. Pawel Norway and his attempts to visualize dreams by gathering biometric data is a fable, attempts to visualize the content of individuals' dreams are alive and well today. Several neuroimaging research centers, including the Gallant Lab at UC-Berkeley, have begun to investigate whether it is possible to find patterns of brain activity that correspond to the viewing of particular images or sequences of images. According to a 2011 press release from UC-Berkeley[57] (which is worth quoting at length here):

> [Subjects] watched two separate sets of Hollywood movie trailers, while fMRI was used to measure blood flow through the visual cortex, the part of the brain

that processes visual information. On the computer, the brain was divided into small, three-dimensional cubes known as volumetric pixels, or "voxels."

"We built a model for each voxel that describes how shape and motion information in the movie is mapped into brain activity," Nishimoto said.

The brain activity recorded while subjects viewed the first set of clips was fed into a computer program that learned, second by second, to associate visual patterns in the movie with the corresponding brain activity. Brain activity evoked by the second set of clips was used to test the movie reconstruction algorithm. This was done by feeding 18 million seconds of random YouTube videos into the computer program so that it could predict the brain activity that each film clip would most likely evoke in each subject.

Finally, the 100 clips that the computer program decided were most similar to the clip that the subject had probably seen were merged to produce a blurry yet continuous reconstruction of the original movie.

Just like in the examples of FitBit, sleep-tracking technologies, and mood-tracking products, to suggest that someday we will be able to gather enough data to "see" people's dreams is to assume an equivalence between data and world. Once a computer can "show" you your "dreams," will you ever trust your own memory of a dream if it isn't in the dream "data" presented back to you?

The consequences of a pervasive ideological commitment to the equivalence between "data" and "world" are massive and far-reaching. Scholars and theorists in a vast array of disciplines, especially in post-1968 Critical Theory and Cultural Studies, have grappled with what it *means* for "data" and "world" to be seen as one and the same. These studies often begin by describing the privileging of measurement as the primary way of knowing—echoing Bridgman's operationalist dictum. But these theorists also show how the imperative to quantify is supported by capitalism's reliance on the "market." And, further, they show how the idea that "data" equals "world" changes an individual's experience of everyday life by changing what people think they can know about themselves and the world around them.

Philosopher and social theorist Henri Lefebvre, in his 1981 *Critique of Everyday Life, Vol. 3* proposed that in "informational capitalism," everyday life must be fragmented into quantifiable bits and connected through systems of equivalence such that everyday activities could have relative monetary values ascribed to them. He keenly understood that when this happens, everyday life comes to be experienced not as a coherent whole but as a "sequence of moments," which can be quantified and compared with one another and that operate as a "function" and have "no other reason or purpose."[58]

Perhaps more insidious than everyday life becoming a fragmented yet fundamentally undifferentiated sequence of quantifiable moments, however, is that, under such circumstances, "*to be is to be seen and measurable.*"[59] Writing around the same time as Lefebvre, the philosopher and media theorist Vilém Flusser wrote:

> Modern science ... contains *quantification* within its program. The extended thing has a punctual structure: bodies may be decomposed into planes, planes into lines, and lines into points. The thinking thing must therefore possess a structure adjustable to points. It must be composed of clear and distinct elements, of concepts and numbers ... *To know is above all to enumerate.*[60]
>
> (emphasis his)

Flusser created a phrase for this: the "inversion" of "the vector of signification." He meant that instead of numbers standing to represent certain aspects of people, people themselves come to represent numbers. People serve only to verify the reality of the number. Indeed, beginning at an early age (even before birth), individuals are put into percentiles that demonstrate acceptable deviations from a given "norm" in terms of weight or height. Soon after birth, however, the numbers that serve to represent people (or that individuals themselves serve to represent) take on a different quality. IQ tests measure intelligence, grades measure competence at a specific discipline or task, EEG data demonstrates ability to concentrate, "steps" show fitness level and by proxy overall health. Cameras track the numerical dimensions of the triangles created by one's eyes, mouth, and nose, and from all those measurements, evaluate what facial expressions and make inferences about emotional states, which themselves are measured in percentages of things like "joy," "anger," or "frustration." As these various quantities increase in variety and thus enhance the potential for the capture of different aspects of the self as data, they no longer serve as a proxy for the self. *It is the self, and the subjective embodied experience that becomes merely a tool for the verification of the numerical truth.*

Quantitative data—biometric, physiological, and behavioral—when faced with a sufficient amount of it, is easily confused with an internal reality that is subjective and unique. Am I depressed if an algorithm that's scanning my Instagram account—measuring and classifying the objects and frequency of the appearance of those objects in my posts—tells me that I am?[61] Or if an app that tracks my keystrokes and other interactions with my mobile device does?[62]

What is so remarkable about this is that we no longer trust what we know about ourselves, our own narratives. This emptying of one's confidence in what one can know about oneself or one's world happens when users encounter the interfaces to the computational products that show us "data" and "world" are equal. If individuals come to believe they cannot know themselves or their world unless they capture as much data as possible, a compulsion to capture any "missing" data may arise. In the next chapter, we will address the strange insecurity this creates and why more computing appears to resolve this insecurity.

Notes

1   Sonification is the process of converting data to audio. See, for example: the work of Robert Alexander: "Listen to Solar Storm Activity in New Sonification Video," *University of Michigan News*, March 13, 2012, https://news.umich.edu/listen-to-solar-storm-activity-in-new-sonification-video/.

2   Amber Walsh, "Inquiries at the Intersection of Design and New Materialism" (Conference Presentation, Frontier: the AIGA Design Educators Conference, Montana State University, Bozeman, MT, October 9, 2016).

3   See, for example: Jane Bennett, *Vibrant Matter: A Political Ecology of Things* (Durham: Duke University Press, 2010).

4   Empirical, generally speaking, means that a phenomenon be verified through observation.

5   "360 Smart Bed—Smart & Effortless Comfort—Sleep Number," accessed October 15, 2017, https://www.sleepnumber.com/pages/360.

6   https://www.sidewalklabs.com/.

7   Matteo Pasquinelli, "Abnormal Encephalization in the Age of Machine Learning," *E-Flux Journal* 75 (September 2016), https://www.e-flux.com/journal/75/67133/abnormal-encephalization-in-the-age-of-machine-learning/.

8   Stanley Aronowitz and Robert Ausch, "A Critique of Methodological Reason," *The Sociological Quarterly* 41, no. 4 (2000): 699–719.

9   P. W. Bridgman, *The Logic of Modern Physics* (New York: MacMillan, 1927): 5.

10 Hasok Chang, "Operationalism," in *The Stanford Encyclopedia of Philosophy*, ed. Edward N. Zalta, Fall 2021 (Metaphysics Research Lab, Stanford University, 2021), https://plato.stanford.edu/archives/fall2021/entries/operationalism/.

11 Aronowitz and Ausch, "Critique of Methodological Reason," 708.

12 George C. Rosenwald, "Why Operationism Doesn't Go Away: Extrascientific Incentives of Social-Psychological Research," *Philosophy of the Social Sciences* 16, no. 3 (September 1986): 303, doi:10.1177/004839318601600302.

13 Bridgman, *LMP*, viii.

14 Bridgman, *LMP*, viii.

15 Chang, "Operationalism."

16 Bridgman, *LMP*, 67.

17 Bridgman, *LMP*, 10.

18 Bridgman, *LMP*, 28.

19 Aronowitz and Ausch, "Critique of Methodological Reason."

20 Gerald Holton, "Candor and Integrity in Science," *Synthese* 145, no. 2 (2005): 282.

21 Holton, "Candor and Integrity in Science," 277–94.

22 Rosenwald, "Why Operationism Doesn't Go Away," 315.

23 Rosenwald, "Why Operationism Doesn't Go Away," 321.

24 Paul Humphreys, *Extending Ourselves: Computational Science, Empiricism, and Scientific Method* (New York: Oxford University Press, 2004).

25 Peter Markie and M. Folescu, "Rationalism vs. Empiricism," in *The Stanford Encyclopedia of Philosophy*, ed. Edward N. Zalta, Fall 2021 (Metaphysics Research Lab, Stanford University, 2021), https://plato.stanford.edu/archives/fall2021/entries/rationalism-empiricism/.

26 David Golumbia, *The Cultural Logic of Computation* (Cambridge, MA: Harvard University Press, 2009).

27 Martin Davis, *Engines of Logic: Mathematicians and the Origin of the Computer* (New York, NY; London: Norton, 2001).

28 Gottfried Wilhelm Leibniz, *New Essays on Human Understanding*, in Gottfried Wilhelm Leibniz and George Henry Radcliffe Parkinson, *Philosophical Writings*, New rev. ed, Everyman's University Library (London: Dent, 1973): 150–1.

29 Mark Fuller, "Review of Martin Davis, Engines of Logic," *The Review of Modern Logic* 9, nos. 3–4 (December 2003): 124.

30 See: "FitBit Alta HR User Manual Version 1.4," 2017, https://staticcs.fitbit.com/content/assets/help/manuals/manual_alta_hr_en_US.pdf.

31 "Help Article: How Does My Fitbit Device Calculate My Daily Activity?," January 27, 2018, https://web.archive.org/web/20180127030643/https://help.fitbit.com/articles/en_US/Help_article/1141.

32 Leland Teschler, "Teardown: Inside the Fitbit Charge," *Microcontroller Tips*, September 27, 2016, https://www.microcontrollertips.com/inside-fitbit-charge/.

33 Alexander G. Krause et al., "A High-Resolution Microchip Optomechanical Accelerometer," *Nature Photonics* 6 (October 14, 2012): 768.

34 "Accelerometer API," *FitBit Developer*, February 8, 2019, https://web.archive.org/web/20190208210247/https://dev.fitbit.com/build/reference/device-api/accelerometer/.

35 "SleepIQ® Technology in the Sleep Number 360™ Smart Bed," *Sleep Number Newsroom*, December 3, 2018, https://web.archive.org/web/20181203133247/http://newsroom.sleepnumber.com/phoenix.zhtml?c=254487&p=irol-product_siq.

36 Which may be more accurately referred to as "capta." See: Johanna Drucker, *Graphesis: Visual Forms of Knowledge Production*, MetaLABprojects (Cambridge, MA: Harvard University Press, 2014).

37 Matthew Fuller and Andrew Goffey, *Evil Media* (Cambridge, MA: MIT Press, 2012): 19.

38 See: Edward R. Tufte, *The Visual Display of Quantitative Information*, 2nd ed. (Cheshire, CT: Graphics Press, 2001); and, Edward R. Tufte, *Envisioning Information*, Fourteenth printing (Cheshire, CT: Graphics Press, 2013).

39 "LIS2DH—3-Axis MEMS Accelerometer, Ultra-Low-Power, ±2g/±4g/±8g/±16g Full Scale, High-Speed I2C/SPI Digital Output, Embedded FIFO, High-Performance Acceleration Sensor—STMicroelectronics," *ST Microelectronics*, June 9, 2018, https://web.archive.org/web/20180609091902/https://www.st.com/en/mems-and-sensors/lis2dh.html.

40 Frank Pasquale, *The Black Box Society: The Secret Algorithms That Control Money and Information* (Cambridge: Harvard University Press, 2015).

41 Nick Srnicek and Laurent De Sutter, *Platform Capitalism*, Theory Redux (Cambridge, UK; Malden, MA: Polity, 2017): 53.

42 Rick Osterloh, "Google Completes Fitbit Acquisition," *Google: The Keyword*, January 14, 2021, https://blog.google/products/devices-services/fitbit-acquisition/.

43 Roland Barthes, *Mythologies*, trans. Richard Howard and Annette Lavers (New York: Hill and Wang, 2013).

44 Jessica Helfand and William Drenttel, "Wonders Revealed: Design and Faux Science," *Émigré* no. 64 (2003): 73–85.

45 Helfand and Drenttel, "Wonders Revealed," 78.

46 "World's First Emotion Sensor & Mental Health Advisor," *Myfeel.Co*, October 20, 2018, https://web.archive.org/web/20181020144036/https://www.myfeel.co/.

47 "World's First Emotion Sensor & Mental Health Advisor," *Myfeel.Co*, October 20, 2018, https://web.archive.org/web/20181020144036/https://www.myfeel.co/.

48 It is not within the scope of this work to address, but CBT is deeply linked to both the traditions of rationalism and neoliberalism, and it has served as part of the apparatus to maintain docile subjects under increasingly difficult economic circumstances. See, for example: Farhad Dalal, *CBT: The Cognitive Behavioural Tsunami: Managerialism, Politics, and the Corruptions of Science* (Abingdon, Oxon; New York, NY: Routledge, 2018).

49 "Upmood," *Upmood*, October 13, 2018, https://web.archive.org/web/20181013023538/http://www.upmood.com/.

50 "Upmood."

51 Edwards, *The Closed World*, 147.

52 Clare Carlisle, "Creatures of Habit: The Problem and the Practice of Liberation," *Continental Philosophy Review* 38, nos. 1–2 (July 10, 2006): 29, doi:10.1007/s11007-005-9005-y.

53 Elizabeth Grosz, "Habit Today: Ravaisson, Bergson, Deleuze and Us," ed. Tony Bennett et al., *Body & Society* 19, nos. 2–3 (June 2013): 226, doi:10.1177/135703 4X12472544.

54 Carlisle, "Creatures of Habit," 28.

55 Grosz, "Habit Today," 225.

56 Henri Lefebvre, *Critique of Everyday Life: The One-Volume Edition*, One-vol ed. (London: Verso, 2014), 743.

57 Yasmin Anwar, "Scientists Use Brain Imaging to Reveal the Movies in Our Mind," *Berkeley News*, September 22, 2011, https://news.berkeley.edu/2011/09/22/brain-movies/.

58 Neil Curry, "Review: Critique of Everyday Life, Volume 3: From Modernity to Modernism," *Capital & Class* 33, no. 98 (2009): 171.

59 Aronowitz and Ausch, "Critique of Methodological Reason," 701.

60 Vilem Flusser, *Post-History*, Flusser Archive Collection (Minneapolis, MN: Univocal, 2013), 45.

61 See: Adele Peters, "This Algorithm Can Tell if You're Depressed Just from Your Instagram Posts," *Fast Company*, August 8, 2017, https://www.fastcompany.com/40449192/this-algorithm-can-tell-if-youre-depressed-just-from-your-instagram-posts.

62 See: Rachel Metz, "The Smartphone App That Can Tell You're Depressed before You Know It Yourself," *MIT Technology Review*, October 15, 2018, https://www.technologyreview.com/2018/10/15/66443/the-smartphone-app-that-can-tell-youre-depressed-before-you-know-it-yourself/.

3 PREDICTION AND THE STABILIZATION OF IDENTITY

Introduction: The Scrambling of Algorithmic Anticipation

Imagine encountering, perhaps in a museum or even in someone's home, a very modern-looking device—a small, white, acrylic box, its smooth facade only broken by the affordance of a single red button, with a small microphone protruding from its left side. A stream of receipt paper cascades to the floor, which documents its activities. *Whisper*, as the object is called, is a product of collaboration between myself and Dr. Gabi Schaffzin (Figures 3.1, 3.2, and 3.3). It is a piece of art, designed and produced in 2013, that masquerades as a consumer product, like a Google Home or Amazon Echo. It includes voice recognition similar to Alexa or Siri, but *Whisper* has a very specific and subversive function—when a user presses the red button, *Whisper* asks the user to tell it how they feel, and then intentionally misinterprets those feelings and orders products from Amazon.com based on the scrambled data that it generates. The process by which the data becomes scrambled—through a word-association algorithm—as well as the product the system ends up ordering, is displayed on the receipt paper that cascades to the floor.

For example:

> You said tired.
> Whisper thought of banal.
> Whisper thought of commonplace.
> Whisper thought of humdrum.
> Whisper thought of unvariedness.
> Whisper is searching for invariability …
> I promise I am working …
> breaking algorithms takes time …
> Whisper ordered *Pyrrho, His Antecedents, and His Legacy*: $95.76.

FIGURE 3.1 The *Whisper* prototype in a museum exhibition, 2014. Courtesy the author.

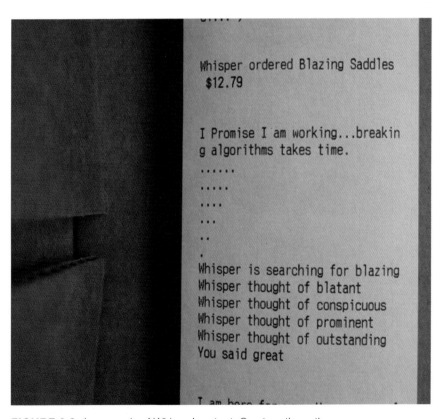

FIGURE 3.2 An example of *Whisper*'s output. Courtesy the author.

Or:

> You said "great."
> Whisper thought of outstanding.
> Whisper thought of prominent.
> Whisper thought of conspicuous.
> Whisper thought of blatant.
> Whisper thought of blazing …
> I promise I am working …
> breaking algorithms takes time …
> Whisper ordered *Blazing Saddles*: $12.79.

To be sure, the absurdity of such a project elicits a chuckle. But through this humorous experience, the object begs the question: what if you liked the thing that *Whisper* ordered for you? Would you have found out about it otherwise? Would it ever have come across the "Recommendations for you in Books" or "Additional Items to Explore" on your Amazon homepage? Are you who Amazon thinks you are? And if you are, is that the "you" that you want to be? In short, *Whisper* is about

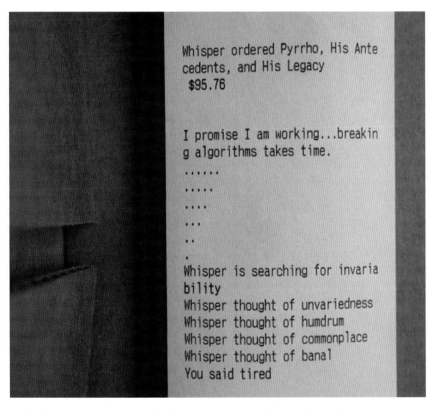

FIGURE 3.3 Another example of *Whisper*'s output. Courtesy the author.

reintroducing surprise and serendipity into lives that have become increasingly "algorithmically anticipated." As an increasing amount of everyday life is captured as data, inference and recommendation algorithms—ranging from those used by Netflix to those in "smart" household objects—begin to shape the identities of users. They "configure life by tailoring its conditions of human possibility."[1]

Whisper's original intent was to subvert one "tailoring" of possibility—the ability of Amazon's inference and recommendation algorithms to "accurately" predict the user's preferences and interests. Furthermore, if installed in someone's home, it is possible that users who Amazon has determined to be "similar" (i.e., "people who bought this also bought") to Whisper's user might be recommended products that reflected this scrambling process as well, extending the effects of the surprise and serendipity beyond the individual Whisper user themselves. Whisper suggests people must actively work to reintroduce surprise and serendipity into their algorithmically anticipated lives by subverting those systems that predict preferences and produce compelling recommendations. Such systems seem almost to "know us," but in effect close off avenues of potential. Whisper is a small effort to reopen those avenues.

***

Whisper is a project that began as a tactical attempt to resist algorithmic inference and recommendation. It also illustrates the facet of the computable subjectivity to which this chapter is devoted: the aspiration to be both legible to, and predictable by, computers. This aspiration soothes the feeling of fragmentation that accompanies an adherence to the belief that "data" equals "world." And like the last chapter, this chapter will describe some of the origins of this particular characteristic, its consequences, and the role of UX in propagating it.

In order for "data" to become equal to "world," as we looked at in the last chapter, there are two processes that need to occur: first, the "smooth space" of everyday life, undifferentiated and qualitative, needs to become "striated," fragmented into discrete pieces to be quantified; second, some kind of transformation must happen to those quantified pieces such that they become commensurable with one another—a particular system of equivalence must be applied. Strangely, it seems, the fragmentation of the normally smooth space of everyday life becomes an attractive prospect for individuals who adopt the computable subjectivity. Why is this?

In this chapter, I will argue that not only is the fragmentation of everyday life a matter of logistics, but, indeed, it is much more so a matter of psychology and *ontology*. Beginning in the early twentieth century, scholars from an array of disciplines suggested that modernity was defined by alienation, fragmentation, and abandonment, resulting in an "ontological insecurity." Because of the fragmentation and alienation experienced by people living under modernity, those individuals desire to become whole again. Computation offers that possibility by demonstrating that individuals are truly "knowable," if only all the "data" about them can be captured.

This "homogeneous fragmentation"[2]—homogenous because of the quantitative equivalence to which data is subjected—presents a strange coherence. Predictive analytics and systems of algorithmic inference and recommendation, through the interfaces in which users experience them, present users with a coherent version of themselves and thus provide a new ontological security.

There is no small irony in this: by becoming subject to the computational systems that fragment and quantify them, users see themselves as becoming more ontologically stable, while opening themselves up to incisive biopolitical control via systems of algorithmic anticipation. There is an additional layer of irony here as well: the "self" presented back to users via the interfaces of various products and services is predicated on categorization and the linking of data about one user with data about others. This "self" represented to a user in the interface is often not singular, but rather an accumulation of data that puts a user in relationship to others determined to be "similar."

Before moving on, it will be useful to review the term "ontology," because, if you are a designer like me, this term might not be something you encounter regularly.[3] Ontology is the study of the nature of being or existence. The entry "Logic and Ontology" in the *Stanford Encyclopedia of Philosophy* has a wonderfully brief "first approximation" of a definition of the term: "ontology is the study of what there is."[4] While a much more complex elaboration of this definition could follow (and does in the *SEP*), for our purposes here, considering "ontology" and the "ontological" as questions of "what there is" or the "nature of existence" will be sufficient.

Some scholars of design have begun important conversations about "ontological designing." I love this idea because it acknowledges that "we design our world, and our world designs us back."[5] This means that design—including UX design—has an effect on how people understand the very nature of their beings. Design *is* ontological, whether designers and users know it or not. And since design is tied up in the political-economic situation of a given time and place[6]—in the case of this writing, neoliberal capitalism—the political-economic situation reflected by the artifacts that designers create is thus also a factor that shapes someone's *ontological understanding*. In other words, *because design and political-economy are deeply interrelated, they both produce and are produced by people's ideas about who they are*, the nature of their being and their existence.

This complex situation—in which people's ideas about the nature of their existence and design and political economy all feed into and mutually constitute each other in different ways—is also acknowledged by a term highlighted in the first two chapters of this book: *governmentality*. This term refers to the governing rationality, the dominant problem-solution framework in a given society at a given time. The neoliberal governmentality produces a particular problem-solution framing of society that eschews anything but a market-based solution. This makes perfect sense in a context where people are assumed to operate as simplified economic models of themselves. Furthermore, when advanced computation makes information transfer *appear* seamless, the model begins to *appear* as reality, and ambient intelligence and algorithmic anticipation, in the guise of convenience-enhancing tools and technologies, aid in the production of a self that is ever more pliable to the needs of capital while at the same time fostering confidence in one's self-optimization. Indeed, self-optimization as a kind of goal or imperative is predicated on the models, which now not only "model" people, but toward which individuals aspire—the very thing on which we model ourselves.

Through the manipulative capacities of the interface, users come to believe they can become their most authentic selves by "self-optimizing," producing a mathematically efficient and coherent version of themselves (even if this isn't their primary objective). Seeking to engage in such self-optimization, treating oneself as the Cyberneticists treated the market or warfare, individuals prepare their entire selves for "markets," facilitating capitalism's ongoing quest for the augmentation of surplus value at every turn. The aspects of the self that can be reified into "commodity" form transcend mere "labor"—they are every movement, every sneeze, every orgasm, every drop of blood—ready to be sold back to individuals as products and services that help them self-optimize more. *The fragmentation we experience becomes the answer to the problem it itself creates.*

The Digital Production of Fragmentation and Alienation

Algorithmic recommendation systems are used everywhere, all the time, by products and services large and small. Individuals are subject to these systems at nearly every turn throughout the day: Google Maps, Amazon, Netflix, Instagram, YouTube, fitness trackers, new "smart" devices and household objects, and so on. These systems, which infer things about their users and then present users with recommendations based on those inferences, soothe the ontological insecurity of a fragmented self. They help create a perception of a wholeness-of-the-self in a world where everything is constantly broken down into tiny quantifiable bits, in which individual lives become assessed numerically on an increasingly granular level, and, in which aspects of everyday life that once appeared unquantifiable begin to fall under the domain of computation. The computational creation of ontological security—this wholeness-of-the-self—results from the way technologies present users, *through the interface*, a version of themselves that is *computable* and therefore ultimately *knowable*.

As I demonstrated in Chapter 2, scientism and a commitment to methodology, as well as Cybernetics and its disciplinary offspring, gave rise to an assumed equivalence between "data" and "world," an equivalence which caters to the neoliberal governmentality and enables granular biopolitical control of individuals. For "data" to become equal to "world," life must be carved up into distinct domains, quantified, and then subjected to some kind of system of equivalence. These fragments of everyday life become "data" once they are captured by some computational technology or other. Then they become external to the user themselves. No longer is that piece of data part of a continuous stream of experience in someone's life. Instead, this life has been broken into chunks that are made legible to computation, and then they are re-presented to the user in the interfaces of products such as FitBit or the Feel mood monitor. This re-presentation is also a capture, repackage, and selling of the user's data back to them through computational products and services. The user is thus *alienated* from the very activities that constitute their everyday life. This profound "alienation" has two components: (1) alienation from one's labor; and, (2) alienation from one's everyday life.

Computation and Alienation in the Realm of Labor

The concept of *alienation* in the way I'm using it here has its origins in Marx's ideas about what happens to people's labor as the result of industrialization. Marx argued that the conditions and changes wrought by industrialization and the specialization of labor produced an effect in which workers were distanced— *alienated*—from the actual results of their work. Marx wrote that the labor of the worker becomes detached from the worker and becomes rendered in material reality as the commodity, an idea he called *reification*. Thus, a worker's labor, once *alienated* from them, is *reified* in the products that are the eventual result of that labor, a result that is produced apart from the worker themselves, not immediately visible to them, through industrialized and distributed processes. Key theorists of "modernity"[7] build on this notion of reification. Lukács, for example, writes that "the worker's own activity is estranged and turns into a commodity subject to the nonhuman objectivity of market laws. Labor alienated from the worker takes on a life of its own."[8] While the process of alienation and reification is certainly still operative today, I am interested here in the role computation and interfaces play in the alienation of labor from its end product and the consequences of this alienation. Computation and the interfaces to computational tools used in industry produce a specific kind of alienated laborer: the *functionary*. Functionaries are separated from the moral responsibility they have to other humans, and the proliferation of functionaries in society is directly correlated with the datafication of everything.

When removed at increasing distances from the material results of their work through the rendering of every aspect of work as data, the functionary's quest for efficiency and optimization becomes an end in and of itself. This is one of the most dangerous features of modernity. Zygmunt Bauman equates this particular kind of technological distancing of someone from the products of their labor with the bureaucracies characteristic of modern industrial society. Because one cannot possibly understand the results of one's labor, because one is so alienated from the actual things or material conditions one participates in producing, the only barometer of value in one's work is their *technical* ability. Thus the "bureaucracy" that Bauman describes is predicated on technical responsibility—that one is faithful first and foremost to the maintenance of the technical system. "Technical responsibility differs from moral responsibility in that it forgets that the action is a means to something other than itself."[9] Indeed, more technology has come to be seen as an end in itself in nearly every domain of society today. *Make the objects "smart" and they will be inherently somehow "good"*—once invested with computing, tools seem to take on a moral trajectory unrelated to their social effects (see, for example, Chris Gilliard's terrific scholarship on "luxury surveillance"[10]). Again, an astute reader might ask, *well, even though workers are more and more alienated from the material effects of the work they do, how do interfaces to computational products and services fit into this idea of workers becoming functionaries?*

Zygmunt Bauman calls this particular result of alienation—in which technique or technical progress is seen as an end in itself because one is so far removed from the actual, material result of their labor—the "social production of distance." Supply chain logistics, for example, and, in particular, the workers who make those supply chains work—and the extraordinary complexity and material consequence thereof—are reduced in the interface for SAP's management software to entries in spreadsheets, little icons, or dots or lines on graphs.[11] Meanwhile, gig economy workers delivering food for Uber Eats or Doordash are not seen as people, but instead flattened to uniform icons on a map, timed and rated, not subjectively experienced as a human being.[12] The social production of distance is everywhere today and it emerges in part because many individuals experience each other through the very same kinds of interfaces through which they become alienated from themselves.

The apotheosis of the social production of distance, Bauman argues, is genocide. This may feel like a bridge too far, but he makes a convincing case for understanding the atrocities of the Holocaust not as an exception to the rule of modern rationality but as its pinnacle. And I think he's right. Which is why I believe the transformation of the political subject into a computable subject is such an important thing to discuss. Bauman writes that "the civilizing process is, among other things, a process of divesting the use and deployment of violence from moral calculus, and of emancipating the desiderata of rationality from interference of ethical norms or moral inhibitions."[13] The kinds of distance produced by the alienating effects of the interface—distance from our own selves and from one another—also create a separation between moral responsibility for one another and "rational coordination of action."

The Alienation of Individuals from Everyday Life

Lukacs's concept of alienation extended that of Marx, in that he believed modernity's "rational mechanization extends right into the worker's 'soul': even his psychological attributes are separated from his total personality and placed in opposition to it so as to facilitate their integration into specialized rational systems and their reduction to statistically viable concepts."[14] In today's digital products and services, users' entire lives—not just their labor—become externalized, *alienated* from them, through computational technologies that claim to make things easier or more convenient by datafication and optimization.

There is an immediate problem, however, with the analysis that I have started to propose here, and that problem has to do with the original intent of the term "alienation" in the Marxian tradition. That term's use was based on the idea that one's *labor* was separated from oneself and then reified into commodities to be consumed. One could argue, compellingly I believe, that the datafication of every aspect of everyday life *is not the same* as "labor" under capitalism. Indeed, whether this giving up of one's "data" to tech companies might be considered "labor" is a question that countless scholars have debated. *That is less of an issue here to me than the question of what happens when our lives must become external to us, when our experiences are categorized, quantified, visualized, and packaged into neat little applications and interfaces.*

When every aspect of life is externalized, quantified, and sold back to users by tech companies ranging from FitBit to SmartPlate, human lives are *reified*, made into something objective and independent of the people living them. Once externalized, such informational commodities and the companies capturing and storing them can not only enable capitalism to continue its quest for the augmentation of surplus value,[15] but they also exert subtle and incisive biopolitical control. In this way, I think replacing "labor" with "life" and "worker" with "person" when reading certain texts on alienation can become a productive way of gleaning new insight about today's consumer technologies, regardless of the question of whether or not data and labor are one in the same:

> Subjectively, the *PERSON'S* own activity is estranged and turned into a commodity, subject to the nonhuman objectivity of market laws. *LIFE* alienated from the *PERSON* takes on a life of its own. Thus, capitalistic commodity production makes *LIFE* into an abstraction that becomes incorporated into commodities.[16]
>
> It is here where one's *LIFE* becomes reified, made into something objective and independent of the *PERSON*; it is something that controls the *PERSON* and at the same time is an alien object having power over the *PERSON*.[17]

These statements, adaptations of two passages from Roger Salerno's *Landscapes of Abandonment*, indicate the core of my concern around the effect of alienation as produced by the computable subjectivity and the acceptance of the fragmentation that its adoption necessitates. In short: individuals open themselves up to biopolitical control when they come to believe that the data about them is more real than their subjective experience of everyday life, when "data" comes to be seen as equivalent to "world" *precisely* because one is alienated from one's own subjective experience of that very world.

Ontological Insecurity: One Consequence of Fragmentation and Alienation

The aspiration to be legible to—and predicted by—computers emerges as a result of the fragmentation and alienation of individuals from their lives and labor. It soothes the feeling of insecurity that is produced when "data" becomes equivalent to "world," and yet individuals are perpetually unsure if they have surrendered all the data they possibly can to the computational systems that purport to know them. The fragmentation, datafication and capture, and resulting alienation and reification of one's everyday life in the interfaces to computational products and services result in what cultural critic Rob Horning calls "ontological insecurity." Horning describes "ontological insecurity" as an individual lacking "an overriding sense of personal consistency or cohesiveness."[18] Horning's critique is centered on social media, but I would argue that its scope should expand to any computational product or service that alienates one's life from themselves, externalizing it and reifying it as a commodity in the interface to those products and services. Horning describes his borrowing of "ontological insecurity" from influential psychiatrist R.D. Laing:

> Laing defines [ontological insecurity] as when one lacks "the experience of his own temporal continuity" and does not have "an overriding sense of personal consistency or cohesiveness." Without this stable sense of self, Laing argues, every interaction threatens to overwhelm the individual with the fear of losing oneself in the other or of being obliterated by their indifference. "He may feel more insubstantial than substantial, and unable to assume that the stuff he is made of is genuine, good, valuable," Laing writes of the ontologically insecure. "And he may feel his self as partially forced from his body."[19]

When every aspect of one's everyday life is quantified, fragmented, and reflected back to them in an interface, how can one be sure of anything unless it has become "data?" This very question *is* the ontological insecurity that Horning is addressing.

But there is a strange irony to invoking R.D. Laing here. Some of Laing's most pioneering work argued that the traditional psychiatric establishment, deeply Freudian at the time, was subjective, biased, flawed, and not "scientific." The psychiatric establishment had its own politics and Laing sought to correct it, but—and this is the great irony—he did so through appeals to *Game Theory* which seemed to provide an objective *anti-politics*. As we saw in Chapter 1, Game Theory is one of the historical foundations for the computable subjectivity. For Laing, sowing mistrust in the institution of psychiatry also required bolstering trust in some kind of corrective, which became systems of categorizing symptoms without worrying about root causes.[20] By viewing people as self-interested autonomous agents—as computers—Laing's provocative anti-psychiatry ended up helping contribute to the sort of control he was attempting to wrest away from the psychiatric establishment itself.[21,22] To me *as a designer* this is instructive: designers must be wary of the kind of *anti-politics* that seemingly objective things like computation seem to possess.

The Digital Mirror Self: Soothing Ontological Insecurity with Computation

In suggesting that once a user's entire life is datafied and re-presented in the interface, users can be ultimately knowable, the digital interface appears to offer a remedy for the ontological insecurity that it produces. In other words, the psychological harm of datafication is resolved only through more datafication. The manner in which this happens hinges on UX. But a brief detour through some psychoanalytic theory and semiotics is necessary in order to make this connection clear.

In some branches of psychoanalytic theory, it is assumed that there are certain absences for which individuals spend their lives seeking to compensate. Jacques Lacan—a psychoanalyst whose work is as influential as it is difficult to understand—suggests that one specific kind of "loss," which defines how people view themselves, happens when a child sees for the first time its reflection in a mirror. He calls this the "mirror stage," and argues that the child perceives the reflection as having a "coherence which the subject itself lacks—it is an *ideal* image."[23] Because it is so familiar yet not of itself, "the subject defines itself entirely in relation to it … [The subject] loves the coherent identity which the mirror provides. However, because the image remains external to it, it also hates that image."[24] In writing about Lacan in the domain of *semiotics*—the study of language, images, and culture as signs that produce meaning—Kaja Silverman underscores the importance of not taking the "mirror" too literally. The "ideal" image described by Lacan is one that is culturally constructed, with the term itself only being able to have meaning within a given system of values. Our identities, from the get-go, are culturally mediated. "That mediation may be as complex and diffuse as the introduction into the child's environment of various representations (dolls, picture-books, trains, or toy guns) which determine the way in which it will eventually regard itself."[25] Today, such mediation is increasingly computational.[26] In other words, the "complex and diffuse" mediation to which Kaja Silverman refers in her explanation of Lacan's work is effectively a space of *representation*. The spaces of representation that dominate life today are those of the interfaces that represent every aspect of everyday life back to users—heart rates, calorie intakes, trips to work and school, as well as "sleep IQ"[27] and other measures of seemingly qualitative experience. Such interfaces not only represent people as computational, but they also represent people as predictable and suggest that to be predictable is something to which one should aspire, in part because of the ontological coherence that these representations promise.

Because capitalism uses psychoanalysis to produce objects that appeal to people's inner drives, the perpetual lack suffered by the Lacanian subject appears as a great opportunity for savvy marketing. By producing commodities that seem to unite individuals with something that ameliorates a self-loss, capitalism manufactures desire. "Not only does language provide the agency of self-loss, but cultural representations supply the standard by which that loss is perceived. We look within the mirror of those representations—representations which structure every moment of our existence—not only to discover what we are, but what we can never hope to be and (as a consequence) hopelessly desire."[28]

And if we think about "reification" in the more expansive sense, in which we replace "labor" with "life," in which all aspects of everyday life are fragmented, quantified, and reified via computational technologies, we can begin to draw a series of connections—to a new kind of computational "mirror," one that individuals can own if they are able to purchase them: the FitBits, the smart mattresses, and so on; and, thus, to a new kind of commodity fetishism, wherein individuals desire technologies that seem to connect them deeply to this mirror image of themselves in a way in which they weren't able to connect with it before. These technologies, by fragmenting individuals into quantifiable bits then turn around, and through their interfaces, present them as coherent and knowable selves.

This mirror—the reification of oneself via technologies that capture and visualize data about every aspect of everyday life—produces an ontological security, a coherence that emanates from the "knowability" an individual possesses. In this way, computational products and their interfaces suggest that, if indeed people are computational beings, computation could precede language and that, by becoming fully knowable to computers—by capturing all data that can be captured, completely striating the smoothness of everyday life—individuals can return to their pre-languaging selves, achieving a unity with the Lacanian mirror and compensating for the loss they experience in childhood. Because of the supposed equivalence between "data" and "world," the more "data" one can capture about oneself, the more "knowable" one is, and the more one is able to approach the idealized version of themselves that, before, never seemed reachable. None of this ever needs to reach the level of a user's "consciousness" to have a profound impact on how they perceive themselves. In other words, aspiring to be knowable to, and predicted by, computers is what soothes the ontological insecurity that results from the use of computational tools that make life easier, more convenient, or optimal.

The Role of UX in Producing, then Soothing, Ontological Insecurity

As has been the refrain throughout this chapter, more computational fragmentation presents itself as the answer to the problem that it originally created. As such, UX is key both in the ontological insecurity produced by the fragmentation of everyday life, but also in presenting additional computational intervention as the answer to this issue. I present some examples here to help analyze this particular facet of the computable subjectivity and its consequences. By examining certain consumer technologies, we can gain some insight into the process by which individuals are incentivized to see themselves as knowable by becoming legible to computation.

When viewed through the interface, the smooth space of everyday life becomes striated[29] and the individual self—a whole, a unity—becomes a series of discrete data points. And, the interface suggests to a user, without those data points, one can know nothing at all about oneself, because the tool's purported "accuracy" relies on the collection of as many data points as possible. Thus, the collection of more data points, and the continued fragmentation of the individual into tiny bite-sized pieces of data is incentivized.

The more individuals view their daily lives—sleep habits, exercise habits, food, activities, friendships, mood, mental health—through interfaces that purport to know them, but only through this delimiting of life into discrete data points and through the physical and psychological destruction of the continuous *individual* into what Deleuze called a "dividual," the more users come to believe themselves to be the way these products see them: as computing and computable.

Optimizing, or, Fragmenting and Reifying Sleep

Think for a moment about sleep. Different people have different preferences for the environments in which they sleep as well as different abilities to change the situation in which they attempt to get some rest at night. Furthermore, sleep as an activity itself is not discontiguous from the rest of everyday life. Things that happen to people during their waking hours impact their sleep, as do the ratios of different chemicals in the brain, food intake and general nutritional health, and so on. Sleep also is deeply linked to the unconscious. Some people dream nightly, while others rarely do.

And yet, both startups and established tech companies alike suggest that not only does sleep not possess its own internal continuity, but that it is instead full of discrete data points to be mined for analysis (and capitalization) and that it can be analyzed on its own terms, apart from any continuities it has with the rest of everyday life. This suggestion is made through the interface. The sleep-tracking startup, Beddit, for example, suggested (prior to being acquired by Apple[30]) that one can only understand one's sleep through measuring it.[31]

Like other quantified-self products that we have examined throughout this book, the Beddit app presented itself as "scientific," using charts and graphs to suggest the neutrality of its data collection and analysis hardware and software. The interface to the Beddit app was not dissimilar to what has, since Beddit's acquisition by Apple, supplanted it: the "sleep tracking feature" of the Apple Watch and its companion interfaces in iOS and Watch OS. Even prior to being acquired, Beddit was used in a number of academic sleep studies and flouted its scientific credentials. But, just like the early FitBit model we examined in Chapter 2, the Beddit relied on establishing an equivalence between "data" and "world." Interestingly, the original Beddit app relied on data collected not by a wearable (which was one of its selling points), but rather a very thin and soft sensor that sat "hidden under your sheet." Ultrathin sensors are not uncommon, and the Beddit used a combination of humidity and temperature sensors (outside the strip, powered by USB) along with a capacitive touch sensor and a piezoelectric sensor—which is typically used to detect vibrations, and can be purchased at different sizes with varying sensitivities. This vibration data then must be correlated with user input and other inferences made by the app itself to become "useful" and translatable into the terms by which a user will understand it. Looking at the Beddit interface—and now Apple's sleep tracking interface—however, it might seem incredible that anyone before our new age of connected computational products had ever managed to achieve a good night's sleep. And perhaps this is the interface's most important function.

Indeed, to argue whether or not the Beddit "data" was in some way "real" or "accurate" is perhaps giving Beddit and other QS products too much credit. It doesn't matter if these computational products are "accurate" or not. The space in which I think it is more useful to question the role these tools play in our lives is the space in which we discuss the *nature of the activities themselves*. The friendly—yet scientific- and authoritative-looking—interfaces, through which users interact with the myriad sensors, processors, algorithms—and the assumptions embedded within those things—suggest, quite simply, that the nature of the activities that these systems analyze *is* computational.[32] It follows, for these companies, that if humans are by our very nature computational, then users *need* these computational products in order to actually understand themselves. By merely taking on claims of accuracy versus inaccuracy in the computing of, say, sleep data, one cedes a more fundamental ground, which is that the nature of oneself or one's sleep is itself computational.

Google's Nest Hub, meanwhile, might be seen as making the case for a "unified-self" approach to the Internet of Things, wherein the data about your sleep is stored and analyzed within the same system as your other activities (fitness, voice interaction queries with Google Home products, and so on), but, it is important to note—harkening back to Chapter 2—that for Google, "data = world," and when this is the case, all of life can be broken down, fragmented into the discreet data points that Google needs you to believe is all that constitutes everyday life in the first place. "Sleep is difficult to track and *decode*" (emphasis mine), says the video explaining how the Nest Hub's patented Sleep Tracking works.[33] Again, when the Nest Hub was launched, the interface and its accompanying copywriting made a very forceful claim to a user that their sleep—and perhaps they themselves—is fundamentally computational in nature.

Similar to the Beddit, the Google Nest Hub (Figure 3.4) does not require a user to wear anything in order for their sleep to be tracked. Instead, the Nest Hub uses Soli, a proprietary and hypersensitive radar system designed by Google to "turn it into a futuristic sleep tracker. By combining Soli data with locally processed audio, the smart display monitors tossing and turning, breathing, snoring and coughing to generate sleep reports."[34] The tech publication *Protocol*, reporting on the second generation Nest Hub, wrote that:

> Soli was originally conceived as a way to track small finger movements to control mobile devices, but it turns out that the radar tech can also monitor an entire body ... Placed on the bedside table, the Nest Hub is able to focus just on the person next to it—and ignore partners sleeping in the same bed.[35]

Additionally, "Data and insights gathered by the display can be fed into the Google Fit app for a more comprehensive picture of a consumer's personal health" (Figure 3.5).[36]

And yet, all this very complex and sophisticated technology disappears at the level of the interface. A user is not bombarded with code or a stream of *Matrix*-style zeros and ones. If that were the case, as we discussed in Chapter 2, the *translation* of "world" to "data" and the *mechanism of translation* would become obvious to the user. It would be a rhetorical failure because it would make clear the kind of proverbial gymnastics needed to suggest that people are computational in nature. Instead, our computational companions, such as the Google Nest Hub, speak to us in simplified charts and graphs, they listen to us using natural language input and then speak ever more naturally back to us.

I want to return here to the idea that formed the first half of this chapter: when people view themselves through interfaces as fragmented points of data, alienated from both their lives and their labor, they come to believe not only that they are computable and computing in nature, but that they can only achieve an ontological stability by becoming completely knowable to the very technologies fragmenting them. Google thus produces the Nest Hub as part of a campaign to capitalize on the ontological insecurity that they have helped produce. And yet, could we, if we were *not* computational in nature, find other ways to improve our own sleep? Did no one understand what made them sleep well *before* the Beddit or the Nest Hub?

FIGURE 3.4 Google's Nest Hub interface. Courtesy Google. © 2021 Google LLC. All rights reserved.

FIGURE 3.5 Google's Nest Hub data integrated with its Google Fit mobile application. Courtesy Google. © 2021 Google LLC. All rights reserved.

One of the key selling points for both the defunct Beddit and Google's Nest Hub is the fact that the user does not need to be wearing any kind of wristband or other device for their sleep to be tracked and analyzed. And, in late 2020, the market for wearables cooled down a bit,[37] owing perhaps to the consolidation of market share effectively in Apple's Watch and Google's FitBit. There were, however, some unique players on the margins of the wearables space that sought to stake their claims on various forms of differentiation from the two major wearable manufacturers. One of these is Ōura.

A glowing review from TechCrunch in 2020 described Ōura as follows:

The Oura Ring is a health tracker that's unlike just about any other wearable with a similar purpose. It's a ring that's virtually indistinguishable from an actual ring … [and] has sensors located on the inside surface, but these barely add to its overall thickness and are totally hidden when the ring is worn.

…

It measures sleep … as well as various other metrics under two broad categories: Readiness and Activity. Sleep, Readiness and Activity all provide one overall summary score out of 100 to give you a topline sense of where you are, but each is actually calculated from a range of sub-metrics that add up to that larger score.

Ōura's sleep tracking is much more in-depth than the forthcoming Apple Watch sleep tracking that Apple is releasing with its next watchOS update in the fall. It monitors when you go to sleep, how long you sleep, how much of that qualifies as "deep" and how much is "REM," and gives you a metric or you [sic] sleep efficiency, your time in bed, your total sleep time and more. Readiness tracks your ambient body temperature, heart rate variability, respiratory rate and your resting heart rate, while activity automatically measures calorie burn, inactive time, your steps and how close you are to your overall activity goal.[38]

Just like other wearables, Ōura was designed to communicate with an app on a user's phone (Figures 3.6 and 3.7). And this app, just like all other manner of quantified-self products and smart home gadgets, has an interface that seems both friendly and scientific. It's an interesting rhetorical sleight of hand—three simple metrics, in terms that people can easily understand. The sensors establish an equivalence between "world" and "data" and the application and its interface then turn around and suggest that "data" is equal to "world" through an easy-to-understand, "human-readable" system.

The interfaces to Beddit, Google's Nest Hub, and Ōura all suggest that humans are little more than agglomerations of metrics that, given the right technologies, can be accurately measured and predicted. There are few taglines that better encapsulate both what these technologies promise—as well as the dangers in believing this promise as I have laid out above—than the Ōura ring: "Know why you feel how you feel."

Only through externalizing and making "objective" that which was once internal and "subjective"—only by becoming legible to a computer and thus admitting that you *yourself* are computing and computable—*only then* can you truly know *why you feel how you feel.* Supposedly.

Life, Predicted

Key to the argument made in the first half of this chapter is that not only is the individual ontologically soothed by seeing themselves as knowable to computers, but that this desire for computational knowability engenders a desire to be

FIGURE 3.6 The interface for Ōura's app, including "readiness" (November 2021). Courtesy Ōura. © 2021 Ōura Health Oy. All rights reserved.

FIGURE 3.7 The Ōura website's hero image as of October 2021. Courtesy Ōura. © 2021 Ōura Health Oy. All rights reserved.

predicted. This desire, of course, dovetails with the goals of hegemonic institutions under neoliberalism and will be channeled to ensure its manifestations benefit those in places of power. Let's return to the Google Nest Hub for a moment, to help us unpack this a bit further. While it utilizes sophisticated sensing technology to capture data about users' sleep, it also serves numerous other functions in a fully integrated and connected family and home. Nest Hub integrates with Google Fit and FitBit—its fitness tracking platform and hardware—as well as the Nest Doorbell and climate control systems within a user's Google-powered smart home. Such integration allows hands-free voice control of various smart home functions, such as lights, media, and Google Assistant queries. Nest Hub also allows users to interact with content via touch-free "quick gestures" without even having a camera built in, because of its Soli radar functionality. Like Google Assistant needs to be "always listening" for the cue words ("hey, Google"), the Nest Hub's Soli radar system is "always tracking," and even though it is not a camera, it is always sensing, registering movements on both a micro and macro scale. This allows, for example, a user's audio to follow them from room to room in a home with multiple connected Nest objects. Taken together, these data points might provide a seemingly accurate picture of an individual or family's daily activities. I presume Google likely believes as much, since they were granted a patent in 2021 for an AI assistant that predicts activities a user would like to do and then recommends those activities (Figure 3.8).[39] A user will no longer even have to think about what they would actually like to do because Google already knows in advance. And this patent indicates that Google believes such a situation, in which users are completely algorithmically anticipated, will be both profitable *and* desirable to users, who, as Google has sought to ensure, believe themselves to be both computable and computing.

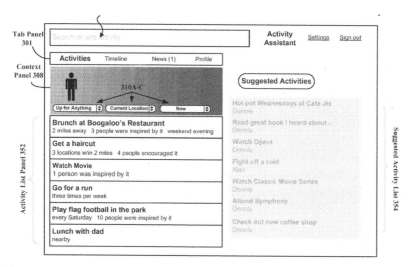

FIGURE 3.8 The interface concept for Google's AI Assistant in the eponymous patent application, 2021. Image USPTO.[40]

Such claims are common in Silicon Valley, and have been for some time. Indeed, Amazon is developing the infrastructure for what it calls "ambient intelligence."[41] In 2021, the blog for Amazon's Developer Team posted an article called "Our Vision: Building a World of Ambient Computing Together."[42] In it, they demonstrated clearly what Amazon's ambitions were: "Better sensors, AI, connectivity, and edge computing are starting to come together to give us homes and neighborhoods that are smarter in ways that matter: our latest devices and services are already able to understand the context of your home, predict your needs, and *act on your behalf*" (emphasis mine). Why would a user want to actually *ask* Alexa for something when Alexa already knows what the user wants?[43] "[A] truly ambient experience means you'll talk to Alexa less, or in some cases not at all." As of 2021, the authors argue, "Already, 1 in 4 Alexa smart home interactions are initiated by Alexa—without customers saying anything—thanks to predictive and proactive features like Alexa Guard, Routines, and Hunches." Thus, Amazon's aspiration seems to clearly be *total prediction based a user's belief in becoming totally knowable to Amazon's computing systems.*

Meanwhile, Jeff Bezos—the founder of Amazon—and his venture capital organization, Bezos Expeditions (an incredibly apt name for something that seeks to quite literally colonize all of everyday life), invested in Mindstrong, a platform that *Scientific American* called a "mood-predicting smartphone app."[44] Mindstrong's "science"[45] appears quite sound. They have a scientific advisory board full of important sounding physicians and researchers. It should be noted, however, that SABs are compensated (quite handily) for their work, and as such have a material stake in the success and growth of the company they advise.[46] Mindstrong uses what they call "digital phenotyping" to "understand" a user's mental state.

> To identify the digital phenotyping features that could be clinically useful, Mindstrong used powerful machine learning methods to show that specific digital features correlate with cognitive function, clinical symptoms, and measures of brain activity in a range of clinical studies.
>
> Research volunteers completed extensive neuropsychological testing, clinical assessments of mood and cognition, and, in some cases, neuroimaging with fMRI. The results revealed a set of digital biomarkers from human-smartphone interactions that correlate highly with select cognitive measures, mood state, and brain connectivity. These interactions were comprised of taps, swipes and other touchscreen activities which were completely content-free and not reliant on capturing personal information.

Mindstrong's assumptions about how people use their phones rely on a particular model of a person, and there is a strong likelihood that this person might be considered "normal" by various standards. As such, individuals not conforming to that model might be considered outliers, and thus marked as having particular tendencies toward specific mental illnesses, regardless of whether that's true. This could have significant material consequences for those individuals.

Again, the question of accuracy is less useful to us here than the question of whether the very nature of our mental health is computational in the first place, and, furthermore, that those computational processes become evident in the way we type on our phones, with our bodies becoming extensions of our mind-computers. Only when we yield completely to the intrusion of computing on every facet of our lives can we then truly "know" ourselves—we only become knowable when computers fully know us.

And yet, the interfaces suggest that complete computational knowability and predictability is possible for each and every individual. Mental health is reduced, in the interface, to apparently quantifiable and separate characteristics: cognitive control, working memory, processing speed (makes someone definitely sound like a computer, right?), and so on (Figures 3.9 and 3.10). Users see a small graph—in Edward Tufte's terms, a "sparkline"—that suggests the relative change in each of these categories, which, again, here are presented as fragmented and separate data points, and not as interrelated parts of a *whole individual, complex, and ultimately never fully knowable*. Once externalized, these data points present themselves as essential to understanding one's own feelings—they appear as neutral and scientific, but also friendly and inviting. And the user thus aspires to maintain or even enhance the data collection because the interface naturalizes the assumptions about the user that the Mindstrong technology makes, namely, that a user's mental health state can be inferred through the data they are capturing, and that, in this case "data" does equal "world." Through its "matter-of-fact" presentation and its appeals to modernism in its simplicity and flatness, the interface suggests that mental health is literally nothing more than the agglomeration of those metrics, and, therefore, accurate and continual measurement and data capture is the only way to self-understanding. The user is thus encouraged to respond to this interface by adopting, and perhaps adapting, to the very model of people built into the Mindstrong system itself.

Mindstrong's promotional rhetoric and interface designs have been effective in convincing people that, indeed, even our mental states can be subject to algorithmic anticipation. For example, Mindstrong received a contract from Los Angeles county to test a "digital fire alarm for mental distress."[47] In all of these cases—the Nest Hub, Amazon's ambient intelligence systems, and Mindstrong—individuals are algorithmically anticipated, predictable because they submit their lives to the fragmentation that then presents itself back to them as a coherent whole, but only if they come to believe that they themselves are computing machines not unlike the tools modeling and predicting their behavior.

This type of thinking—made to seem like common sense by its vociferous advocates in Silicon Valley who financially benefit from individuals' adoption of this idea—leads to outlandish claims such as an op-ed titled "One day wearables will save your marriage," which bears the subheading, "Smart devices are already

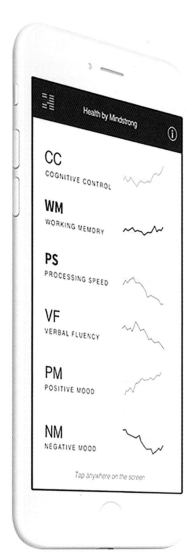

FIGURE 3.9 One screen from Mindstrong's patient-facing interface. Courtesy Mindstrong.

FIGURE 3.10 Mindstrong user interface for providers. Courtesy Mindstrong.

equipped to collect physiological data. Could they use it to predict a fight with your spouse?"[48] In a society full of computable subjects, wherein each individual is completely predictable, sure. But is such a society desirable in the first place?

Consequences: Soft Biopower and the Proscription of Potential

The ease with which we might unite with our Lacanian-mirror selves is a persuasive force. Inferences made by algorithms, "artificial intelligence," and "machine learning" acquire an authenticity that makes subsequent predictions or recommendations seem only natural. And it is the interface through which this naturalization occurs. If the stability produced by understanding the self as computable appears to compensate for a lack, then the recommendations made by computational systems—or actions taken by them on a user's behalf—become harder to resist (if resisting them even crossed one's mind in the first place).

Strangely, however, this apparent possibility of merging with one's mirror self, a truly authentic self, is built on technical systems that are deeply social and categorical.

Although computational products and services constantly capture data about you—whether through your Facebook feed, Amazon searches, your FitBit, or your Nest thermostat—and infer things about you based on their interpretations of your actions, such inferences are often cross-referenced with existing data about other users determined to be similar to you. Then, products, restaurants, films, "friends," etc., are recommended to you. Your responses to such suggestions are cataloged, added to the entry you occupy in a given system's database, and used to help the algorithmic system better define the categories to which you "belong." Your actions help shape the categories to which others belong, and *you* therefore impact what products, experiences, or services, are recommended to others who are determined to be in the same categories as you. Your algorithmic identity is therefore both dynamic and responsive to your actions and to the actions of those whose database entries are determined to be similar to yours. As such, one's aspiration to complete computational legibility and predictability has consequences for those with whom one is associated in these various databases. This aspiration therefore has a normative force that it exerts through the computational products and services that capture and utilize data about their users, supposedly to "help" them—it subtly encourages other users to see themselves in the same way, as aspiring toward total computability. The more users accept the recommendations delivered to them, the more they become like the Lacanian "mirror" self, that which is reflected back to them in the interfaces to the technologies they use everyday. It is thus that those technologies "configure life by tailoring the conditions of human possibility." In a world of what Katja de Vries called "ambient intelligence," layers of computational mediation, operating subtly, shape users' identities and at the same time leverage this shaping of identities to shape the identities of other users. If individuals, indeed, are becoming "algorithmically anticipated,"[49] and algorithms are using as the input the data they have anticipated or influenced, only to make further inferences and anticipate subsequent actions, we have perhaps found ourselves in a programmed and programmatic society, what Vilém Flusser called "inhuman," an "absurd game."

Some UX professionals, however, seem to not think it so absurd at all. As some of the technologies discussed in this chapter demonstrated, examples of contemporary UX design that seek to anticipate users abound. As far back as 2015, "anticipatory design" was a term that signaled the cutting edge of interaction design, and was the topic of a feature in *FastCompany*, in which it is heralded as helping people suffering from "decision fatigue," making life easier and more convenient. The digital agency HUGE developed a heuristic and system for determining when clients should "deploy" anticipatory strategies.[50] Other examples of anticipatory UX and design strategies have cropped up periodically since then.[51] "Anticipatory design will supposedly help us avoid decision fatigue by actually limiting the number of choices we face."[52] At the interface level, as we have seen, algorithmic anticipation often involves a disappearance—of the mechanisms that translate "world" to "data" as well as the complex processes required to infer and predict users—mimicking the shift in a user's agency. This shift must be legitimated with a business case but also via promotional discourses that help the user understand such anticipations are to benefit them. Through the interface, UX design aids in both the rhetorical and technical promotion of the idea that one should become legible to, and predictable by, computers, and in doing so, users can ultimately become ontologically coherent and knowable.

Conclusion: Becoming Cyborgs

In 1960, Manfred Clynes coined the term "Cyborg" as a shorthand for "cybernetic organism." Astute readers will note both the reference to Cybernetics, a topic that occupied much of our attention in Chapter 1, as well as the date of this term's invention, which was during the Cold War and the rise to prominence of Game Theory and Rational Choice. The basic idea of the cyborg as Clynes described it will be familiar to readers because it echoes the flattening of ontological difference that Cybernetics requires: a "self-regulating man-machine" *system*. The idea that a singular entity could be composed of two different things that were so dissimilar in nature is a central feature of both the computable subjectivity writ large and the particular facet of it that this chapter addresses, namely, that the success of Clynes's idea of the cyborg was predicated on an individual human being completely legible to the machines to which they were connected.

Today, people whose material conditions afford them the opportunity to engage with the sorts of computational products and services described here are very much *cyborgs*,[53] or at least they aspire to be as such. But what kind of cyborgs do people become when they adopt the computable subjectivity, when their ideological commitment to the equivalence between "data" and "world" produces an intense insecurity about what they can really know about themselves, and which can only be resolved through succumbing to more invasive computational surveillance? What kind of lives does that lead people to live? And what does that mean for how people treat each other, what kind of ideas about morality or ethics they adopt, and how does that impact society? The next chapter will build on the insights developed here and will examine the last question in detail.

Notes

1   John Cheney-Lippold, "A New Algorithmic Identity: Soft Biopolitics and the Modulation of Control," *Theory, Culture & Society* 28, no. 6 (November 2011): 164–81, doi:10.1177/0263276411424420, 169.

2   An adaptation of Henri Lefebvre's "homogeny of fragmentation."

3   Although perhaps you have heard something about the relatively recent interest in "ontological designing" is the design disciplines on account of the work of Arturo Escobar, Anne Marie Willis, and Tony Fry. See, for example: J. P. Hartnett, "Ontological Design Has Become Influential in Design Academia—But What Is It?," *Eye on Design*, June 14, 2021, https://eyeondesign.aiga.org/ontological-design-is-popular-in-design-academia-but-what-is-it/.

4   Thomas Hofweber, "Logic and Ontology," in *The Stanford Encyclopedia of Philosophy*, ed. Edward N. Zalta, Spring 2021 (Metaphysics Research Lab, Stanford University, 2021), https://plato.stanford.edu/archives/spr2021/entries/logic-ontology/.

5   Arturo Escobar, *Designs for the Pluriverse: Radical Interdependence, Autonomy, and the Making of Worlds*, New Ecologies for the Twenty-First Century (Durham: Duke University Press, 2018), 4.

6   The first chapter of this book sought to demonstrate this as well. One might also make reference here to the somewhat vulgarized Marxist concept of "base-superstructure" in the sense that political economy (e.g., capitalism) has some capacity to determine the nature of other institutions in society (e.g., the design disciplines).

7   Roger A. Salerno, *Landscapes of Abandonment: Capitalism, Modernity, and Estrangement*, SUNY Series in the Sociology of Culture (Albany: State University of New York Press, 2003).

8   Salerno, *Landscapes of Abandonment*, 130.

9   Zygmunt Bauman, *Modernity and the Holocaust* (Cambridge: Polity Press, 2008), epub, Chapter 4.

10 See, for example: Chris Gilliard, "Luxury Surveillance," *Real Life*, https://reallifemag.com/luxury-surveillance/.

11 See Miriam Posner's insightful and deeply researched work on SAP software, including: Miriam Posner, "The Software That Shapes Workers' Lives," *The New Yorker*, March 12, 2019, https://www.newyorker.com/science/elements/the-software-that-shapes-workers-lives. SAP Ariba, *SAP Ariba Supply Chain Collaboration Demo NAMER/LATAM Session*, 2019, https://www.youtube.com/watch?v=Ad1iqMR5wHg. SAP Ariba, "Supply Chain Collaboration," *SAP Ariba*, accessed November 14, 2021, https://www.ariba.com/solutions/solutions-overview/supply-chain/supply-chain-collaboration. SAP, "Supply Chain Planning Software Systems," *SAP*, accessed November 14, 2021, https://www.sap.com/products/supply-chain-management/supply-chain-planning.html.

12 Peter Jakubowicz, "I'm a Lyft Driver. My Passengers Act Like I'm Part of the App," *Wired*, accessed October 11, 2021, https://www.wired.com/story/im-a-lyft-driver-my-passengers-act-like-im-part-of-the-app/.

13 Bauman, *Modernity and the Holocaust*, epub, Ch. 1.

14 Lukács, cited in Salerno, *Landscapes of Abandonment*, 130.

15 Verso Books, *Understanding Rosa Luxemburg's Life and Work | Peter Hudis*, 2020, https://www.youtube.com/watch?v=7jNjGsjNbF0.

16 Salerno, *Landscapes of Abandonment*, 130. (Adapted)

17 Salerno, *Landscapes of Abandonment*, 130. (Adapted)

18 Rob Horning, "Sick of Myself," *Real Life*, accessed November 9, 2018, https://reallifemag.com/sick-of-myself/.

19 Horning, "Sick of Myself."

20 See the section on the DSM III in chapter 2.

21 Gerald Alper, "The Theory of Games and Psychoanalysis," *Journal of Contemporary Psychotherapy* 23, no. 1 (1993): 47–60, doi:10.1007/BF00945922.

22 Adrian Chapman, "'Knots': Drawing out Threads of the Literary Laing," *PsyArt: An Online Journal for the Psychological Study of the Arts*, November 11, 2014, https://psyartjournal.com/article/show/chapman-knots_drawing_out_threads_of_the_literar.

23 Kaja Silverman, *The Subject of Semiotics*, 16. print. (New York: Oxford University Press, 1984): 157.

24 Silverman, *The Subject of Semiotics*, 158.

25 Silverman, *The Subject of Semiotics*, 160.

26 Norm Friesen, "Doing with Icons Makes Symbols; or, Jailbreaking the Perfect User Interface," *CTheory*, April 17, 2012.

27 "SleepIQ Sleep Tracker—Sleep Number," https://www.sleepnumber.com/pages/sleepiq-sleep-tracker.

28 Silverman, *The Subject of Semiotics*, 177.

29 David Golumbia, invoking Deleuze and Guattari. See Chapter 6 in: David Golumbia, *The Cultural Logic of Computation* (Cambridge, MA: Harvard University Press, 2009).

30 Sam Byford, "Apple Acquires Sleep-Tracking Hardware Company Beddit," *The Verge*, May 10, 2017, https://www.theverge.com/2017/5/10/15604528/apple-buys-beddit-sleep-tracking-company.

31 See https://beddit.com or https://web.archive.org/web/20210410193141/https://www.beddit.com/

32 This particular discussion dovetails with David Golumbia's concept of "computationalism," examined in some detail in Chapter 1.

33 Made by Google, *How Sleep Sensing Works on the Second-Gen Nest Hub from Google*, 2021, https://www.youtube.com/watch?v=oKRA6GhlthM.

34 Janko Roettgers, "Google Built a Radar for Your Bedroom. It May Just Be the Company's First Step to Monetize Wellness," *Protocol—The People, Power and Politics of Tech*, March 16, 2021, https://www.protocol.com/nest-hub-sleep-tracking-radar.

35 Roettgers, "Google Built a Radar for Your Bedroom."

36 Roettgers, "Google Built a Radar for Your Bedroom."

37 See: Brian Heater, "Wearable Growth Slowed—but Not Stopped—by Pandemic," *TechCrunch*, June 3, 2020, https://social.techcrunch.com/2020/06/03/wearable-growth-slowed-but-not-stopped-by-pandemic/.HYPERLINKError! Hyperlink reference not valid.

38 Darrell Etherington, "Oura Ring Health and Sleep Tracker Review," *TechCrunch*, August 12, 2020, https://social.techcrunch.com/2020/08/12/the-oura-ring-is-the-personal-health-tracking-device-to-beat-in–2020/.

39 Mike Murphy, "Google Wants to Help You Get a Life," *Protocol—The People, Power and Politics of Tech*, February 28, 2021, https://www.protocol.com/google-personal-asistant-patents.

40 Stephen Chau et al., Activity assistant, United States US10929486B1, filed October 23, 2017, and issued February 23, 2021, https://patents.google.com/patent/US10929486B1/en?oq=10%2c929%2c486.

41 Katja DeVries wrote presciently about ambient intelligence and algorithmic anticipation in 2011, in her article called "Identity, Profiling Algorithms and a World of Ambient Intelligence." See: Katja de Vries, "Identity, Profiling Algorithms and a World of Ambient Intelligence," *Ethics and Information Technology* 12, no. 1 (March 2010): 71–85, doi:10.1007/s10676-009-9215-9.

42 Amazon Developer Team, "Our Vision: Building a World of Ambient Computing Together," *Alexa-Blog*, July 12, 2021, https://developer.amazon.com/en-US/blogs/alexa/alexa-skills-kit/2021/07/building-a-world-of-ambient-computing-together.html.

43 Dieter Bohn, "Amazon's Race to Create the Disappearing Computer," *The Verge*, September 28, 2021, https://www.theverge.com/22696187/amazon-alexa-ambient-disappearing-computer-limp-interview.

44 Kate Sheridan, "Can a Mood-Predicting Smartphone App Work?," *Scientific American*, October 4, 2018, https://www.scientificamerican.com/article/can-a-mood-predicting-smartphone-app-work/.

45 Mindstrong, "Science," *Mindstrong Health*, accessed October 4, 2021, https://mindstrong.com/science/.

46 See: Bruce Booth, "Biotech Scientific Advisory Boards: What Works, What Doesn't," *Forbes*, September 10, 2012, https://www.forbes.com/sites/brucebooth/2012/09/10/biotech-scientific-advisory-boards-what-works-what-doesnt/?sh=1deadfa5388c. And Jake Mendel, "Building Your Startup Advisory Board | Silicon Valley Bank," May 25, 2021, https://www.svb.com/startup-insights/startup-strategy/building-startup-advisory-board#

47 Benedict Carey, "California Tests a Digital 'Fire Alarm' for Mental Distress," *The New York Times*, June 17, 2019, sec. Health, https://www.nytimes.com/2019/06/17/health/mindstrong-mental-health-app.html.

48 Gary Eastwood, "One Day Wearables Will Save Your Marriage | CIO," *CIO*, May 7, 2017, https://web.archive.org/web/20170802022444/http://www.cio.com/ article/3195086/artificial-intelligence/one-day-wearables-will-save-your-marraige. html.

49 Katja de Vries, "Identity, Profiling Algorithms and a World of Ambient Intelligence," *Ethics and Information Technology* 12, no. 1 (March 2010): 71–85, doi:10.1007/ s10676-009-9215-9.

50 Aaron Shapiro, "The Next Big Thing in Design? Less Choice," *Fast Company*, April 15, 2015, https://www.fastcompany.com/3045039/the-next-big-thing-in-design-fewer-choices.

51 See, for example: Sarah Doody, "Productized 19 Notes: Anticipatory Design & the Future of Experience," *Medium*, March 30, 2021, https://productized.medium.com/ productized-19-notes-anticipatory-design-the-future-of-experience-sarah-doody-e239eb7e149f.

52 Brenda Taulbee, "Is the Future of UX Screenless? Savy Weighs in on UX Trends of 2021 and beyond," *Branding, Web Design and Digital Marketing Agency*, May 25, 2021; https://savyagency.com/ux-trends-of–2021/.

53 Since the 1991 publication of Donna Haraway's "Cyborg Manifesto," in *Simians, Cyborgs, and Women: The Reinvention of Nature*, ed. Donna Jeanne Haraway (New York: Routledge, 1991), the idea of the cyborg in academia has had a liberatory and feminist quality. But this optimism about the possibilities of a subject's relationship to technology is devoid of a critical reading of the political economic conditions under which those technologies were developed as well as the racial politics of the figure of the cyborg (and, again, the racialized histories of the technologies on which the idea of the cyborg is constructed). See: Julia R. DeCook, "A [White] Cyborg's Manifesto: The Overwhelmingly Western Ideology Driving Technofeminist Theory," *Media, Culture & Society* 43, no. 6 (September 2021): 1158–67, doi:10.1177/0163443720957891, 1161.

4 THE MORAL IMPERATIVE OF NORMALITY THROUGH COMPUTATIONAL OPTIMIZATION

Introduction: The Optimized Professor and the Pressures of Optimization

Imagine the following scenario: *You're a new professor at a large research university. After a long afternoon of teaching, you open an app and view your student engagement statistics. Scientific-looking charts and graphs populate the screen, accompanied by friendly animations that seem to soften their sterility. As you scroll through the data visualizations, you notice that the "student distraction rate" seems to have decreased. This inference is based on the data from skin conductance sensors on students' wrists, data from sensors in the seats, as well as from eye-tracking and body language information gathered from the camera system in the room. Your "compellingness" score is also a little higher, owing to some additional variation in tone and volume when you spoke. A red dot above the "research" icon in the interface indicates an alert. You open it and see a new recommended publication for dissemination (which is in the 6th percentile in its field), the aspect of your research best suited for this publication, and suggested next steps in order to efficiently produce this new article. Just below this, a small chart shows how such a publication might positively affect your overall faculty productivity score as well as the predicted increase in percentage chance of being promoted that such a publication would produce. Below that are some suggested changes to the way you manage your activities in order to accommodate this new project. This includes an additional afternoon of childcare, but it seems as though the benefits would outweigh the cost given the merit-based salary increases that the publication might produce over the coming year. You acknowledge these suggestions and add the new project to your research portfolio.*

In 2018, an analytics company called ScholarStat published an "advertorial" in *Art Journal*, a highly regarded scholarly publication for art and design academics. Advertorials are common in popular magazines, such as *Bon Appetit*, and are generally longer-form advertisements that look and feel like journalistic content

FIGURE 4.1 ScholarStat's Faculty Productivity Index "Ticker," a device similar to a stock ticker that would sit outside professors' offices. Courtesy the author.

and seem to fit more seamlessly within a publication. In its advertorial, "Advanced Analytics for a Better University," ScholarStat demonstrates its vision for the future of universities.

ScholarStat's advanced analytics system works on both the research and teaching aspects of a professor's work. Tracking research output as well as connecting with technologies, such as wearables and smart furniture, that quantify an individual professor's behavior and health, the system builds detailed models of professors which can then be used as both "evaluative metrics" and a "predictive tool in hiring and promotion." This predictive component—based on models generated from data about "similar" professors across the globe—can also provide recommendations for funding sources, research areas, and publication outlets for individual professors. In addition to both professor- and administrative-level dashboards, data about professors' productivity would be publicly visible through constantly updating "tickers" that would sit outside their offices (Figures 4.1 and 4.2).

In the realm of teaching, ScholarStat claims its advanced text analysis of student writing, which uses machine learning (ML) to adapt to subject and learning outcomes, will enable better evaluation both of student work and of writing assignments themselves. Meanwhile, its networked cameras and microphones, complete with sophisticated voice recognition, sentiment analysis, and facial expression recognition, will measure the effectiveness of classroom discussions and give that feedback in real time to teachers through the ScholarStat teaching dashboard.

When I presented about ScholarStat to a group of faculty at my institution, my colleagues seemed both distressed yet unsurprised, perhaps because it represents a synthesis of various trajectories that have emerged in academia and society

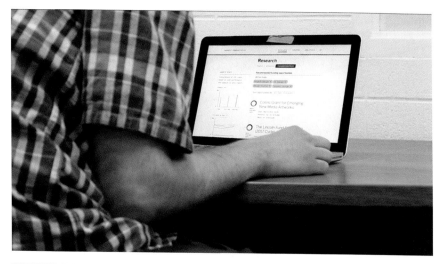

FIGURE 4.2 A still from a film in which ScholarStat's faculty-facing interface is featured. Courtesy the author.

across the last half-century. In reality, however, ScholarStat is a *parafiction*. "Like a paramedic as opposed to a medical doctor, a parafiction is related to but not quite a member of the category of fiction as established in literary and dramatic art. It remains a bit outside. It does not perform its procedures in the hygienic clinics of literature, but has one foot in the field of the real."[1] I created ScholarStat as a way to materialize my concerns about the future of higher education based on what I was learning about the technologies being developed and deployed at research institutions like my own. These trends map to the following:

1 Research evaluation and prediction/recommendation

  a Basic bibliometric[2] indicators and peer comparison.

  b Contextual indicators through interoperability with wearables and voice UI tools.

  c Predictive analytics and recommendations for publications, conferences, grant opportunities, collaborations, research topics.

2 Teaching evaluation, feedback, and responsiveness

  a Text analysis for assessing student learning outcomes powered my Machine Learning (ML) models.

  b Real-time analysis of voice/conversation/discussion using Natural Language Processing (NLP) and sentiment analysis.

  c Facial expression recognition to gauge alertness and emotional response and giving instructors real-time feedback.

These trends speak to two ideas that—as part of an increasing emphasis on "accountability" in higher education—have risen to prominence:

1 Holistic and systems-oriented evaluation/assessment that considers factors that affect productivity and not just productivity itself (this might include health and wellness initiatives and insurance). These evaluative tools might include metrics for the evaluation of teaching as well as research. Indeed, ScholarStat suggests the integration of sensors and biometrics in the classroom as indicators of teaching efficacy.

2 The use of predictive analytics and recommendation systems for scholarship and productivity, which become increasingly enmeshed in the institutional infrastructure, ranging from promotion and tenure decisions to intranet applications, etc.

Given the arguments put forth in the preceding chapters, there should be no mistake here that these trends and tendencies are evidence of the computable subjectivity penetrating the very heart of academia. There are far more examples of these trends than I can possibly address here, but I will aim to offer some evidence for the ways that the various aspects of ScholarStat's technological platform are not "fictions" at all, but are actively being developed and deployed by companies and academics across the globe. ScholarStat was perhaps more than anything else a way for me to compress these trends into a single object for critique. Indeed, a colleague from the UK once asked me if the "fiction could keep pace with reality."[3]

Beginning around 2010, companies like Academic Analytics and Simitive established themselves as major players in the "academic accountability industry" by using similar rhetoric to ScholarStat, focused on the relationship between the measurement of performance, feedback, and exchange of information. In 2018, for example, Simitive's "Academic Solution," claimed to provide "a platform for the engagement of management, academics, non academic staff and students in the performance of the university." Simitive's Workload Allocation Management System was a university-wide planning tool which took data from departments and automatically produced plans and processes for the institution. The system provided "a holistic approach to personal as well as organisational development." With it, "Past performance trends, current delivery progress and future planning options are all simultaneously available."[4]

Meanwhile, beginning around 2017, Academic Analytics touted its "benchmarking" and "discovery" tools, which allowed universities to:

aggregate, curate, visualize, and contextualize data on the research created by scholars and we provide powerful, user-friendly business intelligence tools to visualize and identify patterns from those data. Our tools give institutional leaders a new understanding of the research accomplishments of scholars, departments, programs, and the entire institution—and they point to directions in which to grow the research footprint strategically and in line with the university's mission. We help senior administrators view research activity in an appropriate context for the issues being addressed, identify new funding opportunities, form expert teams to win funding, and increase the visibility of the institution's research enterprise to companies, foundations, and potential collaborators.[5]

There have also been a number of efforts to realize some of the more ambitious tools represented by the ScholarStat parafiction. These efforts are generally focused on the utilization of highly invasive surveillance technologies that are supposed to improve the efficacy of the educator. These include using sentiment analysis on student writing to help instructors "shape course content," using facial expression recognition and posture detection to determine "audience response" and "engagement," because instructors are "the sensors in a classroom" but "are not scalable."[6] There is no clearer evidence that the dominant view of educators in many areas of educational technology and higher-education policy is that they are nothing more than fleshy computers. Indeed, ANS, a tech company that specializes in cloud computing, declared that chatbots are "the future of higher education."[7]

Efforts at analyzing and predicting the research output of faculty members tend to be less well-known than the efforts at shaping classroom experiences using predictive analytics, and these efforts have tended to, with the exception of companies like Academic Analytics, emerge from within academia itself, specifically from the disciplines of bibliometrics and scientometrics. Take, for example, a study called "Tenure Analytics: Models for Predicting Research Impact," published in 2015 in the journal *Operations Research*.[8] The authors, from MIT's Sloan School of Management, suggested the following: "Tenure decisions, key decisions in academic institutions, are primarily based on subjective assessments of candidates," and that "analytics can complement the tenure decision-making process in academia and improve the prediction of academic impact," implying of course that the bibliometric database they used to train their prediction models is somehow objective. In a promotional piece on Sloan's website, titled "'Moneyball' for Professors?" the authors suggested that predictive analytics are the future of hiring and tenure decisions, thus completely optimizing academia.[9]

In 1997, long before the "Moneyball for Academia" study, Dean Keith Simonton, publishing in the journal *Psychological Review*, wrote an article called "Creative Productivity: A Predictive and Explanatory Model of Career Trajectories and Landmarks," in which he claimed to have developed a (computational) model that can derive "several precise predictions that cannot be generated by any alternative theory."[10] Included in the article are a number of equations and charts and graphs, along with a host of citations that, in spite of his references to artists and writers, tend to focus on the "productivity" of research scientists. On the surface, Simonton's claim seems patently absurd. But if we consider one of the arguments that I've made throughout this book thus far, that becoming legible to computational systems is itself an aspirational ideal in society, then the more legible a professor becomes to systems that quantify and categorize them, the more likely they'll be able to be predicted by computational models like Simonton's.

While synthesizing many of the aforementioned developments through a fictional company and thus suggesting their existence under "one roof," ScholarStat is very much a reality regardless of whether itself as a company exists or not. The way I chose to manifest this reality, using *design* to provoke colleagues and others to think about the ways that professors are computed, modeled, and predicted, reflects my belief in the power of the *interface*—the visual manifestation of the underlying computational systems to which we are beholden—to catalyze discourse. How do systems like ScholarStat, Academic Analytics, and those such as EduSense—that use facial expression recognition, posture detection, and sentiment analysis to "optimize" the delivery of instruction—shape how faculty conceive of themselves, each other, and of the students who they teach?

The consequences of the metrics and analytics systems permeating universities are far-reaching. Professors are encouraged to see themselves as they are seen by the metrics systems to which they become beholden. Perhaps they fear not producing "impact" in their fields, thus endangering their employment, or maybe they are applying for a grant that looks at specific metrics in its evaluation process. No matter what, they are incentivized at every turn to become completely legible to the systems of metrics and analytics used in their fields and institutions. Meanwhile, because metrics that measure "impact" purport to evaluate quality of research, "good" research, meaning that which contributes to knowledge and society, becomes equated with higher metrics. Thus the metric takes on a moral dimension as well, with higher "impact factors" becoming indicative of research with a better return-on-investment for society as a whole. Consistently concerned about the legibility of their work to such metrics and thus whether their work will be considered impactful and therefore fundamentally "good," professors experience an increasing anxiety, one which will only be exacerbated with the proliferation of metrics and predictive analytics that bolster the continued obsession with return-on-investment in neoliberal universities.[11] This obsession with ROI and the anxiety produced by the metrics on which this obsession relies is part of the neoliberal rationale for the increasingly precarious nature of teaching in universities today.[12]

This chapter will address these themes as part of its examination of the third characteristic of the computable subjectivity: *a belief in computational optimization as both normal and as a moral good.* Adopting the computable subjectivity bolsters the production of normality and morality via quantification and categorization, and at the same time produces feelings of anxiety that result in a need for *more* quantification and categorization. When complete self-optimization seems possible, and when it seems as though one can achieve an ontological security through technologies that purport to "know" them via the "data" they offer for capture, the quest for self-optimization becomes a moral imperative. If you can capture data that will help you live a "healthier" life, reducing your cost to insurers and making you a more reliable mother or father, then you appear morally bankrupt if you do not do so. When individuals are assumed to be computable *and* computing, they reveal a moral shortcoming if they do not take the opportunity to compute more accurately or become more legible to computational systems that model them. Such moralizing contributes to the creation of intense anxiety in individuals, producing yet another force strongly guiding them toward succumbing to the inferences and recommendations made by anticipatory technologies and shown in the interfaces of the computational products and services—apps and websites—that people use every day. This chapter will examine the moralizing dimension of the computable subjectivity, the way designers create the visual and interactive experience of systems that purports to help individuals self-optimize, and the consequences of the manner in which these interfaces support the purported morality of self-optimization. What the interface reveals and conceals is of paramount importance to the normative force exerted by computational technologies. Designers must appreciate the gravity of their role in producing the idea that self-optimization through computation is normal, moral, and necessary.

Measurement, Normality, and Morality: Two Origin Stories

I want to introduce two histories that have helped naturalize the idea that it is morally good to computationally optimize oneself. These two histories are about the role of measurement in society and they are also about the relationship between normality and morality—the way normality became something to aspire to. The first history is about the relationship between quantification and categorization, the way the advent of statistics produced new "kinds" of people. The second history is that of dramatic change in the psychiatric establishment, which would reverberate throughout society, and which would echo the Cyberneticists' privileging of a system's behavior over its essence.[13]

The Influence of Statistics on Optimized Normalcy

The idea of "normal" as something toward which one should aspire owes its rise to the incredible influence of statistics on every aspect of everyday life. It is the reason so many of us take for granted that "social laws will be cast in statistical form."[14] Lennard Davis, in his introduction to the *Disability Studies Reader*, writes that,

> it was the French statistician Adolphe Quetelet (1796–1847) who contributed most to a generalized notion of the normal as an imperative. He noticed that the "law of error," used by astronomers to locate a star by plotting all the sightings and then averaging the errors, could be equally applied to the distribution of human features such as height and weight. He then took a further step of formulating the concept of "*l'homme moyen*" or the average man.[15]

Strangely, Quetelet's idea of the average man became transformed into an imperative—something for which the population should strive. Davis writes, "with the concept of the norm comes the concept of deviations or extremes. When we think of bodies, in a society where the concept of the norm is operative, then people with disabilities will be thought of as deviants. This … is in contrast to societies with the concept of an ideal, in which all people have non-ideal status."[16] In the late nineteenth century, just as Emile Durkheim was attempting to distinguish the "normal" from the "pathological," "Karl Pearson, a founding father of biometrics, eugenics, and Anglo-American statistical theory, called the Gaussian distribution the *normal curve*"[17] (emphasis mine). Therefore, "many of the modern categories by which we think about people and their activities were put in place by an attempt to collect numerical data." Statistics and its need for quantification led to the production of categories, which led to *new kinds of people* being created. To *be* normal, you have to *be counted*.

It is essential for designers and students of design to understand the connection between quantifiability, statistics, and eugenics that creates an uncomfortable linkage between the efforts of early eugenicists and the projects of quantifying, predicting, and recommending all aspects of human activity via technologies such as FitBits, "SmartPlates,"[18] the Sleep Number Smart Mattress, and so on. Interfaces to such products are the means by which the norm, along with our relationship to it, becomes feedback mechanisms in a cybernetic loop of quantified normalcy.

Ian Hacking's work, reflected in the title of his highly influential *Taming of Chance*, is also about the shift from determinism to chance and the study of statistics and probability. The history he tells is a useful prequel to the cybernetic obsession with prediction and control, which tames chance through modeling probabilistic scenarios. Today, it seems, chance is perpetually being tamed in new and ever-more "innovative" ways. Predictive analytics are embedded in nearly every computational system with which people interact, powering the inferences and recommendations that shape users' everyday lives. Just as the ScholarStat parafiction suggests, publishers such as Springer and Elsevier have produced recommendation systems to help researchers find the correct dissemination venue for their work.[19,20] To become the best researcher I can (and therefore be as responsible to those that employ me and the taxpayers of Michigan), at least according to the metrics on which I am evaluated, I should advantage of services that tame chance, that use probabilistic modeling and predictive analytics in order to ensure that I am as productive as possible, that I fall within an acceptable percentile distribution on the curve when compared with my peers.

If chance itself can be tamed through probabilistic methods, through computing and cybernetic feedback loops, the possibilities of self-optimization must not be lost on the users of the technologies that *do* this taming. Communicating to the user the moral imperative to self-optimize is done *by design*. It is done through interfaces, where users meet the computational versions of themselves. This interface-level communication of normalcy *and* computational optimization as an aspirational ideal is the domain of user-experience design.

The DSM-III and the Computerization of Normal

Normality came to have a moral dimension attached to it, in part through the historical interlocking of statistics and eugenics. Becoming "normal," then, became an aspiration precisely because it was seen as a moral good. It came to be this way through the advent of the kinds of quantification that are themselves ancestors of today's "smart" technologies. One highly influential example of this process— the role of quantification, categorization, and technology in the production of a morally charged idea of "normal"—is the third edition of the *Diagnostic and Statistical Manual of Mental Disorders* (DSM-III). The DSM-III is also an early example of the use of computing to process data about large groups of people and analyze patterns for "normality" or "non-normality."

Psychiatry's shift, after the introduction of the DSM-III, to an emphasis on the *symptom* as opposed to the *person*, epitomizes both the false equivalence between "data" and "world" and lays the groundwork for the moral imperative of "normality" through enumeration and computing. Prior to the introduction of the DSM-III, psychiatry as a discipline viewed symptoms not as definitive but rather as inroads to a deeper analysis of the *whole* person. But after the DSM-III was introduced, psychiatry was "reorganized" to focus on symptoms and diagnoses. "The basic transformation in the DSM-III was its development and use of a model that equated visible and measurable symptoms with the presence of diseases. This symptom-based model allowed psychiatry to develop a standardized system of measurement."[21] External data became equivalent to internal world, and the mechanism of translation, once again, disappeared. Robert Spitzer, who led the writing of the DSM-III, writes, "The psychiatric diagnosis of Major Depression is based on the assumption that symptoms alone can indicate there is a disorder; this assumption allows normal responses to stressors to be mischaracterized as symptoms of disorder."[22]

The diagnostic and classificatory system of the DSM-III had more far-reaching consequences that its authors did not anticipate.

1 The opening of the door to the pharmacological establishment through quantification of disease the subjection of this quantification to capital.

2 The imperative that the population felt to adhere to the norm such that they came knocking on doctors' doors. This norm is that which is established through quantification.

Like other anticipatory systems that have been discussed thus far, the DSM-III utilizes the combination of quantification and classification to produce its intended effect: predictability and normativity. Indeed, *some researchers believed that computers crunching the results of checklists were equally adept at diagnosing patients* (based on the DSM-III criteria) as clinicians.[23]

Is it possible that the DSM-III medicalized—and therefore suggested was outside the norm—everyday "normal" human emotional experience? Most people, at that point, became "abnormal," and in need of medication or other treatment.[24]

Once people became able to be categorized through quantification, and certain categories perceived as "abnormal," a quantifiable norm became not only an aspiration but a societal imperative—to remain a "productive" or "contributing" member of society meant that one must seek medical help to become and remain "normal." It is hard to overemphasize this point, because this idea—that, computerization, quantification, and categorization produce predictability and normativity, and that this process is socially desirable—has made its way into so many other aspects of everyday life. Quantification yields particular kinds of information which can be plotted on a curve, analyzed for deviancy, and "solutions" that correct this deviancy can be sought, as well as allowing this deviancy to be predicted and modeled for future reference. When you can be easily diagnosed, even perhaps by a computer, and the pharmaceutical industry is at the ready to provide drugs that push you statistically toward what is quantitatively defined as "normal," why wouldn't you want to become normal?

The "innovation" of the DSM-III might be seen as a predecessor to research devoted to identifying whether or not an individual is depressed from the content of their Instagram posts. In their study, "Instagram Photos Reveal Predictive Markers of Depression," Reece and Danforth suggest that "Photographs posted to Instagram can be analyzed using computational methods to screen for depression. Using only photographic details, such as color and brightness, our statistical model was able to predict which study participants suffered from depression, and performed better than the rate at which unassisted general practitioners typically perform during inperson patient assessments."[25] Of course, this research is predicated on a particular idea of depression. Indeed, the idea of "depression" that the researchers have in mind is precisely the kind of behaviorally oriented, context-independent, diagnostic ideal first espoused by the authors of the DSM-III.

> Danforth now hopes to study the potential for a similar tool to predict suicide risk. "That's one of the hardest prediction problems that there is," he says. "There's a lot of risk factors associated with suicide, but trained psychiatrists whose job it is to assess risk still really struggle with it. Maybe there's something in our social media that could be helpful."[26]

This passage is representative of a number of ideas that have been discussed thus far in this book. It demonstrates a commitment to the cybernetic ideal of the perfect system of prediction and control given the right feedback and frictionless information transmission. It also represents a commitment to the idea that we are, at our core, computable and able to be understood through computation. Perhaps it's no coincidence that seemingly early literature on predicting the creative output of researchers and professors over their careers came from the field of psychology.

While all this information about the evolution of psychology and the role of computing in this evolution has seemingly very little to do with "design," it is essential in helping designers understand what might be considered as "symptom-based computing"—in which the data captured about us are equated with the world in which we live, without an appreciation for context or that which was not captured. "Data" that can be captured about us by our FitBits, smart furniture, or other computational systems, are effectively just like the behavioral symptoms used by the DSM-III—they are used to make generalizations about us or the world (or about a person's mental state), but are free of any kind of context and rely on specific ideas about people which are already embedded in the software (or the diagnostic in the case of the DSM-III). These ideas, the assumptions they make about users, and the ways they frame certain norms as aspirations, are then reflected back to the users of these technologies through the interface. They persuade users to believe in normality as a moral good that can only be achieved through computational self-optimization.

The Moral Imperative of Self-Optimizing Technologies: The Case of the Amazon Halo

In 2020, Amazon launched the Halo, its first foray into the wearables market, and, loosely speaking, a competitor with the likes of the Apple Watch and FitBit. The second chapter of this book discussed the early iterations of the FitBit at length—its underlying technologies, and the way the ideas driving those technologies produce an ideological commitment to "data" being the same as "world." Even though the first version of the Halo object lacked a screen-based interface, the Halo is similar to the Apple Watch and the FitBit in some respects: it tracks "activity," such as steps, it differentiates between types of activity (e.g., walking vs. running), and it has an incentive system for users to be more "active"; it also tracks "sleep" and gives a user a score, just like the FitBit and Apple Watch do. However, the Halo also differentiates itself through its emphasis on being more of a service than an object, with the Halo mobile app having more sophisticated functionality than the wristband alone. The key differentiators between the Halo and other wearable product-service systems are "body" and "tone."

Amazon's press release announcing the Halo hailed its "body" feature as revolutionary:

> The tools that measure body fat percentage can be expensive or difficult to access. Using new innovations in computer vision and machine learning,

Amazon Halo lets customers measure their body fat percentage from the comfort and privacy of their own home, making this important information easily accessible. The Amazon Halo body fat measurement is as accurate as methods a doctor would use—and nearly twice as accurate as leading at-home smart scales.[27]

While you wear nothing but your underwear, the Halo app takes four pictures of you—front, back, and each side—then uploads these images to Amazon's servers where they are assembled into a 3D scan of your body. Amazon's proprietary ML systems then analyze this scan and determine your body fat percentage, which, along with the scan, is returned to your phone. In the interface to the app, you can then manipulate your own body using a simple slider, to experience what you would look like with "more" or "less" body fat.

Like many of the other technologies discussed in this book, "personalization" is effectively correlations run on massive datasets in which inferences are made about a user based on their similarity to other users (i.e., quantification and categorization). The resulting inferences and recommendations, regardless of their clinical validity, serve to enforce particular norms about health and well-being, while only considering that which can be made legible to the system in the first place. The Halo's "body" feature should thus be seen as a direct descendant of early eugenics programs and the influence Quetelet had on them. Other questions arise, such as the validity or diversity of the datasets on which the ML systems were trained. A mantra in computer science is "garbage in, garbage out," and much of the critical discourse around AI and ML technologies is centered on bias in training sets. If one gets bogged down in questions about the validity of the training data, however, it obscures Amazon's bigger project, which is to convince you that you are able to be understood by a computer and that to become healthier, you *should* subject yourself to these kinds of computational systems and the norms toward which they guide you.

The Halo's "tone" feature, meanwhile, at least when it was announced, felt somewhat more audacious. Amazon's press release again:

> The globally accepted definition of health includes not just physical but also social and emotional well-being. The innovative Tone feature uses machine learning to analyze energy and positivity in a customer's voice so they can better understand how they may sound to others, helping improve their communication and relationships. For example, Tone results may reveal that a difficult work call leads to less positivity in communication with a customer's family, an indication of the impact of stress on emotional well-being.[28]

After you opt-in to the use of the "tone" feature, the microphone on the Halo wearable will begin to recognize your voice and subsequently intermittently judge it on a variety of metrics, including "positivity" and "energy." Writing about the

Halo immediately after its launch, *Verge* columnist Dieter Bohn said, "It picks up on the pitch, intensity, rhythm, and tempo of your voice and then categorizes them into 'notable moments' that you can go back and review throughout the day. Some of the emotional states include words like hopeful, elated, hesitant, bored, apologetic, happy, worried, confused, and affectionate."[29]

As the reader might imagine at this point, my response is not only one of skepticism, but also one of deep concern about the ramifications of technology like this becoming an accepted facet of interpersonal interaction. Can my interactions with another person be judged through computational metrics? What kind of people do we become when we believe this is possible? How does the "tone" feature of Amazon's Halo further entrench the direct equivalence between "data" and "world" and will the data it captures become more "real" than the emotions that a user actually feels or the quality of a conversation as experienced by the participants?[30]

How Emotional "Data" Becomes Equal to Emotional "World" and Its Impact on the Moral Imperative of Normality through Computational Optimization

The patents for the various technologies underlying the Halo, and in particular its "tone" feature are numerous. One patent that Amazon was granted in 2019 is helpful to understanding the convoluted relationships between "world" and "data" that must be naturalized in order to make it *seem* as though the Halo really does *understand* your "tone" and thus your emotional state or the qualitative experience of a conversation with a friend or loved one. Indeed, Amazon's advertising for the Halo includes taglines such as "See how you sound to your *partner*: Maintain relationship health with tone of voice analysis," "See how you sound to your *interviewer*," and "See how you sound to your *boss*."

Amazon's patent for emotion detection through voice input is mind-numbing to read. The mind-numbingness of patents is partly what allows technologies that emerge from them to take on a kind of naturalization.[31] That which becomes useful but is not able to be inspected or understood can become uncritically accepted if only in part because attempts to understand it tend to be fruitless.[32]

The "tone" and emotion-recognition system for the Halo, according to one Amazon patent,[33] proceeds roughly as follows: When a user "enrolls" in the system— meaning when they enable the "tone" feature of the Halo device and app system— the system asks users to speak different sentences so they can determine a "baseline neutral emotional state." Concerning most things, including the determination of the baseline emotional state, the patent filing is long and contains quite a bit of detail while remaining ambiguous enough to not give too much away. Some comments on audio baselines and how they get compared to subsequent audio/ voice data that is captured are probably of use here, especially when considering how these get translated into the types of feedback a user *sees* in the interface: For audio files to be compared with one another by ML systems, and to have particular aspects of them identified as being consistent and thus representative of particular emotional states, the sound wave samples need to be standardized and formatted in a way that a machine can read and analyze. This is generally done through the use of spectrograms, which are a way of visualizing a soundwave that show the presence of different frequency ranges of sound over the duration of the wave form. They look kind of like heatmaps. One variant of spectrogram that is often used in ML projects about sound utilizes *Mel-frequency cepstral coefficients (MFCC)*, which implements a particular scale for the frequency bands that supposedly does a better job of approximating the human auditory system.

Once the audio files are rendered in a way that a ML system can extract relevant features—in the case of the sound waves above, the sound waves are represented by *images* generated through the MFCC processing—the features need to be identified and audio files classified. "Features" here refer simply to a measurable property of an individual soundwave that can be compared across other sound waves within a dataset. Thus, the ML system might compare the appearance of high levels of specific frequency bands at different times within a given set of audio samples, and thus determine that some samples are more similar to others given the presence of certain levels of energy in specific frequency bands at specific timestamps. These features are translated into terms we associate with the sound of human vocalizations (e.g., accent, pitch, intonation, tone, stress, rhythm, speed), and these are the properties with which certain values are stored when a "baseline" is determined for a given user.

Of course, the ability for nuanced differences in the presence of different frequency ranges to be detected by any spectrogram generator requires the sound in question to have been captured with a certain fidelity, and this is dependent then on the microphone used by the device capturing the audio. And different microphones have different "frequency responses,"[34] which means that different microphones will respond differently to the exact same sound, and thus transmit sound as electrical signals in ways that will end up being represented differently in the spectrograms that eventually get generated with any ML sound classification system.

Nonetheless, once the "baseline" is determined, then any "input audio" can be captured and analyzed relative to the (supposedly) emotion-neutral baseline, thus enabling the system to determine particular emotional states of the user (again, supposedly). When input audio is captured by the Halo for the purposes of its "tone" feature, the audio needs to be analyzed first and foremost to determine if it is a vocalization and if that vocalization was indeed made by the user. This is done by comparing the audio captured to the "baseline" audio that was stored when the user enrolled in the system. This comparison process can be done through various ML techniques, and outputs a series of scores that indicate the confidence with which the system has made its determination about whether the audio is indeed the user's voice. These confidence scores determine whether the analysis of the user's voice proceeds to the tone and/or emotion detection algorithms.

If the audio is determined to have a confidence score beyond a given threshold (which means it's still possible that it's not even the user's voice), then the system may retrieve the baseline audio for processing and comparison, in order to determine the user's emotional state.

This is where things seem to get *really* complicated. The determination of the user's emotional state is done through a series of ML processes, which use "trained models" as tools for making classification determinations based on weighted likelihoods of particular properties having specific corresponding values. This is effectively a probabilistic approach to analyzing and classifying emotion. Such an approach should recall the work of Ian Hacking, who, as we discussed earlier, famously describes the "taming of chance" in the history of statistics, in which life became understood not in deterministic terms but in probabilistic ones. Hacking sees the shift from determinism to probabilistic modeling in tandem with what he calls the "making up" of people, in which individuals are remade in the image of that which measures them and calculates various facets of their life chances.[35] Today, individuals have become seen as information processors, with new measurable characteristics being discovered every day—such as "tone" or "emotion."

The "trained model" that is used to determine the user's emotional state from their vocalizations refers to a variety of models that can include Neural Networks— Support Vector Machines, Deep Neural Networks, Recurrent Neural Networks, or Convolutional Neural Networks. Before the model can be applied to new input audio (meaning anything a user says subsequent to their enrollment in the system), it itself has to be trained. It's difficult to tell how the model is initially trained and how frequently it gets updated after the user's enrollment. For example, questions arise around what kinds of human vocalizations comprised the original training data set and from who did those vocalizations come? How are emotions identified in that data set and what features are correlated with those emotions? The patent is very vague about the types of ML techniques used by the system in question, and they say nothing about the actual content of the original training data for the models prior to the user's enrollment in the system. Once the user is enrolled, however, the training data includes audio data representing the user's neutral and non-neutral emotional states, as well as contextual data, which "may" include GPS/location data, interaction type and/or setting (family gathering, sporting event, work meeting, time of day, action in which the user was engaged (indicated perhaps by other sensors in the device), weather information, physiological data about the user, and more.[36]

The establishment of emotional state through vocalization might also, according to the patent, be surmised in part through the actual words a user says. In this case, voice recognition software is applied to extract the content of a user's speech and analyze the words for their emotional content. Similar ML techniques are used to determine not only whether a user has actually spoken certain words, but the weighted emotional qualities of those particular words in particular contexts. Thus, both acoustic model processing and language model processing then combine to establish an "understanding" of a user's emotional state.

"For a given input to the neural network, it outputs a number of potential outputs each with an assigned score representing a probability that the particular output is the correct output given the particular input."[37] The "top scoring" output then is passed along in the process, eventually establishing the "correct" emotional state of the user. This emotional state is reflected back to the user in the interface to the Halo app (Figure 4.3).

This digression into the details of Amazon's patent filings might seem absurd. One could imagine an auctioneer reading it at light speed and taking a deep breath afterwards, exhausted by the technical jargon. The absurdity, however, is part of the point—it is here, in the patents. But it must disappear for users to be incentivized to adopt Amazon's technologies, to embrace the idea that "world" and "data" are the same, that because of this equivalence they can only be understood through computing, and that this belief is a moral obligation.

If I can optimize my tone in order to "maintain my relationship health," then what kind of person am I if I actively *choose not to?* I may be seen as morally deficient and wasting the opportunity to enhance my relationships with others and better society. "Maybe I should sound less sad," I might tell myself, "so that my colleagues think more highly of me or so that my relationships with my family can be better," even though maybe I do *feel* sad. Or maybe I feel sad but don't sound it, so I'm told that I seem emotionally well-adjusted. Amazon's advertising and promotional materials for the Halo are quite clear about the moral and ethical implications of using or not using the Halo's "tone" feature. This is biopower at work, through the interface.

FIGURE 4.3 An image of the Amazon Halo App interface. Courtesy Amazon Press Center.

How the Morality of Self-Optimization Is Leveraged in Neoliberal Healthcare

It is worth mentioning one additional feature of the Amazon Halo product-service ecosystem, especially as it pertains to the development of norms regarding health and well-being, and the relationship between these ideas and biopower within neoliberal governmentality: the landmark partnership between Amazon and John Hancock Life Insurance that was launched in late 2020.[38] By subjecting yourself to constant surveillance and aspiring to be completely legible to the Halo's computational system, you will reap the rewards of lower premiums on your insurance and gain an advantage over others who desire similar life insurance benefits. This suggests one of the key features of neoliberal governmentality and the way it manifests in the biopoitical dimension of everyday life—that you, the individual, are solely responsible for your health and well-being, that your future is in *your* hands, and in order to reduce costs to your employer or to society at large, you *must* aspire toward complete computational-legibility and achieve optimal health efficiency. This consumerized notion of personal health and well-being strategically does not account for asymmetries of power and privilege in society, the way that race, income, and other factors keep people from being able to make the kind of personal lifestyle changes that Amazon and John Hancock Insurance claim are possible for anyone. Together, Amazon and John Hancock suggest that there are technological solutions to what are, at the core, fundamentally political problems. But Amazon and John Hancock are wrong, in that health is *not* an individual matter, but rather a systemic one. If consumers to know this, however, it would shake the neoliberal entrepreneurial individualism on which Amazon and John Hancock make their fortunes. The interfaces to the Halo app and to one's own insurance policy, for example, serve to conceal then the systemic nature of health, its deep interconnectedness to political economy and the histories of science and technology that have been examined throughout this book thus far.

In her book, *The Quantified Self*, Deborah Lupton emphasizes the normative implications of an acceptance of a computable subjectivity, connecting it to self-help literature in the cultivation of docile neoliberal subjects. "The materials that contribute to self-help literature reproduce the notion of individuals as atomized actors who are expected and encouraged to work upon themselves in the quest to achieve health, productivity, and happiness."[39] Such literature suggests the existence of an authentic self that should be the aim of one's efforts, and accessing one's authentic self requires different kinds of self-tracking.

Practices of self-optimization encourage individuals to believe in the value of pursuing their own "enlightened self-interest." By pursuing their own self-interest, being a healthy and productive worker, they are regarded as fulfilling their obligations to society, and they appear to be doing so voluntarily. Given a computing and computable individual acting in their own self-interest, once the appropriate knowledge is gained and applied, at least according to the cybernetic ideal, most problems can be resolved.

> Any suggestion that a person's difficulties may be caused by intractable biological problems … or by their position as members of socially or economically disadvantaged groups tends to be discounted for the sake of the focus on personal management and responsibility. Not overcoming difficulties becomes firmly positioned as the fault of the private individual rather than of their relative social and economic advantage.[40]

The Halo, its promotional discourses, its interface, and the partnerships Amazon has developed in conjunction with it provide perhaps the ultimate example of Lupton's assertion. It is deeply embedded in a long-standing neoliberal commitment to the privatization of risk, where individuals pursue, in the words of sociologist Ulrich Beck, "biographical solutions to systemic contradictions." These individuals are alone, without solidarity and without help. In a world in which risk is offloaded onto individuals, self-optimization and the need to be legible to computational systems that infer and predict various aspects of everyday life become moral imperatives—they become the mark of a good citizen, a good parent, a good lover, a good friend.

Consequences: Anxiety, Superfluity, and the Instrumentalization of Interpersonal Interaction

As with the previous two chapters, this chapter not only seeks to describe and explain some of the roots of this particular facet of the computable subjectivity, but it will also examine some consequences that emerge from the moral injunction to computationally self-optimize. There are three consequences that, while also linked to the aspects of the computable subjectivity described in the previous two chapters, illuminate the high stakes of accepting that self-optimization through computing is a moral good: the anxiety associated with compulsory communication, the potential for individuals to feel superfluous, and the instrumentalization of interpersonal interaction. In what follows, I will address each of these, primarily in the context of the preceding discussion in this chapter, but also within the broader narrative arc of the book.

Anxiety Produced by Moralized Datafication and Commanded Communication

When one's morality hinges on self-optimization through complete datafication, people are in effect *commanded to communicate*, to capture their data and transmit it, whether through the giving up of data to Amazon via the Halo or by sharing the image of one's reduced body fat on social media. Your agreement to FitBit's terms of service or to the terms of service for your Nest thermostat, both of which capture data about you and your activities, is an acceding to a form of supposedly "benevolent" surveillance in exchange for convenience, efficiency, or ease. Data about individuals' activities, ranging from the temperature of their households to the firmness of their mattresses, is continuously captured, turning mundane activities into public self-performance in which people have the opportunity to constantly compare themselves to others (or be compared to others through their entries in the databases of corporate and governmental entities[41]). Such performances become nearly inescapable as ambient intelligence and the Internet of Things tips over the precipice of implementation.[42,43]

Not only then can any and everything be datafied and thus communicated, but communication itself becomes effectively compulsory.[44] Opting out is no longer an option, socially, and often, technically.[45,46] Such a system poses an implicit threat of social and structural decoupling as a result of opting out or a desire not to communicate. One's life chances, for example, are negatively impacted by choosing not to use an Amazon Halo or FitBit, taking advantage of insurance discounts pursuant to that use, etc. In a situation where the decision-makers that influence one's life chances believe the numbers about an individual are more real than the individual themselves,[47] the compulsion to communicate, paired with a distributed sense of uncertainty, is a feeling of precarity, and consequently, *anxiety*.

Datafied Superfluity: Bullshit Jobs, Bullshit People, and Teaching from beyond the Grave

Ironically, the moral injunction to computationally self-optimize ends up creating individuals who believe themselves to be superfluous. How is this possible? If one feels as though they are engaging in moral behavior through optimizing their "relationship health," let's say, through an Amazon Halo, how could they possibly come to believe that they are superfluous? Building on the key ideas from the preceding chapters—a commitment to the equivalence between "data" and "world," and the resulting aspiration to be legible to computers in order to be truly knowable—Vilém Flusser and Gabriel Marcel's ideas of people as "functionaries" can help us understand the counterintuitive feelings of superfluity.

Beginning in the 1970s, Vilém Flusser characterized the modern individual as a "functionary," focused on the verification of a person or object through the data that exists about it as opposed through attempts to understand its essence. Like Flusser, Gabriel Marcel, a philosopher and dramatist writing primarily during the early-to-mid 1900s, argued that modern society is characterized by attempts to elide the mystery of being, instead stressing "the activity of verification" and thus ignoring "*presence*" (italics his).[48] This is precisely the shift in psychiatry that happened with the DSM-III, in which the symptom became the most important thing, while the underlying situation within the individual patient became irrelevant because it was, to a computer at least, unknowable. And it is one of the ideas on which early Cybernetics was based.

For Marcel, the defining personality characteristic of our "broken" world is a "misplacement of the idea of function," where "function" takes precedence over an *awareness* of *being* that transcends an individual's vital and social functions. In this broken world, an individual "tends to appear both to himself and others as an agglomeration of functions."[49] The subway token distributor, who serves as Marcel's example, has a job that is itself a collection of functions that could be automated. People treat the token distributor as a machine, and he begins to think of himself in this way, even beyond his job. He sees every aspect of life—activities as a citizen, spouse, parent—as a function operating on a timetable, perhaps even executable by a machine. This person's sense of wonder, and their sense that the world could be any other way, dies.[50]

But as automation and the proliferation of "bullshit jobs"[51] make clear, it is no longer just those whose jobs are akin to the subway token distributor who lose the idea that they are anything but an agglomeration of functions. Instead, people with all kinds of jobs, both at home and at work, are coerced into seeing themselves as agglomerations of machine-readable functions and that this self-perception is morally responsible. Without a sense of mystery or transcendence, when one begins to see oneself as comprised only of computable "functions," one might also find one has become superfluous, replaceable by a machine, or just plain irrelevant to the actual functioning of society, as in the case with those who believe they hold "bullshit jobs." Hannah Arendt was particularly sensitive to the concept of superfluity. In her book *The Origins of Totalitarianism*, she argues that when the feeling of superfluity becomes pervasive in a society, that society is primed for the emergence of totalitarianism.

Totalitarianism, Arendt wrote, "strives not towards despotic rule over men, but toward a system in which men are superfluous ... Total power can be achieved and safeguarded only in a world of conditioned reflexes, of marionettes without the slightest trace of spontaneity."[52] Media theorist L.M. Sacasas writes of Arendt's words, "Superfluity, as Arendt uses the term, suggests some combination of thoughtless automatism, interchangeability, and expendability. A person is superfluous when they operate within a system in a completely predictable way and can, as a consequence, be easily replaced. Individuality is worse than meaningless in this context; it is a threat to the system and must be eradicated."[53]

Individuality, I would add, is different from the neoliberal *individualism* that legitimizes the moral injunction to self-optimize, characterizing all problems as individual and not political. Indeed, digital products and services that claim to personalize recommendations, like the Amazon Halo or Netflix, seem to offer the opportunity to fully realize an authentic self.[54] But as the preceding chapters have demonstrated, this supposed individuality belies a commitment to fragmentation of the self in the service of prediction and control. Sacasas writes: "so-called individuality is irrelevant ephemera so far as the network is concerned. In other words, people, insofar as they are considered as individuals, are, in fact, superfluous."[55] A sense that one is superfluous, replaceable by another within the system, because one is predictable—which is *the very thing that we must desire* when we experience the fragmentation described in the preceding chapters— emerges alongside and in spite of the belief that one *must* succumb to systems of incisive data capture, inference, and recommendation in order to become or remain a productive member of society, a good parent or colleague, and so on. This contraction is part of the anxiety described above.

The perception of every aspect of life as a *function* is where the role of the interface comes into focus. It tells individuals this very fact, that they are indeed nothing but a collection of computable functions. How was your sleep? 8 out of 10? Just like the 8 out of 10 you got in your performance metrics at work that were displayed to you through a different interface. Or perhaps the score your vocal inflection was given in your most recent job interview or your most recent interaction with your spouse as displayed by your Amazon Halo app. Regardless of how different technologies make these determinations, the privileging of such determinations by developers and their manifestation at the level of the interface makes it clear that individuals are nothing but agglomerations of functions which, to be morally responsible, they must seek to optimize through the use of those very technologies.

Because one is a functionary does not necessarily render one superfluous. But what happens when jobs that had previously transcended their codification into functions—college professors, for example—start to take on characteristics reminiscent of the subway token distributor in Marcel's example above?

By bombarding professors with data about themselves, each other, and their students, university technocrats suggest that even though a faculty member might contribute to the success of the university beyond rankings or grant dollars or publications and research, they are effectively nothing more than the collection of data points that the university can gather about them. And if those data points can be replicated or even enhanced by the hiring of someone else, then who really cares what else you did for the institution that might not be captured by that data? Even if you think you know you are important to the institution, the interfaces with which you are confronted may suggest otherwise—even though that is not their intent, and even though you might not realize it. *This* is what Marcel was worried about.

Taken to an extreme, if I as a scholar and teacher am nothing more than the data that my university's technocratic administrators can capture about me through the advanced analytic techniques developed by companies like Academic Analytics (Figures 4.4 and 4.5) or the parafictional company ScholarStat, and if inferences and predictions about future courses of action can then be made about me, what use am *I* as a *being*?

In January 2021, a student at Concordia University tweeted[56] that the professor from whom he was taking an online art history course had been dead since 2019.

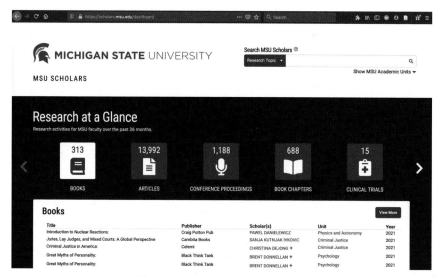

FIGURE 4.4 A screenshot of the interface to the scholars.msu.edu dashboard. Courtesy Academic Analytics, © 2005–21, Academic Analytics, LLC. All Rights Reserved.

FIGURE 4.5 A screenshot of the interface to the scholars.msu.edu dashboard. Courtesy Academic Analytics, © 2005–21, Academic Analytics, LLC. All Rights Reserved.

The university was still using his lectures and course materials, and the grader for the course didn't even know that the professor had passed away. The online course was offered through eConcordia, which is actually a "joint operation between the university and KnowledgeOne, a Montreal-based consulting-services company" (Bartlett, 2021).[57] This story seems, on the surface, to have less to do with the datafication of a faculty member and more to do with intellectual property and the ownership of course materials. "A policy statement on online education put out by the American Association of University Professors says vaguely that 'provision should … be made' so that the creator of a course can 'exercise control over the future use' of recorded materials."[58]

But there is a more complicated role that this scandal plays in the minds of faculty and administrators everywhere. If, because professors must believe in the inherent value of becoming legible to the computational systems that shape their everyday lives, they become more and more like the agents in the computational models that simulate them, then there are stark consequences. The more focused on the technocratic assessments of research and teaching that university administrators become, the more professors and students begin to look like computers. If all aspects of teaching and learning can be quantified, modeled, and optimized, then perhaps most teaching can be done with at least the assistance of computational (AI) instructors if not done entirely by a computer? Even if this isn't the case, there are already those who think it *should* be, and society can thus do away with the eccentricities of professors who engage in low-impact research or do not adhere to "evidence-based" practices in the classroom. Whether or not a professor is *replaced* is somewhat irrelevant when the transcendence of being is emptied and the professor *themselves* reduced to a mere functionary. As has become a common refrain in this book, the individual person—in an effort to meet those metrics to which they are beholden and to which they aspire, believing themselves to be morally just in doing so—starts to become more like the computational model of themselves.

The Instrumentalization of Interpersonal Interaction

The last consequence I'll discuss here, of the moral injunction to computationally self-optimize, is what I will call the "instrumentalization of interpersonal interaction." Individuals come to treat one another as the same type of individual—a computable one—that they perceive themselves to be. In seeing each other as functionaries, with specifically delimited duties that serve particular ends, one person might see another person as an instrument of the various compartmentalized activities that comprise their purview of everyday life. This isn't necessarily a selfishness in which everyone sees each other as either helping or hindering their own satisfaction (although that might often be the case). Instead, it's a bit more complicated.

Let me illustrate with another example. In October 2020, Microsoft announced a new feature in their "365" workplace suite of software (i.e., the interconnected and cloud-based versions of MS Office products such as Word, Excel, Outlook, etc. and internal communications channels such as Teams). This feature was the "Productivity Score" and it was closely connected to other emerging technologies that the company had been developing. It caused something of a stir, and we'll get to why momentarily.

I had an inkling that something was up with my Microsoft 365 products, because I had been receiving emails from a software called "MyAnalytics" for several months leading up to the fall of 2020 (Figure 4.6). These emails told me about the percent of my time that was "Collaborative" or "Focused." I can only assume that the MyAnalytics algorithms were using my Outlook calendar (where I stored no information about meetings or classes) to determine these "scores." I found these emails odd, and also, quite disturbing. What if my superiors were seeing these scores? What would they expect from me based on the calculations MyAnalytics was making about how I was using my time? What if I were forced to use Outlook as my calendaring system and MyAnalytics could access metadata about Word documents and Excel spreadsheets on which I was working? What kind of picture would it paint of my productivity? Seeing too many *Black Mirror* episodes or my general skepticism prompted additional questions—what if Microsoft could track my activities in physical space? Or listen to the tone of my voice? How would MyAnalytics assess my work? And what would the consequences be?

Turns out my fears weren't unfounded. The launch of the "Productivity Score" (Figure 4.7)[59] and the questions it raised became a small PR crisis for Microsoft. In November 2020, Geekwire reported on a Microsoft patent application called "Meeting Insight Computing System,"[60] which was connected to the Productivity Score launch. The system, "as described in patent filings, would use cameras, sensors, and software tools to monitor the people and the conditions in a meeting, as well as post-meeting surveys, to create a 'quality score' for the meeting."[61] The patent application describes a system for:

> deriving and predicting "overall quality scores" for meetings using data such as body language, facial expressions, room temperature, time of day, and number of people in the meeting. The system uses cameras, sensors, and software tools to determine, for example, "how much a participant contributes to a meeting vs performing other tasks (e.g., texting, checking email, browsing the Internet)."
>
> The "meeting insight computing system" would then predict the likelihood that a group will hold a high-quality meeting. It would flag potential challenges when an organizer is setting the meeting up, and recommend alternative venues, times, or people to include in the meeting, for example.[62]

These insights would be shown in the interface to meeting scheduling technologies, ranging from physical screens outside conference rooms to digital/remote meeting spaces such as Microsoft Teams.

The blowback from the launch of the productivity score technology and its unsavory future as part of a massive corporate surveillance apparatus prompted Microsoft to apologize in December 2020, and they pledged to wipe individual usernames from the productivity score.[63] This anonymizing of productivity score data was primarily in response to concerns from privacy experts. While this concession is important, the overall function of the productivity score system,

FIGURE 4.6 A screenshot from one of the Microsoft MyAnalytics emails that were sent to me. Courtesy Microsoft.

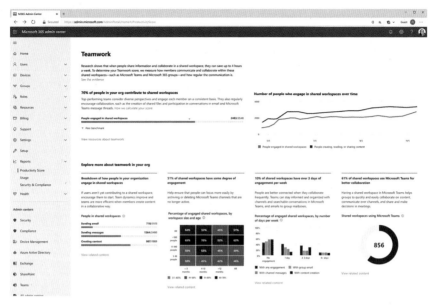

FIGURE 4.7 Microsoft Productivity Score administrative UI. Courtesy Microsoft.

and its ability to shape behavior at both an individual and organizational level, was basically unchanged.

Even as late as 2021, their productivity score technology remained much the same as before the PR kerfuffle, and, regardless of whether or not their "meeting insight computing system" comes to be precisely in the way imagined by the patent application, Microsoft's desire to subject users to incisive metrics that flatten the richness and variation of human experience are quite obvious. An employee, for example, might think a meeting was quite productive because the discussion focused on implicit bias, vulnerability, care work, or other things that affect someone's everyday working life, but if these concepts aren't embedded in the model of "productivity" used by Microsoft, then the meeting will receive a low score and similar meetings will be deemed unproductive and any meeting that the system predicts to have a similar outcome will be modified or canceled accordingly. And even if Microsoft chooses to enhance the sophistication of its models, the goal remains the same—a number or a metric, a proxy for the thing and not the thing itself.

In a press release on the heels of their "apology," Microsoft claimed that "research has shown that when people collaborate and share content in the cloud (instead of emailing attachments), they can save up to 100 minutes a week."[64] As detailed in Chapter 1, convenience has been the door through which technologies have become fetishized, and Microsoft continues to exploit the "value of convenience" today. Regardless of whether employee-level productivity scores are anonymized, becoming successful at work under such a regime requires employees to see each other the way the system sees them, and become *legible* both to the systems and to one another in the same ways. *Technological interfaces are what mediate these relationships—how else can employees understand the way the system (and by association, peers, friends, colleagues, etc.) perceives them?*

This scoring of workplace interaction extends into the domain of language, in which work and collaboration software, such as Slack or Microsoft Teams, as well as educational software, such as TurnItIn, offers certain affordances that allow users to engage in particular "speech acts" while not offering the opportunity to engage in others.[65, 66] Meanwhile, Outlook not only checks my spelling and highlights misspellings and/or jargon-y neologisms that are specific to my fields but maybe not in its core dictionary, but also it has started to make suggestions, double-underlined in blue, to help me with "clarity, conciseness, formality," and "inclusiveness." Does an increased conciseness help my organization's "productivity score?" Perhaps. Does it enhance the ease with which computational models trained on vast amounts of data, maybe including the text of these very emails,[67] can read and supposedly "understand" what I'm saying, and therefore more accurately anticipate text for their anticipatory text suggestion, autocomplete, and autorespond features? Maybe.

Microsoft has to build models of people in order to identify the benchmark against which things like a meeting's "productivity score" might be judged, or against which an email is considered to be more or less "inclusive." These models often include (but are not limited to) techniques of Natural Language Processing (NLP). While NLP has helped computers "understand" human language, making search queries easier, for example, NLP is often used in "sentiment analysis" (another thing that can help employees send more "inclusive," "collaborative," or "pleasant" emails). This dimension of its use has also "helped" with "risk-prediction" in a plethora of domains, ranging from anti-terrorism to predicting risks posed by psychiatric patients. NLP also forms the backbone for things like AI chatbots, and now, GPT-3—a rather famous AI that utilizes NLP techniques—can write novels with a single sentence as a prompt.[68] In modeling and then feeding back to users those models as aspirational ideals, in, for example, email best practices, Microsoft's NLP models shape language use. But such models have shaped much more than just what people say to one another.[69,70] As individuals work to become legible to these systems, receiving feedback about this legibility via the interface, they also "read" and "speak" to each other on the system's terms.

Even more troubling, perhaps, is that when individuals "read" each other on the terms of the computer systems to which they have become legible, the difference between individual people and between people and companies or other computers becomes irrelevant. Like the cybernetic systems developed for warfare, output is privileged over essence. This erases not only the distinction between individual people, but between individuals and society. While not totally separate—individual people can only become individuated by living in a society—the idea that the core essence of anything is irrelevant is to succumb to a technocratic stagnation in which the political possibilities produced by the mutually constitutive interactions of people and society are eschewed in favor of equilibrium.[71]

When individuals succumb to the moral injunction to self-optimize via computation, they aim to satisfy metrics—in, for example, interfaces to university administration tools or Microsoft's Meeting Insight system. They aim at a proxy, at "data" that will equal a supposedly better "world," at least according to the projections displayed in the interfaces to those very products. But that better world never happens, because human interaction has been turned into an instrument of the metrics that measure it.

When normativity via computational self-optimization appears as a moral imperative, all aspects of human interaction are turned into instruments of something that has nothing to do with the people in a society themselves. Instead, people become instruments of the metrics to which biopolitical governing structures adhere in the ongoing evaluation, inference, and prediction of individual activities. It's important to differentiate this from fatalism or technological determinism. It doesn't really matter *what* you do so much as that what you do can be integrated into a computational model so that the outcomes of your actions can be inferred and predicted, so that you can have "tailored" recommendations delivered to you and so that various metrics can be met—whether that metric is profit or a productivity score.

Conclusion: Fighting for Servitude as if It Were Salvation

The "paradoxical answer" to Spinoza's question of "why people fight for their servitude as if it were salvation," Jason Read writes, is that "it is precisely because we actively strive to interpret the world according to inadequate ideas of our freedom and autonomy that we are subject to it." In other words, "We interpret our subjection as freedom."[72] The inadequate ideas of freedom and autonomy through which individuals attempt to interpret the world emerge through the interfaces to computational products and services. Not only do these interfaces seem to free people to be their most authentic selves, but they exert a moralizing force by demonstrating that full self-optimization is both possible and responsible.

The ongoing merging of individuals with the computational models of themselves used by corporations and governmental entities leads to feelings of anxiety, precarity, and perhaps even superfluity. We've seen that this is connected to an evaporation of ontological security, wherein individuals feel alienated from themselves and fragmented, and yet the continued subjection to computational products and services that further this fragmentation purports to soothe this ontological insecurity. But the wholeness promised by technologies such as the Amazon Halo is always just out of reach, requiring more computational products, more interfaces with more metrics to reassure users that, yes, they are becoming whole again. But this reassurance never comes, instead producing subjects that constantly seek more ways to self-optimize through becoming legible to computation in new ways, attempting to arrive at a quantified state of normalcy. These individuals and their interactions become instruments of systems seeking only a particular quantitative optimal state, and have nothing to do with the people in a society. And yet, as I have sought to demonstrate, such systems, like the analytics systems to which professors are subjected, have massive and predominantly deleterious effects.

Two key questions might emerge from the analysis presented here in this chapter and the two preceding it: (1) what is the role of design in intervening to "solve" this problem?; and, (2) why is the computable subjectivity itself the problem and not the political-economic system from which it emerges, namely, capitalism? In what follows, I will begin to address these questions.

Notes

1   Carrie Lambert-Beatty, "Make-Believe: Parafiction and Plausibility," *October* 129 (August 2009): 51–84, doi:10.1162/octo.2009.129.1.51, 54.

2   Bibliometrics is the process of using statistical methods to analyze and measure scholarly productivity and impact. For a relatively comprehensive overview, see: Blaise Cronin and Cassidy R. Sugimoto, eds., *Scholarly Metrics under the Microscope: From Citation Analysis to Academic Auditing*, ASIST Monograph Series (Medford, NJ: Published on behalf of the Association for Information Science and Technology by Information Today, Inc, 2015).

3   Alan Finlayson, "E-Introduction & the Neoliberal University," Personal email communication, March 31, 2018.

4   Simitive, "University Staff and Students," *Simitive*, accessed November 10, 2018, https://www.simitive.com/university-staff-and-students.html.

5   Academic Analytics, "Academic Analytics," December 14, 2018, https://web.archive.org/web/20181214002527/https://academicanalytics.com/.

6   Virginia Alvino Young, "EduSense: Like a Fitbit for Your Teaching Skills—News—Carnegie Mellon University," November 14, 2019, http://www.cmu.edu/news/stories/archives/2019/november/edusense-fitbit-your-teaching-skills.html.

7   ANS, "Are Chatbots the Future for Higher Education? | ANS," Blog, *ANS Blog*, (April 12, 2021), https://www.ans.co.uk/are-chatbots-the-future-for-higher-education/.

8   Dimitris Bertsimas et al., "OR Forum—Tenure Analytics: Models for Predicting Research Impact," *Operations Research* 63, no. 6 (December 2015): 1246–61, doi:10.1287/opre.2015.1447.

9   Erik Brynjolfsson and John Silberholz, "'Moneyball' for Professors?," *MIT Sloan Management Review*, December 14, 2016, https://sloanreview.mit.edu/article/moneyball-for-professors/.

10 Dean Keith Simonton, "Creative Productivity: A Predictive and Explanatory Model of Career Trajectories and Landmarks," *Psychological Review* 104, no. 1 (January 1997): 66–89, doi:10.1037/0033-295X.104.1.66.

11 Vik Loveday, "The Neurotic Academic: How Anxiety Fuels Casualised Academic Work," *LSE Impact of Social Sciences*, April 17, 2018, https://blogs.lse.ac.uk/impactofsocialsciences/2018/04/17/the-neurotic-academic-how-anxiety-fuels-casualised-academic-work/.

12 Loveday, "The Neurotic Academic"; and, Sharon McCulloch, "The Importance of Being REF-Able: Academic Writing under Pressure from a Culture of Counting," *Impact of Social Sciences*, February 9, 2017, https://blogs.lse.ac.uk/impactofsocialsciences/2017/02/09/the-importance-of-being-ref-able-academic-writing-under-pressure-from-a-culture-of-counting/.

13 See Chapter 1.

14 Ian Hacking, "How Should We Do the History of Statistics?," in *The Foucault Effect: Studies in Governmentality*, ed. Graham Burchell, Colin Gordon, and Peter Miller (Chicago: University of Chicago Press, 1991), 182.

15 Lennard J. Davis, "Introduction: Normality, Power, and Culture," in *The Disability Studies Reader*, ed. Lennard J. Davis, 4th ed. (New York: Routledge, 2013), 2.

16 Davis, "Introduction: Normality, Power, and Culture," 3.

17 Hacking, "How Should We Do a History of Statistics?," 183.

18 Yes, this, as of late 2021 at least, is a thing: https://www.getsmartplate.com/

19 See, for example: https://journalfinder.elsevier.com/

20 Dinh V. Cuong et al., "A Framework for Paper Submission Recommendation System," in *Proceedings of the 2020 International Conference on Multimedia Retrieval*, ICMR '20 (New York, NY: Association for Computing Machinery, 2020), 393–6, doi:10.1145/3372278.3391929.

21 Rick Mayes and Allan V. Horwitz, "DSM-III and the Revolution in the Classification of Mental Illness," *Journal of the History of the Behavioral Sciences* 41, no. 3 (2005): 251, doi:10.1002/jhbs.20103.

22 Robert Sptizer, "Foreword," in *The Loss of Sadness: How Psychiatry Transformed Normal Sorrow into Depressive Disorder*, eds. Allan Horwitz and Jerome Wakefield (New York: Oxford University Press, 2007), vii.

23 K. Maurer et al., "On the Way to Expert Systems: Comparing DSM-III Computer Diagnoses with CATEGO (ICD) Diagnoses in Depressive and Schizophrenic Patients," *European Archives of Psychiatry and Neurological Sciences* 239, no. 2 (March 1989): 127–32, doi:10.1007/BF01759586.

24 Mayes and Horwitz, "DSM-III and the Revolution in the Classification of Mental Illness."

25 Andrew G. Reece and Christopher M. Danforth, "Instagram Photos Reveal Predictive Markers of Depression," *ArXiv:1608.03282 [Physics]*, August 13, 2016, http://arxiv.org/abs/1608.03282.

26 Adele Peters, "This Algorithm Can Tell If You're Depressed Just from Your Instagram Posts," *Fast Company*, August 8, 2017, https://www.fastcompany.com/40449192/this-algorithm-can-tell-if-youre-depressed-just-from-your-instagram-posts.

27 "Introducing Amazon Halo and Amazon Halo Band—A New Service That Helps Customers Improve Their Health and Wellness," *Amazon.Com Press Center*, August 27, 2020, https://press.aboutamazon.com/news-releases/news-release-details/introducing-amazon-halo-and-amazon-halo-band-new-service-helps/.

28 "Introducing Amazon Halo."

29 Dieter Bohn, "Amazon Announces Halo, a Fitness Band and App That Scans Your Body and Voice," *The Verge*, August 27, 2020, https://www.theverge.com/2020/8/27/21402493/amazon-halo-band-health-fitness-body-scan-tone-emotion-activity-sleep.

30 Amazon's attempts to subject all facets of social life to computational metrics are not necessarily unique. See: Nicolas Perony, "How Amazon Could Improve Halo," *OTO Blog*, September 30, 2021, https://www.oto.ai/blog/how-amazon-could-improve-halo.

31 Matthew Fuller and Andrew Goffey, *Evil Media* (Cambridge, MA: MIT Press, 2012).

32 Anyone working in ML and with neural networks in particular will readily admit the complexities of the systems involved. Amazon's own patent states that: "… values for the input data/output data of a particular layer are not known until a neural network is actually operating during runtime …" Daniel Kenneth Bone, Chao Wang, and Viktor Rozgic, Emotion detection using speaker baseline, United States US20210249035A1, filed February 18, 2021, and issued August 12, 2021, https://patents.google.com/patent/US20210249035A1/en?q=tone&assignee=amazon&before=priority:20191231&after=priority:20190101&page=2.

33 Bone et al., Emotion detection, patent, 2021.

34 Davida Rochman, "Mic Basics: What Is Frequency Response?," *Shure: Louder*, August 10, 2017, https://web.archive.org/web/20210116003833/https://www.shure.com/en-US/performance-production/louder/mic-basics-frequency-response.

35 Ian Hacking, "Making Up People," *London Review of Books*, August 17, 2006.

36 Bone et al., Emotion detection, patent, 2021.

37 Bone et al., Emotion detection, patent, 2021.

38 "Amazon Halo Now Available for John Hancock Vitality Members," *John Hancock Insurance | News*, December 14, 2020, https://www.johnhancock.com/about-us/news/john-hancock-insurance/2020/12/amazon-halo-now-available-for-john-hancock-vitality-members.html.

39 Deborah Lupton, *The Quantified Self: A Sociology of Self-Tracking* (Cambridge, UK: Polity, 2016), e-pub, Chapter 2.

40 Lupton, *The Quantified Self*.

41 See: John Cheney-Lippold, "A New Algorithmic Identity: Soft Biopolitics and the Modulation of Control," *Theory, Culture & Society* 28, no. 6 (November 2011): 164–81, doi:10.1177/0263276411424420.

42 Plan C, "We Are All Very Anxious," *We Are Plan C*, April 4, 2014, https://www.weareplanc.org/blog/we-are-all-very-anxious/.

43 Katja de Vries, "Identity, Profiling Algorithms and a World of Ambient Intelligence," *Ethics and Information Technology* 12, no. 1 (March 2010): 71–85, doi:10.1007/s10676-009-9215-9.

44 Plan C, "We Are All Very Anxious."

45 While this may be a somewhat antiquated example, it is not uncommon for new facets of technologies to be rolled out and reshape our perceived "privacy" or incentivize the sharing of specific information. See Kamdar, 2013 for more details on what was happening with Facebook Graph Search at the time. (Adi Kamdar, "The Creepy Details of Facebook's New Graph Search," *Electronic Frontier Foundation*, January 18, 2013, https://www.eff.org/deeplinks/2013/01/facebooks-graph-search.)

46   P. J. Rey, "Social Media: You Can Log Off but You Can't Opt Out," *Cyborgology*, May 10, 2012, https://thesocietypages.org/cyborgology/2012/05/10/social-media-you-can-log-off-but-you-cant-opt-out/.

47   See Chapter 2 as well as David Golumbia, *The Cultural Logic of Computation* (Cambridge, MA: Harvard University Press, 2009), 159.

48   Gabriel Marcel, *The Philosophy of Existentialism* (New York: Citadel Press, 1995).

49   Marcel, *The Philosophy of Existentialism*, 19.

50   Brian Treanor and Brendan Sweetman, "Gabriel (-Honoré) Marcel," in *The Stanford Encyclopedia of Philosophy*, ed. Edward N. Zalta, Winter 2016 (Metaphysics Research Lab, Stanford University, 2016), https://plato.stanford.edu/archives/win2016/entries/marcel/.

51   David Graeber, *Bullshit Jobs* (New York: Simon & Schuster Paperbacks, 2019).

52   Hannah Arendt, *The Origins of Totalitarianism*, New ed. (New York: Harcourt Brace Jovanovich, 1973), 457.

53   L. M. Sacasas, "Superfluous People, the Ideology of Silicon Valley, and the Origins of Totalitarianism," *L.M. Sacasas*, January 3, 2018, https://thefrailestthing.com/2018/01/03/superfluous-people-the-ideology-of-silicon-valley-and-the-origins-of-totalitarianism/.

54   This echoes the utopian aspirations of those from the counterculture who adopted computing as the apex of their individualist anti-politics (see Chapter 1).

55   Sacasas, "Superfluous People, the Ideology of Silicon Valley, and the Origins of Totalitarianism."

56   https://twitter.com/AaronLinguini/status/1352009211501289472.

57   Tom Bartlett, "Dead Man Teaching," *The Chronicle of Higher Education*, January 26, 2021, https://www-chronicle-com.proxy2.cl.msu.edu/article/dead-man-teaching.

58   Bartlett, "Dead Man Teaching."

59   "Microsoft Productivity Score," *Microsoft Adoption*, accessed March 10, 2021, https://adoption.microsoft.com/productivity-score/.

60   Matthew Vogel, United States Patent Application: 0200358627, US Patent & Trademark Office, accessed March 12, 2021, https://appft.uspto.gov/netacgi/nph-Parser?Sect1=PTO1&Sect2=HITOFF&d=PG01&p=1&u=%2Fnetahtml%2FPTO%2Fsrchnum.html&r=1&f=G&l=50&s1=%2220200358627%22.PGNR.&OS=DN/20200358627&RS=DN/20200358627.

61   Todd Bishop, "Microsoft Patents Tech to Score Meetings Using Body Language, Facial Expressions, Other Data," *GeekWire*, November 28, 2020, https://www.geekwire.com/2020/microsoft-patents-technology-score-meetings-using-body-language-facial-expressions-data/.

62   Bishop, "Microsoft Patents Tech to Score Meetings."

63   Alex Hern, "Microsoft Apologises for Feature Criticised as Workplace Surveillance," *The Guardian*, December 2, 2020, https://www.theguardian.com/technology/2020/dec/02/microsoft-apologises-productivity-score-critics-derided-workplace-surveillance.

64   Jared Spataro and Corporate Vice President for Microsoft 365, "Our Commitment to Privacy in Microsoft Productivity Score," *Microsoft 365 Blog*, December 1, 2020, https://www.microsoft.com/en-us/microsoft-365/blog/2020/12/01/our-commitment-to-privacy-in-microsoft-productivity-score/.

65 Rashmi Dyal-Chand, "Autocorrecting for Whiteness," in SSRN Scholarly Paper (Rochester, NY: Social Science Research Network, March 8, 2021), https://papers. ssrn.com/abstract=3800463.

66 Ezekiel Dixon-Román, T. Philip Nichols, and Ama Nyame-Mensah, "The Racializing Forces of/in AI Educational Technologies," *Learning, Media and Technology* 45, no. 3 (July 2, 2020): 236–50, doi:10.1080/17439884.2020.1667825.

67 Erez Barak, "How Azure Machine Learning Powers Suggested Replies in Outlook," *Microsoft Azure Blog*, March 23, 2020, https://azure.microsoft.com/en-us/blog/how-azure-machine-learning-service-powers-suggested-replies-in-outlook/.

68 Will Douglas Heaven, "Gpt-3," in *MIT Technology Review* (Cambridge, MA: Technology Review, Inc., April 2021).

69 Alex LaPlante, "How Natural Language Processing Is Reshaping the World of Finance," *Global Risk Institute*, January 15, 2017, https://globalriskinstitute.org/publications/natural-language-processing-reshaping-world-finance/.

70 "How Natural Language Processing Impacts Professions," *Wolters Kluwer | Expert Insights*, April 29, 2020, https://www.wolterskluwer.com/en/expert-insights/how-natural-language-processing-impacts-professions.

71 Jason Read, *The Politics of Transindividuality*, Historical Materialism Book Series 106 (Leiden; Boston: Brill, 2016).

72 Read, *The Politics of Transindividuality*, 258.

5 THE QUESTIONS OF POLITICAL ECONOMY AND THE ROLE OF DESIGN EDUCATION

Introduction

The previous chapters articulated the historical foundations, described the characteristics, and examined the effects of the *computable subjectivity*. I have argued throughout that both the characteristics of this subjectivity and its consequences are dangerous for individuals and society. This chapter will turn toward two questions about *how exactly* to counter the dangers I have presented or whether they are dangers first place. These two questions—(1) whether capitalism is to blame; and, (2) how to enact a critical approach to technology in design education—will crescendo in the concluding chapter of the book, which will aim to answer the questions that this chapter poses.

The previous chapters in this book have chronicled the rise of the computable subjectivity and the ways in which user-experience design—through the interface— has served to propagate, legitimize, and naturalize it. I have sought to demonstrate some of the dangers of believing that oneself is both computing and computable, but I want to underscore here that these dangers are not (or at least not entirely) the plot of a single nefarious group of individuals seeking to control the whole of society. Given the interests of digital monopolists, such as Amazon and Facebook, it might seem like it. But the reality of the situation is far messier. Indeed, the place at which users encounter ideas about themselves is at the *interface*, meaning that user-experience designers bear an immense responsibility for the propagation of the computable subjectivity and the disastrous impact it has on society. But those user-experience designers are *my students*. And I can tell you with complete certainty that these are good, well-intentioned people who want to make a living in the world, and perhaps want to do something meaningful with their work. They believe creating useful digital products and services will allow them to do this. One point of intervention in resisting the computable subjectivity, then, might lie in the spaces where user experience designers are trained: the university.

Far from being "out of touch,"[1] higher education is deeply intertwined with, and highly influential of, the "real world"[2] invoked by so many neoconservatives to demonstrate the failings of the "ivory tower." Their rhetoric is being used to turn universities into technical schools, whereby the tiny window of time during which students might have the opportunity to imagine a better world disappears into oblivion.[3] Design education, because of its instrumental function in neoliberalism, flies under the radar. It evades politicians' ad hominem attacks and funding strangleholds on the humanities and is perfectly poised to counteract the dangers and tendencies that the first four chapters of the book outline.

Before I discuss the education of the user-experience designer, however, I would like to address a question that perhaps has lingered in the mind of the reader from the very first chapter. I have spent much of this book linking the computable subject to the deleterious effects of neoliberalism on our society. I have argued that the computable subject can benefit and strengthen a neoliberal governmentality. In this way, this book might be seen also as an indictment of the role of UX in the maintenance of neoliberalism's grip on global political economy. A skeptical reader might then ask: *well, would it be so bad for people to believe themselves to be nothing more than fleshy computers if this subjectivity were to serve different political-economic ends? In other words, is it just neoliberalism that's the problem and not the computable subjectivity?*

Question 1: The Issue of Political Economy and Chile's Socialist Cybernetics

Instead of answering this question straight away, I would like to return to what I said earlier about the impact of the computable subjectivity not being the result of a nefarious group of people, user-experience designers included. In a series of lectures delivered over Canadian radio in 1973, Stafford Beer, a cyberneticist[4] who invented "Management Cybernetics," wrote that he operates on the hypothesis that everyone is "well-intentioned," and that what he calls our "failed society" is not a "malevolent society or a cunning trap" but instead, "a function of the nature of the trapped."[5] The idea is not that the nature of humans is to desire or create the biopower that neoliberalism wields through the technologies it deploys, but rather, that the systems within which individuals live shape the kinds of decisions they can make and the kind of people they can become. Beer uses scientists as an example: "[a]t the moment, the scientist himself is trapped by the way society employs him. What proportion of our scientists are employed in death rather than in life, in exploitation rather than liberation? I tell you: most of them. But that is not their free choice. It is an output of a dynamic system having a particular organization."[6]

Stafford Beer's lectures were published together in a book called *Designing Freedom*, and they draw on his central role in *Project Cybersyn*—perhaps the most ambitious computing project of the twentieth century. Beginning in 1971, Project Cybersyn was an attempt to cybernetically manage Chile's economy. It—and the aspirations accompanying it—were dismantled in the 1973 coup that toppled Salvador Allende's democratically elected socialist government. Cybersyn was an attempt to build a decentralized computer system that would, using cybernetic systems principles, enable a near-real-time way for Chile to adapt its economy to the needs of its people. Ever since I heard about Project Cybersyn, it has served as an inspiration for me, a way to think about how technology might serve people differently. It also complicated my own ideas about the dangers of the computable subjectivity that I have presented in this book thus far. Recall that the origins of Cybernetics lay in military operations research, wherein systems are modeled with no differentiation between people and machines, and in which the key subjects— such as nation states—are in adversarial relationships with one another. Thus, as I argued early on in this book, Cybernetics not only forms one part of the origin of the computable subject, but it has come to support the zero-sum neoliberal individualism that has eroded social solidarity today. How, then, could it help create a different kind of society? And does this undermine the assertions I have put forth in this book about the computable subjectivity?

The question of whether the computable subjectivity is itself a problem, or whether the real problem is with capitalism, is a key critique of the main argument of this book. As such, I believe it is important to examine the story of Project Cybersyn in some detail, because it illuminates the possibilities *and* limitations of the uses of Cybernetics, computing, and predictive analytics toward different political-economic ends. The lessons from Project Cybersyn can inspire new approaches to thinking not only about the implementation of computing in the service of a more just society, but how that implementation might make itself known to its users—the way people might *interface* with it.

In her definitive account of Cybersyn, Eden Medina describes the control room for Cybersyn, effectively the *interface* through which Allende and the ministers in Chile's socialist government would interact with this totalizing communications technology:

The hexagonal room reflected the aesthetic of 1970s modernity. In it, seven white fiberglass swivel chairs with orange cushions sat atop a brown carpet. Wood paneling covered the walls. On one wall a series of screens displayed economic data from the nation's factories. A simple control mechanism consisting of ten buttons on the armrest of each chair allowed occupants to bring up different charts, graphs, and photographs of Chilean industrial production and display them on the screens. On another wall a display with flashing red lights indicated current economic emergencies in need of attention; the faster the flashes, the more dire the situation. A third wall displayed an illuminated color image of a five-tiered cybernetic model based on the human nervous system. This abstract model, seemingly out of place in a space for emergency decision making, was there to remind occupants of the cybernetic ideas that had guided the construction of the control room. Cybernetics, the postwar science of communication and control, looked for commonalities in biological, mechanical, and social systems. The room formed part of a larger system designed to help the economy adapt quickly to changes in the national environment.[7]

By creating a real-time, decentralized, computational system that would deliver the right information to the right stakeholders at the right times, Stafford Beer and Salvador Allende believed that the Chilean economy could become a "liberty machine," maintaining the nation's equilibrium through elegant self-regulation. In Cybersyn's nationwide system of monitoring and feedback, "Hundreds of telex machines were installed in newly nationalized factories all over Chile and employed for sending data on everything from production volumes to employee absence rates back to the central command room in Santiago."[8] There were even happiness indicators, which were to be handed to people in the street.

Stafford Beer believed that Project Cybersyn was an "offering of science to the people."[9] It was science that they—the working class—could actually use to better their own working conditions and serve their country. Beer wrote of the way representatives of workers' councils would participate in decision-making, using computational models of their industries, manipulating those models through the interfaces in Cybersyn's operations room:

> [W]e were teaching the workers, for whom this offering of science to the people was created, how to use the most advanced tools yet designed for national economic management. They could sit with their ministers in the economic operations room in Santiago, watching the animated screens, and discussing the alerting signals provided daily by that clever computer program. They had buttons in the arms of their chairs, so that they could command the appearance on other screens of supporting data—to the capacity of 1,200 different colour presentations, focused through sixteen back-projectors. They could also control preliminary experiments in simulation, on a huge, animated model of the dynamic system. These people, arm in arm with *their* science, were intended to become the decision machine for the economy. (emphasis his)[10]

Beer believed that the system, in which Telex machines at factories and other strategic locations across Chile would exchange real-time information about needs and productivity could give power back to the workers, enabling labor to determine the course of its own activities. This is the kind of autonomy that labor often seeks in firms where unions are strong. Indeed, Beer worked closely with unions at United Steel during a project that improved productivity by 30 percent.[11] Beer believed that the downfall of Allende's government was precisely because of the relationship between its socialist politics and its technology, the way it undermined the basic tenets of Western capitalism, thereby threatening its global hegemony.[12]

One of the most compelling features of the *Designing Freedom* lectures is Beer's overt passion for Cybersyn. And, importantly, these passages I have cited complicate the understanding of Cybernetics on which this book relies. Furthermore, they complicate what one might suspect are the political convictions of Beer himself, who pioneered the field of "organizational management," which serves capitalist interests the world over. And, yet, Beer was clearly committed to radical change, celebrating both the democratic process in Chile and the Allende government's broader socialist aims.[13]

But accounts of Project Cybersyn,[14] including Beer's own reflections, are not uniform. Adrian Lahoud's interpretation of Cybersyn, and its eventual destruction at the hands of Pinochet's coup, complicates the ambitions of Beer and Allende. For example, one of the ways Lahoud characterizes the whole of this ambitious and ostensibly socialist project is as "along the lines of a business regulated by ideals drawn from corporate management."[15] Lahoud's take on Cybersyn possesses a critical edge, indicated clearly by the title of his article on the subject: "Error Correction: Chilean Cyberneticists and Chicago's Economists." The term "Chicago School," in reference to economics, is used as a shorthand for a school of thought, with its geographic nexus at the University of Chicago, that helped spawn neoliberalism, with an emphasis on the superiority of the free market and the selfish individual as the ideal economic actor. Lahoud argues that "Chilean cybernetics would serve as the prototype for a new form of governance that would finally award to the theories of the Chicago School a hegemonic control over global society."[16] As I discussed in the opening chapters of the book, Cybernetics and the tenets of Chicago School economics, complemented one another in laying the technological and political groundwork for the computable subjectivity and its exploitation by capital under the neoliberal governmentality.[17] Indeed, Lahoud argues that, in opposition to Beer's apparent political commitments, his efforts to afford workers autonomy and flexibility resonated with the entrepreneurialism that is characteristic of neoliberal workplace management.[18]

Lahoud points out that Beer's ideas about organizations revolved around two key elements: (1) systems should be understood the same way, regardless of scale, from a cell to a nation-state; and, (2) "black-boxing" and the primacy of the "output." For Beer, all systems were also recursive, meaning "the same logic of feedback and response that structured each part also structured the larger component that these sub-parts were contained within, ad infinitum."[19] Beer's Cybernetics flattens the world into systems of equivalence—a wave is just like an institution—a dynamic system, able to be modeled. The scale and nature of the system itself were irrelevant: "For Beer, the question of scale was wholly commensurable across different problems, from a small cellular organism to an entire ecosystem, just as from a clerk's office to a production line."[20] This commensurability of scale and the irrelevance of the nature of the actual system being studied should remind readers of previous chapters, including both the history of Cybernetics itself and the development of the DSM-III. When computation dominates, everything must become legible to it, and, as such, the scale and nature of anything and everything disappears.

Lahoud's analysis of Cybersyn and his reading of Beer's work is incisive. It presents a different lens through which to view this unprecedented experiment in socialist techno-optimism. Beer and Allende both believed that "a cybernetic model of socio-economic management equaled national stability." But the world of Cybersyn, what it could perceive and what it could not, was "wholly determined by those things Allende's economists and Beer's cyberneticians took to be of value between 1972–1973."[21] In other words, only the variables programmed into the system could be accounted for.

In the case of Cybersyn, attempts to plan, predict, and control every aspect of the economy and society were foiled not because of technical inadequacy but because technological solutions are inadequate in the face of fundamentally political problems. This isn't to say that understanding the world through a systems lens—the cybernetic view—is inherently bad. Instead, it's to suggest that there are multiple axes on which an understanding of the world (or of oneself) might operate, and the systems view is but one axis. Furthermore, the systems view is, despite Beer's active role in the Cybersyn project, at least to some degree, an anti-political view. Much of Beer's writing bears this out, that Cybernetics was adopted as a technological solution to political problems.[22]

Ironically, and sadly, one of Norbert Wiener's great hopes was that Cybernetics might change politics. By positing everything in terms of information exchange and feedback, the realm of the political might be reshaped entirely, such that a liberal humanist rationality might prevail, with humans, always provided with the right information at the right time, making the best decisions for themselves and, in turn, society. Such an optimization, for Wiener, was actually coexistential with the flourishing of all human beings. Wiener foresaw the kinds of issues we run into today, suggesting that to leave consequential decisions up to machines could have potentially disastrous outcomes.[23]

**

The contradictions at the heart of Project Cybersyn thus pose, quite poignantly, questions about the relationship between people, computing, and the political-economic frameworks in which computing is developed and operated. It asks us to consider whether any system that seeks the kind of operational efficiency that Beer sought will inevitably fall prey to its own quest for optimization, or whether a better world can indeed be computationally optimized into being.[24] In either case, however, we will have to view these systems—and therefore see how they view us—through their interfaces. It would be of interest, then, to understand that Beer's vision of Cybersyn's interface was based on the metaphor of a Second World

War operations room. Indeed, "[Beer] realised that [Operations Research], so successful during wartime, also had immense possibilities in peacetime."[25]

One passage from Lahoud's article haunts this entire book: "*The ontological and the epistemic promised to merge on the surface of the screen*" (emphasis mine).[26] In other words, by being *knowable to the computer* (epistemic), only then is something or someone able to *exist* (ontological). There are few better ways to articulate the argument of this book, and the importance of the interface that it seeks to highlight.

Instead of capitalism being the problem, then, I argue that the computable subjectivity can emerge in any society that privileges a certain interpretation of the nature of people. This interpretation tends to align with philosophies that hue toward the political right, but that need not always be the case. We must take care, then, in imagining a better world, and be constantly on guard against the seductive power of optimization, against the convenience presented by positing humans as computable and computing. What does an education that positions designers to be critical builders of a different kind of world look like? How might an education in design promote an awareness of the computable subjectivity and help future leaders guard against its continued domination in every sphere of everyday life? And why is *design* such an important component of this resistance?

As I hope to have made clear in the preceding chapters, the interfaces to computational products and services are where many individuals in societies across the globe, but particularly those in so-called Western countries, meet and come to know themselves and others. While computational products and services mediate an increasingly large percentage of interpersonal interaction, it is the *interfaces* to these products and services that *make function meaningful*, and whose meaning initiates their function. It is precisely because of this that the field of user-experience design carries an immense amount of responsibility in the ongoing atomization of individuals in already deeply broken societies.

Question 2: The Role of Design Education in Resisting the "Reality" of the Computable Subjectivity

If, as I suggested above, UX design education is well-positioned to address some of the harms wrought by the profession's propagation of the computable subjectivity, the question of course follows: *but how?* I believe there are, broadly, two approaches to doing so, and they follow the well-worn divisions in attempts to make change in other domains of society: reform versus revolution. This section focuses on the "reform" part of that conundrum, while the Conclusion of the book focuses on the "revolution" part.

Before examining what I will call the "reformist" approach, it is necessary to unpack assumptions about the "real world," to which pre-professional UX programs appeal, and in which their students are very much interested in working. These assumptions about the "real world" structure the work done in the classroom, and circumscribe the possibilities of that space.

The "Real World," and Its Privilege over "the Classroom"

Professional designers tend to believe they experience an unmediated "real world" while students in design programs work within an inferior and professorially mediated fiction. This view has penetrated design academia so thoroughly that faculty in pre-professional design programs spend a great deal of time selling and legitimizing their course content by invoking its relationship to this "real world." I put "real world" in scare quotes here to emphasize something that I believe is very important: no one world is necessarily more "real" than another, although the material effects of someone's "real world" on other people may structure others' reality such that someone's "real world" dominates those of others.

Let's first examine the idea that the "real world" of design practice outside of the purportedly safe confines of the university is somehow more "real" than the reality of the classroom/design studio in which students work every day. This claim, which professional designers often tout to both students and teachers, suggests that perhaps nothing the students learn in college aside from "real world skills" will be useful once students exit the theoretically protective cocoon of the university. Such a claim devastates perhaps the most important asset any student possesses: *imagination*. For organizations—businesses, non-profits, and governments alike—to contribute to the flourishing of humanity and a more just and equitable society (as many claim to), their employees must be capable of *imagining that better world in the first place*. When the idea that the academic world is not real, and as such, has no value beyond its ability to be instrumentalized under capitalism, students' imagination atrophies. They see no value in imagination because it will not help them in their aspirations to make a living or repay their student loans. The concept of the professional as having some kind of privileged access to a "real world" is damaging and has dramatically depleted the ability of tens of thousands of young designers to make the positive change of which they may once have dreamed.

The "Real World" of Capitalism

Students need to pay back their debts or pay their rent when they leave school. So a job in the "real world" of professional life is necessary. A lack of income may have drastic consequences, and capitalism has material effects that do real harm. At the same time, capitalism lives in our imaginations—it is because there is no shared will to believe in something different that something different does not structure our material reality. Mark Fisher—cultural theorist and music critic—described the relationship between capitalism, fiction, and the economy as follows:

> Far from being a system liberated from fictions, capitalism should be seen as the system that liberates fictions to rule over the social. The capitalist social field is cross-hatched by what J. G. Ballard called "fictions of every kind." Ballard was thinking of the banal yet potent products of advertising, PR and branding, without which late capitalism could not function, but it is clear that what structures social reality—the so-called "economy"—is itself a tissue of fictions.[27]
>
> … We must resist any temptation to idealism here: these fictions are not cooked up in the minds of already existing individuals. On the contrary, the individual subject is something like a special effect generated by these transpersonal fictional systems. We might call these fictions effective virtualities. Under capitalism, these virtualities escape any pretence of human control. Crashes caused by arcane financial instruments, automated high-speed trading … but what is capital "itself," if not an enormous effective virtuality.[28]

What Fisher suggests here is that instruments such as derivatives and stock futures, and the ongoing abstraction of material value bundled via complex algorithmic processes into "assets" to be wagered on and bet against, are no more "real" than any other kind of fiction. And yet they profoundly shape the kinds of action one can take in the "real world." They impact 401k plans, determining sometimes when or if individuals are able to retire. They have ripple effects that shape the course of entire families, cities, generations. Even the rules to prevent insider trading are, in the words of one regulator, "useful fictions" that suggest to the public that the system is not rigged, even though it is.[29]

Startup and venture fund discourse is maybe equal to—if not beyond—the world of finance capital in its fictitiousness. And these two are, obviously, closely linked. Scrolling through the pages of startup funding announcements on TechCrunch, for example, one feels as though they've entered another world entirely.

> A stealthy startup co-founded by a former senior designer from Apple and one of its ex-senior software engineers has picked up a significant round of funding to build out its business. Humane, which has ambitions to build a new class of consumer devices and technologies that stem from "a genuine collaboration of design and engineering" that will represent "the next shift between humans and computing," has raised $100 million.[30]

Sentences such as this are uttered without any hint of irony.

Other, more banal fictions, like advertising campaigns, are also important structuring forces of material reality. When Uber's ad campaigns celebrate that teacher who on her off hours drives for them, this fiction (an advertisement) has material effects because it helps reinforce the existence of a "real" world where *actual* teachers who are *actually wildly underpaid* are allowed by the public to continue going underpaid because the PR machinery of Uber successfully shaped what appears "possible" in the domain of politics. Instead of completely reshaping society to more equitably distribute material and financial resources, viewers of Uber's ad see teachers as being underpaid, but the solution is to offer them flexible additional work instead of changing society.[31,32,33] Tech company advertisements, launch events, and other promotional material—and even the very technologies themselves, like Amazon's Halo, which were effectively fictitious in their nascent stages as patent applications or in secret R&D labs—are fictions that have lasting effects on material reality. And when design educators say that a particular piece of science fiction somehow "predicted" something that would end up happening years later (e.g., the user-experience design in the film *Minority Report*), we should ask ourselves to what degree it predicted versus *shaped* the reality that would subsequently appear. When ideas about the future are produced by powerful capitalist interests and make their way into public spaces, they influence the course on which that space travels. They directly affect the selfsame "trajectory" they claim to examine and on which they claim to extrapolate.[34]

In literary terms, "hyperstition" describes "the ways in which fiction structures or produces reality."[35] Hyperstition's power is especially pronounced in tech, where companies use a combination of seductive interfaces and advertising as a way to peddle to us a future full of their innovations—innovations the desirability of which the public has not expressed, much less demanded. In other words, the fictions that begin in the minds of tech company CEOs and founders become "real" because tech companies produce, through the very technologies they make, the world they *want* to be real. People don't ask to be "disrupted," but the promotional discourses of corporations such as Facebook, Apple, and Google serve a dual purpose: they produce a vision of the future that becomes culturally hegemonic and utilize specific rhetorical strategies to make this vision persuasive. Design educators' teaching is infused with those visions because our students accommodate their lives and their career goals to them, and, in the end, we are accountable to our students.

Neoliberalism *and* the computable subjectivity appear to be natural, the "real world" of everyday life with technology, precisely because of the way those ideas *as fictions* have begun to structure reality. A computationally infused future of mass-customization, enhanced convenience, improved efficiency, and increasing ease is one in which individuals seem to gain new "freedoms" (e.g., more time, unlimited cloud storage, etc.), but, in reality, the space in which everyday people have agency to decide what they actually want their future to be like continues to shrink. And yet, if tech companies produce the conditions that—at least in part—lead to the existence of one "real world," who is to say there aren't other possible "real worlds" to be created? Therein lies, I believe, a key tool for teaching design differently.

Capitalism's semblance as reality, its grip on the imagination, comes both from the power of the material effects of our surrender to its "effective virtualities" and from the way these effects shape the contours of what appears to be imaginable in the first place. The idea that people are both computing and computable, the very notion of a *computable subject* is also an effective virtuality. It has, as this book has demonstrated, material and psychological effects that shape the kind of people individuals think they are and can become.

Educating against the Computable Subjectivity from within the Capitalist Realist Academy: The Reformist Approach

User experience designers are both an important cog in the capitalist machinery *and* are central to the propagation of the computable subjectivity. Without UX professionals, products and services—ranging from consumer technologies to medical devices and from cement mixers[36] to coffee makers—could not produce the profits (or capture the data) sought by the firms that employ them. UX programs in colleges and universities thus have a close relationship to industry in ways that many other academic programs do not. UX degrees are "pre-professional," meaning that they do not prepare students for further study in the academy (as a degree in, say, philosophy might), but rather they prepare students to do a particular job.

Design Studies scholar Cameron Tonkinwise writes that a university design education serves three functions: (1) it prepares job-ready graduates for industry today; (2) it anticipates industry's trajectory and helps students become future industry leaders; and (3) it serves a critical function, "warning of the consequences of certain likely futures and deflecting industry from them."[37] I believe that by privileging (3) while weaving (1) and (2) throughout, UX design educators can work against the propagation of the computable subjectivity and at the same time teach students the skills and methods necessary to participate in the computationally-mediated world they will hopefully seek to change. This is what I'll call the "reformist" approach. In this approach, because of its connection to industry and the nature of UX as a pre-professional degree, teaching UX can function like a trojan horse. The technical competencies, methods, and aesthetic sensibilities privileged in the tech sector could be taught easily while utilizing a small fraction of a student's time-to-degree, meaning that UX courses could—using the structure that Tonkinwise lays out—foreground the critical capacity of design education, while teaching designers who are prepared to take on future industry challenges as well as designers who can work with the needs of industry right now. But, ideally, and primarily, these designers will be prepared to do something entirely different, to take on the politics of the industry, or to tear down the structuring edifices of the industry and build something better. UX design educators can educate *against* the computable subjectivity, against the divisive individualist zero-sum thinking that permeates every aspect of their students' lives, and toward something better, all while appearing to remain the handmaiden of industry, smiling and nodding at the advertising agency executives who donate money or to the corporate HR people who are lining up student internships. In what follows, I will offer some examples of my own (admittedly imperfect) attempts to enact this reformist approach in the day-to-day of the UX classroom. These examples will mainly comprise small interventions—modifications to assignments, new assignments, class discussions—that together perhaps demonstrate what this reformist approach might look like.

Graphic Design 1 and the Designer as Computer

Adobe Research, the business unit inside Adobe that engages in high-level computer science research, has, since the mid-2000s, been committed to developing technologies that automate or augment certain activities of professional graphic designers.[38] Adobe's own Sensei platform, for example, is a system that purports to automate certain aspects of the web and user-experience design process, including reconfiguring sites on the fly (and even rewriting copy) for different audience segments.[39]

As we have examined throughout this book, when powerful interests view everything in terms of computing, the world begins to *appear* as computational—even people, and even UX designers, the very people helping legitimize the view of people as computers through interface designs. This particular view of creativity as computational has its roots in work done at RAND corporation in the 1950s.[40] Since then, "studies on computational creativity have become commonplace," and there are research programs about the topic ranging from Spanish poetry to jazz and the visual arts.[41]

When all problems, including problems of visual design and aesthetics, are seen as software problems, in part because "data" has come to equal "world," then the ideas about people become embedded in the choices about what gets measured and how. "This is no less true in computational tools for the generation or improvement of design work,"[42] in which ideas about what is "aesthetically pleasing" that emanate primarily from European Modernism become *codified* in software, erasing other cultural and geographic influence. Once codified, it reifies these biases in the designs that are produced, circumscribing what designers think is both good *and* even possible in the first place.

In small modifications to a section of Graphic Design 1 (GD1) that I taught in 2018, I sought to push back against these dangerous consequences of automating design activity. Our program has multiple sections of GD1—comprised mainly of first and second year students—and consistency across these sections helps students as they advance in the Graphic Design and UX programs. Nonetheless, because the GD1 curriculum was originally centered on adapting Swiss-Modernist form studies, I believed it to be important to tackle some of the ideas about both the cultural hegemony of European Modernism, the way it manifests in the tools designers use today, and the way it is programmed into convenience-enhancing features of tomorrow's design software. Not only is Western cultural hegemony baked into software that, according to Adobe, allows you to "spend more time executing your creative vision," but the very idea of automating some—if not all—aspects of that vision assumes something more deep about people and aesthetics: that there is a universal set of (Western) visual aesthetics that precedes cultural individuation, and, furthermore, that people themselves operate according to the computational principles that would allow such an aesthetics to be encoded in the first place. I have been compelled to resist this notion and to help my students appreciate its pernicious effects.

In addition to classroom discussions on this topic, the culminating activity in the unit on form studies challenged the students to ask themselves whether "beauty" can be encoded, and what happens when people think it can. Students used Processing and JavaScript to try to "encode" what they perceived as their best form study, which was originally drawn by hand and then traced in Adobe Illustrator. They consistently expressed frustration with "the process of identifying precise pixel-level locations where the points that controlled the curves would be placed."[43] This frustration does not point to inadequacies in students' mathematical abilities or in their ability to write simple code. Instead, this simple exercise asks them whether what they perceive to be beautiful can itself be codified, and what that means, or doesn't mean, about them as people. Admittedly a small intervention into a much larger systemic issue, I hope the activity planted a seed for a more critical reading of the "convenience-enhancing" features of design software.

The Absurdity of the Computable Subjectivity: Data-Driven Horoscopes and a World without Mistakes

Vilém Flusser, whose work features prominently throughout this book, thought that when "to know above all is to enumerate," that scientific knowledge itself "becomes absurd." Throughout this book I've positioned this absurdity and its consequences as dangerous to both individuals and society, and I have used my own artistic projects as a mode of communicating both the absurdity and its dangers to the public.[44] As I have illustrated in this chapter, there is also an absurdity to the acceptance of the "real world" that is peddled to us through products that are themselves little more than fictions in the first place. "Machine Learning," for example, is often just doublespeak for the exploitation of individuals in so-called developing countries.[45] The ideological dominance of Silicon Valley's promotional rhetoric seemed to have permeated my conversations with students so thoroughly that I began to wonder if there were ways to surface this absurdity such that we might be able to have conversations about it. Perhaps, I hoped, those conversations would lead to discussing any number of ideas contained within this book about the computable subjectivity, its characteristics, and its consequences.

In 2017, I taught a special topics course, which was open to both Graphic Design and UX majors. Special topics courses, when able to be offered, are another space in which the "reformist" approach to changing design education can take advantage of existing institutional structures. This course looked at different ways that data is captured and used, as well as what the limits of datafication might be. It asked students to experiment with both technologies and ideas about data capture. One student project, *Elixir*, conceptualized and designed by Lorenza Centi, proposed the existence of an internet-connected mood-ring and corresponding app that gave users access to "data-driven astrology" (Figures 5.1 and 5.2). From her project description:

> Elixir is a precision tracking system that allows you to follow your astrological chart in real time and space for a more accurate reading. With updates on positions of the sun, moon and planets astrological aspects, and consideration of sensitive angles to allow for more accurate representation of events within your life. Using smart-fiber woven, textile color-changing technology, the Elixir ring subtly alerts you of a change in astrological location affecting your sign. Paired with app integration, a custom profile is built on your natal chart and personality traits. Changes in lifestyle categories, including career, life, love and health are then indicated by change in color.[46]

Elixir, as a fiction, is a whimsical critique of "data-driven" discourse. The aesthetic treatment is sensitive and prescient, utilizing the visual vernacular of hip wellness products with which many consumers, years later, have become accustomed. Its seductive aesthetic and absurd business proposition produce a kind of "uncanny valley" effect, causing audiences to wonder "is this real?" The pause that it might offer is an opportunity to begin conversations about the growing perception that everything is computational in nature.

FIGURE 5.1 An image from the *Elixir* project. Courtesy Lorenza Centi.

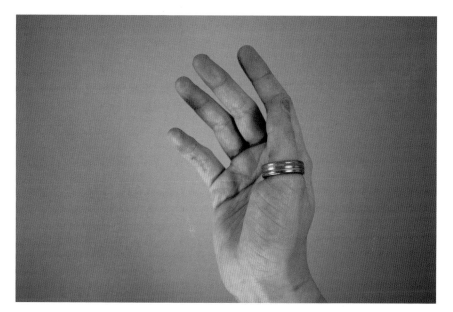

FIGURE 5.2 An image from the *Elixir* project. Courtesy Lorenza Centi.

Such a pause, the moment in which someone questions the veracity of a particular "brand" or campaign, is often associated with successful speculative design[47] projects, which extrapolate on current sociotechnical trajectories and create fictional products or services that aim to provoke discourse about that future.

In the fall semester of 2018, another student in a different course, Erin Campbell, created a speculative design project about a future without mistakes. In a world full of predictive analytics and people who believed themselves able to be predicted by those analytics systems, maybe she thought, we could eliminate "mistakes" altogether. What began as an optimistic exploration became a critique of computational predictability. Do we *want* a world without mistakes? Below are some notes from her project description.

It's 2025. A new tech wearable, ARDA, has just been released to the public. Creators say the name ARDA was inspired by the Zoroastrian phrase Arda Fravash or "Holy Guardian Angels." This guardian angel wearable claims it can eliminate 99 percent of human error with use.

…

It's 2030. The effects ARDA has had on users and society as a whole are being talked about by *The New York Times*. It turns out eliminating 99 percent of human error means fewer car accidents, less "oops!" babies, and, in turn, a drastic decrease in abortions performed this year.

...

It's 2035. A quick Google search for "ARDA wearable" reveals the negative ramifications imparted on the world by the invention and use of ARDA … Maybe a perfect life won't make you happier. Maybe, if you had never made a mistake, you wouldn't be where you're sitting right now. Maybe lives lived without mistakes aren't really lives lived at all.[48]

Perhaps, by becoming completely legible to computing, people could avoid "mistakes" altogether. But what constitutes a mistake and in what ways are they generative of new possibilities? Erin concluded that computational mistake-avoidance would be peddled by Silicon Valley entrepreneurs as a beneficent force for social change but would end up having disastrous consequences. This isn't unrealistic—recall Google's patent for decision-assistance mentioned in Chapter 4. Erin's work echoes Flusser's warning:

> In a society where accident (catastrophe) is forbidden, we limit ourselves only to information that can be produced/deduced from what is already known. Such a (luckily impossible) world may as well be heaven for machines, but for machines only. Throughout his career, Flusser was convinced that we are approaching a society that is unbearably inhospitable to human beings.[49]

A society of computable subjects believing in the elimination of "mistakes" seems somewhat absurd. But, Erin is asking us, is it any *less absurd* than the futures peddled to us by Silicon Valley today?

Social Credit Scoring and Computable Subjects

In the spring of 2018, I taught the introductory interaction design course for our Graphic Design and UX programs. One consistent learning goal—especially as a partner with industry—is to help students see UX as extending beyond the "screen," and being embedded also within products, services, and even physical environments. In this particular iteration of the course, for example, I asked students to produce a proposal and prototype for an interactive museum exhibition, loosely oriented around the relationship between technology and politics. I offered some resources to help students begin their research, and helped students find articles that supported the specific ideas on which they decided to work.

One student in this course, Christina Dennis, focused on the past, present, and future of social credit scoring:

> She wrote a short essay arguing that Ayn Rand's objectivism and the individualist Californian Ideology associated with 1990s Silicon Valley entrepreneurialism that Rand inspired were, paradoxically, similar to both the Chinese Social Credit System and the underlying thrust of two episodes

of *Black Mirror* ("Fifteen Million Merits" and "Nosedive"). This similarity, she suggested, positioned the ideal participant in society as an individual living out selfish desires. In the case of the Social Credit System, this selfish desire is the desire for a higher score; meanwhile, a Randian approach would suggest that to behave in one's own self-interest would inherently make one a better member of society. In neither case, however, is the individual motivated by altruism.[50]

The computable subjectivity is an ideal political subject in societies in which such credit scoring systems might be implemented. Desiring to be legible to these computational systems makes someone more compliant with the behavioral norms for which the systems seek to optimize. Other questions that have arisen throughout this book also were raised in Christina's work: whether individuals can be modeled by computational systems, and if these models assume that people are selfish. Such questions are frequently taken up by Science and Technology Studies scholars in their writing.[51,52]

Christina's proposed exhibition simulated a social credit scoring system deployed by a private company in the United States. For her prototype, she produced what was, in effect, a piece of performance art as interaction design (Figures 5.3 and 5.4). She wanted to provoke students on campus into considering the consequences of social credit scoring. In her prototype, museum visitors entered the space and input their social media handles at an iPad on a pedestal. Then, they were invited to stand in front of a wall across which a moving red line was projected, alluding to a kind of "scan," while the data was "processed." Visitors were then shown their "score," according to the company's "proprietary algorithms," followed by recommendations for improving it.

FIGURE 5.3 Christina Dennis's social credit scoring exhibition prototype and performance piece. Courtesy Christina Dennis.

FIGURE 5.4 The prototypical social credit score shown to visitors as part of Christina's piece. Courtesy Christina Dennis.

Despite the fictive and performative nature of the project, Christina was required to consider a number of user-experience design fundamentals:

> What kind of feedback would she give users to suggest that they had successfully signed in? How would users know which way to orient themselves in the space? Would the score and recommendations be projected publicly or shown only to the user and how would this difference impact the experience for other users? What kind of copywriting would be instructive, but not overwhelm the users, while at the same time maintaining the voice of the fictional company she created?[53]

Interdisciplinarity and the "Reformist" Approach

I would like to offer one final comment about the "reformist" approach: if UX design educators are to work within the existing system while successfully pushing back against the field's propagation of the computable subjectivity and its deleterious effects, the nature of what comes under the umbrella of "UX education" has to change. The kind of epistemic blinders that were required for Graphic Design and UX to become stand-alone fields in industry and higher education in the first place have to be removed. This book itself is an effort to explode those epistemic blinders, a place to begin examining the extremely important connections between UX and other fields that reveal the very deep and often dangerous impacts UX designers have on the world.

Conclusion: Returning to Political Economy and the Limits of the Reformist Approach

I would like to return here to the story of Cybersyn and Stafford Beer. One of the chapter titles in Beer's book, *Designing Freedom*, is "The Future That Can Be Demanded Now." Thinking about how Cybersyn—like the neoliberal governmentality—relies on a particular kind of political subject who believes themselves to be both computable and computing, I wonder: what kind of future can such a subject *really* demand? One that is constrained entirely by that which can be measured and computed? Constrained by the system's existing parameters? Can such a subject really demand *any* future at all?

It's no coincidence that Beer's chapter title is awfully similar to the cover design for Nick Srnicek and Alex Williams's 2015 book, *Inventing the Future*, which bears some of the "demands" that the authors describe in detail in the book itself: "demand full automation"; "demand universal basic income"; "demand the future." The subtitle of Srnicek and Williams's book is "Postcapitalism and a World without Work."[54]

Both Beer's ideas about administering the affairs of a state and Srnicek and Williams's ideas about the coming of a new luxurious world without work are animated by a faith in optimization and a belief that advanced computing will achieve that optimization. Indeed, Srnicek and Williams's book follows in the kind of techno-utopian tradition that has, recently at least, been characterized by the monicker "fully-automated luxury communism." But what kind of future is this? And what happens to people when we get there?

I'd like to conclude with one more story. Written in 1920 by Yevgeny Zamyatin, it is a book, simply called, *We*. *We* is a mathematician's diary chronicling a society in which individual freedom does not exist. Instead, everyone works in the service of the One State, which the reader very quickly realizes is not the communist utopia that its designers sought to create. As one of the translators, Clarence Brown, writes: *We* is "a great prose poem on the fate that might befall all of us if we surrender our individual selves to some collective dream of technology and fail in the vigilance that is the price of freedom."[55] There is an irony here that should not be lost on the reader: that today's advanced technologies of prediction and control and of datafied surveillance that I have described throughout this book are always promoted under the guise of *freedom*—freeing us from certain mundane tasks, anticipating our needs in particular ways to free up our time or resources, and yet, they do precisely the opposite, constraining the space in which we can imagine what is or isn't possible.

Like all characters in *We*, the mathematician-narrator does not have a name. Instead, he goes by D-503. As the reader progresses through D-503's diary, they see the logical and rational mind on which D-503 prides himself deteriorate into a hallucinatory schizoid trance in which he attempts to subvert the One State in the name of individuality and freedom. *We* deftly critiques the computable subjectivity that results from a subservience to technological striation and regimentation. D-503 opens one of the first entries in his diary with a celebration of the quantification of everything. His words sound like those of today's Silicon Valley soothsayers: "the worthiest human efforts are those intellectual pursuits that specifically seek the uninterrupted delimiting of infinity into convenient, easily digestible portions."[56]

Writing *We* during the early days of the Bolshevik regime that rose immediately after the revolution, it is perhaps surprising that Zamyatin's work was not necessarily condemned outright (at first) by The Party. His work was partly funded by the Bolsheviks[57] and to read *We* as a critique of communism as a whole is maybe misguided. It might be better to read *We* as a critique of "Really Existing Communism" or to read it as an attempt at articulating the problems with a Leninism that assumed the Fordist factory to be the production model *par excellence* or Taylorism to be a way towards economic efficiency and an improved standard of living for all (as the later Lenin very much did).[58,59] Both Fordism and Taylorism were built on the ideology of capitalism, and required the kind of fragmentation of individuals that is characteristic of the computable subjectivity. To think that those technological concepts could be put toward the purposes of socialism might be, at least when one is reading *We*, seen as misguided.

For me, Zamyatin's writing underscores the questions posed by Project Cybersyn: can the tools and technologies utilized by capital be turned against it in the service of a better world? And if so, what would it mean for how we perceive ourselves? Can we really *optimize* for justice or for socialism? Or are there dangers in exploiting the computable subjectivity for what seem to be more noble ends?

These questions also reflect what I feel are the shortcomings of the "reformist" approach to changing design education in a way that resists the computable subjectivity and its pernicious effects. The reformist approach takes technological progress as a given, and accepts the existence of the technologies on which capitalism has constructed its hegemony. Any design assignment that takes as a basic assumption the current technological landscape of society will require some acceptance of the ideologies embedded within those technologies, perhaps then limiting the scope of what students feel like they can change. The mandate of a fundamentally *different* design education must be significantly more broad— it must not be only about "critiquing" capital or the computable subjectivity or predictive analytics or algorithmic decision-making. Instead, it must be about *decomputerization*, about *degrowth*, and about a completely different and unfamiliar way of living and being in the world. This is the "revolutionary" approach in the "reform vs. revolution" question to changing design education. I will sketch out some ideas about this in the concluding chapter.

Notes

1. Conservative attacks on the "liberal" higher education establishment are not new (William F. Buckley's first book about his experience at Yale comes to mind) but have been amplified in recent years through conservative media and think-tank ecosystems such as those funded by the Koch brothers. See Isaac Kamola, "Guest Blog: Where Does the Bizarre Hysteria about 'Critical Race Theory' Come From? Follow the Money!," *Inside Higher Ed*, June 3, 2021, https://www.insidehighered.com/blogs/just-visiting/guest-blog-where-does-bizarre-hysteria-about-%E2%80%98critical-race-theory%E2%80%99-come-follow.

2. Gary Hall, *The Uberfication of the University* (Minneapolis: University of Minnesota Press, 2016).

3. See, for example: the systematic dismantling of the University of Wisconsin system, including the elimination of multiple departments at UW-Stevens Point. One helpful reference is Chuck Rybak, *UW Struggle: When a State Attacks Its University* (Minneapolis: University of Minnesota Press, 2017).

4. See chapters 1 and 2 for more information on cybernetics.

5. Stafford Beer, *Designing Freedom* (London: Wiley, 1974), 44.

6. Beer, *Designing Freedom*, 45.

7. Eden Medina, *Cybernetic Revolutionaries: Technology and Politics in Allende's Chile* (Cambridge, MA: MIT Press, 2011), 1.

8. Adrian Lahoud, "Error Correction: Chilean Cybernetics and Chicago's Economists," in *Alleys of Your Mind: Augmented Intelligence and Its Traumas*, ed. Matteo Pasquinelli (Lüneburg: meson press, 2015), 42.

9. Beer, *Designing Freedom*, 24.

10. Beer, *Designing Freedom*, 24.

11. Jeremy Gross, "Stafford Beer: Eudemony, Viability and Autonomy," *Red Wedge*, February 18, 2020, http://www.redwedgemagazine.com/online-issue/stafford-beer-eudemony.

12. Beer, *Designing Freedom*, 48.

13. Beer, *Designing Freedom*, 48.

14. See: Lahoud, "Error Correction" and Medina, *Cybernetic Revolutionaries*, as well as Allenna Leonard, "Stafford Beer and the Legacy of Cybersyn: Seeing around Corners," ed. Dr Raul Espejo, *Kybernetes* 44, nos. 6–7 (June 1, 2015): 926–34, doi:10.1108/K-02-2015-0045.

15. Lahoud, "Error Correction," 38.

16. Lahoud, "Error Correction," 37.

17. See Chapter 1.

18. Lahoud, "Error Correction," 40.

19. Lahoud, "Error Correction," 41.

20. Lahoud, "Error Correction," 41.

21. Lahoud, "Error Correction," 46.

22. Beer, *Designing Freedom*, 3–4.

23 Norbert Wiener, *The Human Use of Human Beings: Cybernetics and Society*, The Da Capo Series in Science (New York, NY: Da Capo Press, 1988 [1954]).

24 I spent much of Chapters 1 and 2 demonstrating some of the ways that Cybernetics as a field had yielded a particular way of seeing people, a way that treated people as automatons, as closed systems that sought to self-optimize, and that, most importantly, could not only be modeled as computers, but perhaps themselves operated by computational principles. This view of people was also informed by a particular technoscientific milieu in which cybernetics came to exist—namely, Second World War and the Cold War. As such, the origins of cybernetics have embedded within them ideas about people and nation states in adversarial relationships. And yet, as N. Katherine Hayles makes abundantly clear in *How We Became Posthuman*, Cybernetics is not a monolithic field, but instead wildly heterogeneous. It underwent three major shifts (we refer to them as "waves") and different cyberneticists studied vastly different topics—ranging from the brain to business and from optics to military operations. Indeed, those who identified as cyberneticists held different worldviews, espoused different politics, and they lived out their ideas about the world in their professional work to differing degrees. Stafford Beer is an interesting example of this, since he seemed quite committed to direct democracy (and even to perhaps a democratic socialism) but also worked with major corporations and is credited with originating the field of management cybernetics. His work might equally have served to enhance the efficiency with which capitalism operates and demonstrate the possibilities of a new kind of socialism infused with cybernetic principles. See: Katherine Hayles, *How We Became Posthuman: Virtual Bodies in Cybernetics, Literature, and Informatics* (Chicago, IL: University of Chicago Press, 1999).

25 Dick Martin and Jonathan Rosenhead, "Stafford Beer," *The Guardian*, September 4, 2002, sec. Education, https://www.theguardian.com/news/2002/sep/04/guardianobituaries.obituaries.

26 Lahoud, "Error Correction," 43.

27 Mark Fisher, "Foreword," in *Economic Science Fictions*, ed. William Davies (London: Goldsmiths Press, 2018).

28 Fisher, "Foreword."

29 Liam Vaughn, "'Most Americans Today Believe the Stock Market Is Rigged, and They're Right,'" *Bloomberg.com*, September 29, 2021, https://www.bloomberg.com/news/features/2021-09-29/is-stock-market-rigged-insider-trading-by-executives-is-pervasive-critics-say.

30 Ingrid Lunden, "Humane, a Stealthy Hardware and Software Startup Co-Founded by an Ex-Apple Designer and Engineer, Raises $100M," *TechCrunch*, September 1, 2021, https://social.techcrunch.com/2021/09/01/humane-a-stealthy-hardware-and-software-startup-co-founded-by-an-ex-apple-designer-and-engineer-raises-100m/.

31 Uber, *Meet Victor—Primary Teacher and Driver Partner*, 2016, https://www.youtube.com/watch?v=6WhC_w6uJRQ.

32 Alissa Quart, "Teachers Are Working for Uber Just to Keep a Foothold in the Middle Class," September 7, 2016, https://www.thenation.com/article/archive/teachers-are-working-for-uber-just-to-keep-a-foothold-in-the-middle-class/.

33 Uber, *Uber—Jenny Is a Full Time Math Teacher Who Drives With … | Facebook*, 2015, https://www.facebook.com/uber/videos/1018996768140608/. This video, produced and circulated on Facebook by Uber, is accompanied by the following copy: "Jenny is a full time math teacher who drives with Uber in her spare time. Adding extra money to her income while subtracting the hassle of a fixed schedule, equals just what she needs."

34 Ahmed Ansari and Jabe Bloom, "Time and Transition," in *Proceedings of Relating Systems Thinking and Design (RSD5) 2016 Symposium* (Relating Systems Thinking and Design (RSD5), OCAD University, Toronto, Ontario, 2016), https://rsdsymposium.org/time-transition/.

35 "Hyperstition" is a complex term with an equally complicated history. Noys' definition boils it down to something that I think can be useful. Unfortunately, this usefulness perhaps belies its history as something used predominantly by the now ultra-right wing accelerationist, Nick Land. Land is a former leader of the Cybernetic Culture Research Unit at University of Warwick and this concept of hyperstition began its life there, at the CCRU, in the 1990s. In an interview with Estselle Gervais, Emily Segal, a member of noted art and trend-forecasting collective K-HOLE, says that "Hyperstition is a term coined in the 1990s to describe fictions that make themselves true. As the CCRU (Cybernetic Culture Research Unit) once defined it: 'There is no difference in principle between a universe, a religion, and a hoax. All involve an engineering of manifestation, or practical fiction, that is ultimately unworthy of belief. Nothing is true, because everything is under production. Because the future is a fiction it has a more intense reality than either the present or the past. Hyperstitions are not representations, neither disinformation nor mythology.'" Estelle Gervais, "Emily Segal: How to Predict Hype," *PHI Antenna*, March 14, 2018, https://phi.ca/en/antenna/hyperstition-or-how-to-predict-hype/.

36 Really, this is a thing … I actually worked on a proposal for a cement mixing technology once.

37 Cameron Tonkinwise, "What Things to Teach Designers in Post-Industrial Times?," *EPIC*, August 24, 2015, https://www.epicpeople.org/what-things-to-teach-designers-in-post-industrial-times/.

38 Zachary Kaiser, "Creativity as Computation: Teaching Design in the Age of Automation," *Design and Culture* 11, no. 2 (May 4, 2019): 173–92, doi:10.1080/17547075.2019.1609279.

39 Adobe Communications Team, "Peek behind the Sneaks: Managing the Challenges of Personalization and Content Velocity," *Adobe Blog*, May 31, 2017, https://web.archive.org/web/20190107115146/https://theblog.adobe.com/peek-behind-the-sneaks-managing-the-challenges-of-personalization-and-content-velocity/.

40 This will, most likely, not surprise readers of Chapter 1.

41 Kaiser, "Creativity as Computation," 180.

42 Kaiser, "Creativity as Computation," 185.

43 Kaiser, "Creativity as Computation," 184.

44 See, for example: *The Dr. Pawel Norway Dream Machine* in Chapter 2 and *Whisper* in Chapter 3.

45 See, for example: the work of Lilly Irani and the Turkopticon project (https://turkopticon.net/), as well as: Rodney Brooks, "An Inconvenient Truth About AI," *IEEE Spectrum*, September 29, 2021, https://spectrum.ieee.org/rodney-

brooks-ai; Parmy Olson, "Much 'Artificial Intelligence' Is Still People behind a Screen," *Bloomberg.com*, October 13, 2021, https://www.bloomberg.com/opinion/articles/2021-10-13/how-good-is-ai-much-artificial-intelligence-is-still-people-behind-a-screen; and, Arvind Dilawar, "The Very Human Labor That Powers Artificial Intelligence," October 27, 2020, https://www.thenation.com/article/society/amazon-mturk-artificial-intelligence/.

46   Course documentation, 2018.

47   In the late 1990s, some designers from the UK who had primarily worked in product/industrial design, began thinking about what their work would look like in the future. They started to think about the kinds of worlds that would exist, what kinds of societies might emerge, what kinds of technologies those societies would have, and how the products they designed would fit within those social-cultural-technological systems. In short, they used objects to tell stories—or more like they used objects to get us to *think the stories they wanted those objects to tell*. They studied cutting-edge technological and scientific research and trends in politics, economics, and culture, and began to extrapolate on what the world might be like in the near (and sometimes far) future, and they started to make designs that could be a part of that future. Through a number of twists and turns, these practices congealed into the discipline that is typically now referred to as Speculative Design. Other names have been used to refer to similar and/or identical practices and projects. These names also include Design Noir, Design Fiction, and Critical Design. At its very best, Speculative Design is a powerful and unique mode of questioning, interrogating, and critiquing the various futures that might emerge from the dynamic interactions of ideologies, social relations, environmental conditions, and technological innovation. Benjamin Bratton writes that "Speculative Design focuses on possibilities and potentials. It confronts an uncertain and ambiguous future and seeks to give it shape." Benjamin Bratton, "On Speculative Design," *DIS Magazine*, March 2016, https://web.archive.org/web/20170503110731/http://dismagazine.com/discussion/81971/on-speculative-design-benjamin-h-bratton/.

48   Erin Campbell's project description, from 2018 course documentation. Used with permission.

49   Konrad Wojnowski, "Telematic Freedom and Information Paradox," *Flusser Studies* 23 (June 2017), http://www.flusserstudies.net/sites/www.flusserstudies.net/files/media/attachments/wojnowski-konrad-telematic-freedom-and-information-paradox.pdf, 13.

50   Kaiser, "Creativity as Computation," 186–7.

51   Luke Stark, "Algorithmic Psychometrics and the Scalable Subject," *Social Studies of Science* 48, no. 2 (April 2018): 204–31, doi:10.1177/0306312718772094.

52   John C. Marshall, "Minds, Machines and Metaphors," *Social Studies of Science* 7, no. 4 (1977): 475–88.

53   Kaiser, "Creativity as Computation," 187–8.

54   Nick Srnicek and Alex Williams, *Inventing the Future: Postcapitalism and a World without Work* (New York: Verso, 2016).

55   Clarence Brown, "Translator's Introduction," in Yevgeny Zamyatin, *We*, Penguin Twentieth-Century Classics (New York, NY: Penguin Books, 1993).

56   Yevgeny Zamyatin, *We* (New York: Random House/Modern Library Classics, 2014 [1921]).

57 Natasha Randall, "Translator's Introduction," in Yevgeny Zamyatin, *We*, Modern Library paperback ed (New York: Modern Library, 2006).

58 Maurice Brinton, "The Bolsheviks and Workers' Control: The State and Counter-Revolution," *Solidarity*, 1970, https://www.marxists.org/archive/brinton/1970/workers-control/05.htm.

59 Arianna Bove, "Notes on Americanism and Fordism," *Generation Online*, accessed November 20, 2017, http://www.generation-online.org/p/fpgramsci.htm.

CONCLUSION

Toward a Luddite Design Education

The Politics of UX and the Computable Subject as the Ideal Political Subject

This book has sought, in part, to demonstrate that user-experience design is never *only* about user-experience design. It is always already political, deeply embedded with histories of science, technology, and political economy from which it can never be extracted, manifesting the dominant ideologies within those histories at every turn. Because of this intertwining, an interdisciplinary approach is essential to understanding the consequences of the work that UX designers do. This book has focused on one of those consequences—the production of the *computable subjectivity*, when people adopt the belief that they are both computable and computing, and the way this subjectivity subsequently becomes an aspirational ideal in society.

Because of the way UX is so deeply intertwined with science, technology, and political economy, the story of how the computable subjectivity rises to prominence is an impossibly large one to tell. Instead of trying to capture every single significant moment, theorist, or technology, this book has been selective in the story it tells. This is perhaps one of the dangers in an interdisciplinary approach to teaching and writing about UX—and it is one of the fundamental critiques of "generalists" (whether in design or other fields): by casting the net so wide, it's impossible to have a "deep" understanding. In opposition to this view, I have never seen interdisciplinarity as anything but essential. Now, more than ever before, designers and scholars (and their students) must examine the politics of design in technology. They must ask what the consequences are of the way design participates in what Rancière calls the "distribution of the sensible"—the delimiting of sensory experience that determines how we are able to participate as political subjects. In citing Rancière, I'm already stepping outside my "field" as a designer. However, I have come to question what constitutes the epistemological boundaries of "user-experience design" as a field, and whether those epistemological boundaries function too often as blinders. Its frequent lack of engagement with

Science and Technology Studies[1] or Political Economy, for example, has also led to my passion for interdisciplinary research and practice. Deep engagement with the diversity of fields that are required to understand—and reckon with—the politics of our technologies is the only way to reimagine how we actually make and use technology today. And this production and use is mediated by the *interface*. It is at the interface, where individuals meet ideas about themselves that propagate Silicon Valley's interests and advance the agendas of the most powerful at the expense of the already marginalized, that various disciplinary threads become so tightly woven that I see it as impossible to untangle them.

In this book, I have described the role of user-experience design in the adoption of the "computable subjectivity": the idea of the self as computing, meaning operating according to computational processes, and computable, meaning entirely understandable by computers. The first chapter laid the historical and conceptual groundwork for the descriptions of the various characteristics of the computable subjectivity that would follow. It synthesized four key historical and conceptual threads—biopolitics, convenience, the countercultural idea of computing, and the rise of Cybernetics—in order to show the way that Western, and particularly American, society was primed for the computable subject to emerge as its political subject *par excellence*. Building on this foundation, Chapters 2, 3, and 4 describe, examine the roots and consequences of, and demonstrate the role of UX in producing the three core characteristics of the computable subjectivity.

In Chapter 2, I examine the first of these three characteristics: the ideological commitment to the equivalence of "data" and "world." I trace this ideological commitment through various histories of the relationship between measurement and meaning. I demonstrate the ways that this equivalence manifests both in the computational technologies that capture data and in the interfaces which present that "data" as the "world" to their users. Through a close reading of the technology inside early iterations of the FitBit, the chapter looks at how "world" is captured and turned into "data," and how the findings from that "data" are subsequently generalized and grafted back onto the world. The disappearance of the mechanism that translates "world" to "data" and back encourages users to falsely equate the two at the moment they encounter their world through the interface.

Once "world" and "data" are seen as one in the same, individuals aspire to be both legible to, and predictable by, computers. This aspiration soothes the feelings of fragmentation that emerge once everything needs to become data in order to be understood. This is the second of the three core characteristics of the computable subjectivity, and it is the topic of the third chapter of the book. This chapter looks at the kinds of alienation that are produced as individuals aspire to become legible to the computers that exert increasing amounts of control over everyday life, and it demonstrates the way UX design makes computational legibility the solution to the problem it itself poses.

When it appears as though one can be completely understood by succumbing to the fragmentation and alienation of constant datafication, the very concept of morality changes, becoming tied to achieving normality through computational self-optimization. This morality at the heart of the computable subjectivity is the topic of the fourth chapter. In it, I chronicle the process by which this type of morality is realized, in which technical prowess is privileged over its material effects on real people. The result of such a shift in morality is a drastic change in the kind of interactions that take place in society, wherein individuals' interactions with one another become instruments of a system that has nothing to do with actual people, but is instead focused exclusively on metrics that were originally only meant to serve as a proxy, but have, sadly, become more real than the people themselves.

Chapter 5 began to address two important questions that emerge from the preceding analysis, questions which I will carry forward into this conclusion: (1) is it really the computable subjectivity that is the problem, or is it actually capitalism's fault? And, (2) what is the solution? In the fifth chapter, I argued that design education is the place from which an attack on the computable subjectivity might be mounted because design education "flies under the radar" of conservative attacks on higher education. I described what I refer to as the "reformist" approach to changing design education, and I offered some examples from my courses that, while small interventions into a much larger problem, might help design educators consider similar small changes in their work. In describing a "reformist" approach, I suggested that there is also a "revolutionary" approach. That approach is what this conclusion will explore.

The Lingering Problem: The Computable Subjectivity and Political Economy

As I demonstrated in Chapter 5, I am convinced that the computable subjectivity and the problems it creates are not limited to neoliberalism. The computable subjectivity is a dangerous way to understand oneself, even under what might be considered a more just political economic system. I offered two anecdotes to support this assertion—one about Chile's experiment in Socialist Cybernetics in the 1970s, which illustrated the limits of believing that everything that matters can be measured; and another about a novel written just after the October revolution in the Soviet Union, which suggested that perhaps a fully planned and technologically advanced communism might not be such a utopia after all.

I'd like to offer some additional support for my suspicion that the dangers of the computable subjectivity are not limited to capitalist political economy. There is a great deal of research that undermines techno-utopian aspirations toward "fully-automated luxury communism."[2] This research centers on three main points, which we'll examine briefly below. First, fully automated luxury communism would be ecologically untenable because of the extractive processes required to produce the amount of computing infrastructure to realize it, and because of the massive amount of energy required to cool and maintain all that computing. Second, the dream of full-automation of all labor is built on a misreading of recent economic history.[3] The cause for job loss in industrial sectors is *not* automation, but rather mass deindustrialization incentivized by finance capital. This has resulted in a decreasing demand for labor, with a shift toward systemic and large-scale underemployment especially as industrial labor shifts to the service sector. And, third, full-automation of labor requires optimization, and optimization requires both commensurability and the circumscribing of possibility via decisions about measurement. Any attempt at optimization requires decisions to be made about what to measure and what not to measure. Something always escapes. And it is that which escapes that makes any effort at optimization *political*.[4] Furthermore, to optimize a system for a particular system state, all the variables within that system need to be subjected to a particular quantitative equivalence (e.g., dollars, in the case of optimizing for something like "return on investment"). Any attempt at optimization requires a flattening of difference. It requires that everything be turned into something that it is inherently not. Full societal optimization, as in fully automated luxury communism, is a false hope of sorts. Can you "optimize" for "social welfare?" Only insofar as you construe social welfare to be a particular agglomeration of metrics and numeric indicators that have some kind of system of equivalence that they all operate with. This is itself a fantasy. It is a kind of technocratic accounting that refuses to call into question the means of optimization, and whether those means are themselves desirable to use—not only as indicators or metrics, but literally whether metrics or indicators should be used *at all*.

So where do we turn? What do we do if it seems like in any political-economic system with sufficiently advanced technology, people will adopt the computable subjectivity and its deleterious effects will follow? This is the question to which the remainder of this chapter will turn.

The Revolutionary Approach: Luddite Design Education

In Chapter 5, I presented what I called a "reformist" approach to changing design education to resist the deleterious effects of the computable subjectivity. What I mean by "reformist" is the seeking of incremental change within existing institutional structures and relations. This approach, as I demonstrated, mostly consists of interventions into UX design curricula at the level of the project/ assignment.

Here, I will present what I refer to as the "revolutionary" approach. This approach requires wholesale change not only of design curricula but of the institutions within which design education is situated and to which it is connected. The reformist approach was inherently piecemeal, but a truly radical shift in the role design plays in how people see themselves would require something more organized. As anthropologist David Graeber wrote, "*The ultimate, hidden truth of the world, is that it is something that we make, and could just as easily make differently.*" Such wholesale change must be driven by a vision of a different society and a different political economic regime. Producing such a vision, perhaps though idealistic, is itself a design activity, but we are then trapped in something of a chicken-or-egg conundrum. How do we *do* design in a new society when that new society doesn't yet exist? But without design, how can we achieve that new society? Instead of getting stuck here, I'd like to focus instead on the kind of society that would expunge the computable subjectivity from its midst, and what might happen when it does. Since design is a goal-oriented activity, part of the revolutionary approach to design education would be to collectively—as a community—*imagine* what this society would look like, what its practices and processes might be, and to begin laying the plans to get there. I will begin by sketching out some basic ideas of the relationship between design and the people within such a society. Because the role of design within a given society is the primary orienting heuristic on which design education is typically based (e.g., the augmentation of surplus value under capitalism), it seems appropriate to examine how that might look if the organization of society itself were both anticapitalist *and* hostile to the adoption of the computable subjectivity (e.g., neither neoliberalism nor "fully-automated luxury communism"). I will use the three core characteristics of the computable subjectivity that I described in Chapters 2, 3, and 4 as dimensions along which to describe the relationship between design and a new kind of society:

1   "Decomputerization, not Data" will take on the computable subject's ideological commitment to the equivalence between "data" and "world."

2   "Wholeness, not Fragmentation" will seek to upend the computable subject's aspiration to be legible to, and predictable by, computers, which soothes the fragmentation required to be seen as such.

3   "Convivial Joy, not Optimization" will address the idea of morality as a computationally self-optimized normality that computable subjects adopt.

Each of these three factors is of course deeply connected, as are the three characteristics of the computable subjectivity. Their separation in this writing is artificial but useful in terms of developing strategies and tactics to build a new society *by design*.

A new kind of design—and a new kind of design education—will inherently address not just the aforementioned characteristics of the computable subjectivity but also the ideologies and histories to which they are connected. It would also address the consequences of the widespread adoption of the computable subjectivity, consequences that I've laid out here in this book. The first step in a new kind of design education is to examine the problems. This book began as a pedagogical project and should be seen as an effort to do some of this work.

I have chosen to conclude the book with imagining the role of design in a different world precisely because it is speculative, a hope more so than a reality. I would like that to change.

One: Decomputerization, Not Data

The computable subjectivity is built on the ideological commitment to the equivalence between "data" and "world." This equivalence, and thus one of the foundations of the computable subjectivity and all its deleterious effects, can be undermined by reimagining the role of computing in society, and more specifically, by *decomputerizing* society. I borrow this term from Ben Tarnoff, who introduces the idea of *decomputerization* as part of a broader approach to rectifying capitalism's harms on the environment. He argues that decreasing the use of technologies that require intensive resource extraction—such as bauxite for aluminum or columbite-tantalite for capacitors—as well as technologies that use more electricity than entire countries—such as cooling data centers or Bitcoin mining—is an essential component of a just society *and* of stopping climate change. Tarnoff argues that we should follow the example set by the Luddites in the early 1800s:

> [W]e should destroy machinery hurtful to the common good and build machinery helpful to it.[5]
>
> Decomputerization doesn't mean *no* computers. It means that not *all* spheres of life should be rendered into data and computed upon. Ubiquitous "smartness" largely serves to enrich and empower the few at the expense of the many, while inflicting ecological harm that will threaten the survival and flourishing of billions of people.

This Luddite future, in which the people demand that computing be applied in the service of the people themselves, is precisely the *democratic control over the design criteria of technology* for which Ivan Illich advocated in the 1970s.[6]

Looking at the technologies and patent applications cited throughout this book—ranging from Amazon's Halo and its "tone" feature to Google's activity recommendation system to Microsoft's productivity score—it's clear that there is no democratic control over the technologies that shape the life chances of millions of people. "If tools are not controlled politically, they will be managed in a belated technocratic response to disaster. Freedom and dignity will continue to dissolve into an unprecedented enslavement of man to his tools."[7] In Illich's conception, tools (meaning technologies, institutions, protocols, infrastructures, and so on) reach thresholds beyond which they become irredeemably damaging to people and the environment. This begins in the colonial era, gains force with the Industrial Revolution, and completely restructures society yielding the individualist, growth-hungry, hypercompetitive and destructive society we live in now. Arturo Escobar writes, "Many technologies or 'tools' based on specialized knowledge, such as medicine, energy, and education, surpassed their thresholds sometime in the early to mid-twentieth century. Once these thresholds were passed, the technologies become not only profoundly destructive in material and cultural terms but fatally disabling of personal and collective autonomy." This is *not* a technologically deterministic account: it means that it is the societal values within which a technology is developed that shape the nature of that technology, which then infuses those very values back into society.

I urge you to imagine what it would look like to judiciously and sparingly use computing for purposes that have been democratically determined. This radical reimagination of the role of computing in society is precisely what Paul Dourish argued that UX's "legitimacy trap"—its claim to legitimacy as a discipline being predicated on usefulness, efficiency, and subservience to capital—precludes.[8] Just think—instead of seeing a glowing news article about an "innovative" technology that just seemed to appear—that literally *no one* ever asked for, that does nothing except extract value, surveil, or exploit individuals, that further entrenches the competitive growth logic of capitalism in products and services that end up as the infrastructure of everyday life—communities would collectively determine their technological futures through decision-making that is not accountable to shareholder profits but to the people of the community themselves. This vision is what Ivan Illich imagined in his 1973 book, *Tools for Conviviality*.

Decomputerization and the autonomous communal determination of design criteria for any new computing technology would also require a sort of "undesign," to put it mildly. Technologies that do not serve the people as they decide they want to be served would be destroyed. By actually decreasing the role of computing in everyday life through actively destroying and refusing to build computational products and services that exploit labor and the planet, the relationship between "data" and "world" would by necessity break down. It would become clear that the "map" is not the "territory,"[9] and this would liberate subjectivity from the shackles of computation.

Two: Wholeness, Not Fragmentation

One of the results of the acceptance that "data" and "world" are one and the same is that individuals become convinced they can only be understood by becoming completely legible to computing. This requires the striation of the smooth space of everyday life, in which every activity becomes fragmented and quantified. When everyday life is fragmented and individuals are alienated from it through its externalization in the interface, more fragmentation presents itself as the solution to the problems it caused. This results in the experience of "ontological insecurity." Chapter 3 addressed this issue of fragmentation of life and the alienation it produces, and it did so through two different lenses: the first is the alienation of individuals from their labor, and the second is the alienation of individuals from their everyday lives.

A decomputerized society that democratically determines the design criteria of its technologies is one that rethinks what constitutes "necessary labor" and how it is divided. This begins the process of making whole those subjectivities that have been fragmented. This is "freedom realized in personal interdependence."[10] Reconceiving of the "realm of necessity," according to economic historian Aaron Benanav, would require the following:

1. Sharing of socially necessary labor, including dissolving the differences between waged and unwaged (hidden/domestic) work

2. Deciding, democratically, what is socially necessary

3. Dividing according to aptitudes and proclivities, such that division of labor "neither leaves important tasks undone, nor reproduces an elite class of technicians"[11]

4. More people participate in necessary work so that the amount any individual has to do is reduced

5. Workweek reduced to as few hours as possible, perhaps under ten

6. Reconceive of the relationships between production and consumption such that one is not divorced from the other, nor obscured by it.

7. Overcome the mentality of scarcity. Abundance becomes is *a mindset cultivated by a practice in relationship with others*

8. Solving (in communally autonomous ways) questions of equitable distributions of resources and the design of tools to achieve this end. This requires using some technologies to coordinate a community/state's needs and activities through the design of algorithms, protocols, and democratic processes for designing, auditing, and changing them[12]

At least part of the alienation that contributes to the computable subjectivity is produced by the increasing specialization and functionary nature of labor, in which technique becomes equated with morality. Benanav's rubric for reimagining the realm of necessity, would, by definition, undo some of that alienation through the explicit sharing of labor that has been deemed necessary through communal decision-making processes. Furthermore, the identities of individuals living within such a community would not be construed around their role in the economy, in part because both necessary labor *and* the tools used in that labor would be a product of communal decision-making and not of capitalist surplus value extraction.

In such a society, the goal would not be "growth" as under capitalism, but instead, "the cultivation of a joyful and balanced renunciation of the growth logic and the collective acceptance of limits."[13] Benanav writes that "*abundance is not a technological threshold to be crossed*," but instead it is "*a social relation*" (emphasis mine).[14] When technologies serve goals democratically determined by a community, the aims toward which a given political-economic system is oriented would shift. Such a political control over the tools used by a society would not only reverse the alienation produced by the specialization of labor, but it would inherently subvert the capitalist logic of growth. What comes to supplant it might then fall under Illich's idea of "conviviality" or the concept of "degrowth."

Three: Conviviality, Not Optimization

Under the regime of the computable subjectivity, morality becomes equated both with technical progress and with a normality produced through computational self-optimization. "Smart" technologies become inherently "good," and so are the people that use them to self-optimize. A different understanding of morality would emerge under a different kind of society, one that cultivates a different subjectivity. This shift, away from an instrumentalized morality in which human interaction serves metrics and not the people in the system themselves, would be catalyzed by decomputerization and democratic decision-making around technology and labor. Such a society would, as demonstrated above, expunge both optimization *and* the capitalist growth logic, emphasizing instead "degrowth," which is the shifting of "productivist ambitions" toward "joyful austerity."

Illich, who employed that phrase "joyful austerity," was concerned with the relationship between the tools a society uses and the impacts of those tools on the people who compose that society. He argued that the tools of our society reflect and subsequently shape what he saw as a deformed cultural imaginary that is obsessed with individualism, competition, and perpetual economic growth. In a society where "our expectations" are "industrially determined," individuals experience an atrophied imagination that leads to "progressive homogenization of personalities and personal relationships." I hope that Illich's words here call to mind the concerns articulated in Chapters 3 and 4 of this book, in which we closely examined biopolitical control and the expectation of computational legibility and predictability that come about when individuals adopt the computable subjectivity.

Illich suggests that this situation cannot be "stemmed without a retooling of society." This retooling of society will entail, at least in part, he suggests, a recognition of the "nature of desirable limits to specialization and output."[15] So, a convivial society, one that prioritizes the communally autonomous political control over tools, is also one that refuses the capitalist commitment to growth. It instead looks to build "institutions, relationships, and persons to live well without growth."[16] If the morality of self-optimization builds on the value of convenience that causes individuals to fetishize technologies that "save time" so they can pursue their "calling" as participants in the market, then degrowth calls that morality into question. A society of degrowth might prioritize: communal autonomy in decision-making, "thriving conviviality among humans and ecosystems," slowness, "the securing of enough for everyone to live with dignity and without fear," the rights of individuals "to experience friendship, love, and health," "to be able to give and receive care," and "to enjoy leisure and nature."[17] It is of the utmost importance to emphasize here that, following the Zapatistas, the preceding sketch is intended to offer a framework for designing "a world where many worlds fit." It is not a prescription nor is it monolithic.

A Provisional Program of Luddite Design Education

Given the preceding discussion, it should be clear that I believe today's design students must become a new generation of Luddites. A decomputerized society, predicated on conviviality and degrowth, is not only the kind of society which opposes the production of the computable subjectivity, but is also one in which justice, equity, planetary sustainment, and human flourishing can coexist. In the brief sketch offered above, I outlined some facets of such a society, paying particular attention to the relationship between that society and design. An education that prepares students to build such a world will look very different than today's UX design education. I have also just described the contours of the manner in which design and society might interact in a different world, not necessarily how to educate designers within or for that world, so a few additional notes might be pertinent here.

There are several primary "design problems"—though I hesitate to use this language—that might be identified and explored as students, educators, and community members alike build the Luddism that can lead toward a convivial new world. I'll try to address these design problems sequentially to some extent, because what I've outlined above as a new kind of relationship between design and society requires a radical and uncomfortable break with what exists right now. But the seeds for such a break need to be sown immediately. Nonetheless, I hesitate to offer the following, even as catalysts for discussion. I hope readers and colleagues will approach these ideas with the generosity of spirit required to realize together that "another world is possible."[18]

1   *Enacting refusal through design collectivism.* Designers today have a
    very hard time refusing to participate in the production of technologies
    that propagate the computable subjectivity, or exploit labor or the
    environment—even if they believe it is the right thing to do. This is, in
    part, because they remain atomized actors, especially when working as
    freelancers. Mutual aid organizations or unions for designers who aspire
    toward a new Luddism would go a long way in ensuring that designers
    feel empowered to refuse to build new extractive and exploitative
    technologies. This is already happening in some spaces, along what might
    be termed a "continuum of collective struggles," toward which a broad,
    design-labor internationalism might be one end. There are both historical
    and contemporary examples of this, ranging from the Detroit Printing
    Co-op[19] to the Tech Workers Coalition.[20]

2 *Figuring out how to identify and destroy existing exploitative technologies and those which are so deeply embedded with capitalist ideology that they are irredeemable.* This requires an intersectional, labor-oriented lens through which to view the world. Like anything in this concluding chapter, it is not something designers can do on their own, if "design" will even exist as such in a degrowth-oriented future. Those who consider themselves designers today, might, however, begin with the technologies with which they work most closely (e.g., the Adobe Creative Suite). We might see the original Luddites as providing a template worth following,[21] while acknowledging the distributed nature of the labor that is exploited through contemporary design technologies, as well as the neocolonialism of the hidden labor woven throughout. We—designers and individuals living in the "Global North"—have a great deal to learn from existing movements of resistance against the seemingly inevitable march of capital and resource extraction, particularly those emerging from indigenous communities across the globe.[22]

3 *How to design systems, processes, protocols, and technologies for the democratic determination of design criteria for any future technology.* There are organizations of designers and technologists already beginning this process, such as the Design Justice Network (DJN)[23] and the Detroit Community Technology Project (DCTP).[24] For example, the DCTP works with communities to build technologies, the priorities and design criteria of which are determined by the very communities who will use it. Designers and design educators in the "Global North" also have a great deal to learn on this front and it is best here to foreground the knowledge and experiences of those in the "Global South" who have been engaged in processes of autonomous communal decision making for a very long time. These include Zapatismo and the well-developed and articulated processes of governance applied therein,[25] as well as the matriarchal cultures that have been displaced by heteropatriarchy through capitalist development.[26]

4 *Envisioning abundance as a social relation and the production of a new "symbolic universe" that assists in producing this vision.* This is perhaps the most traditionally designerly act on this list, in that it is about developing a "vision" for something. We might think of narrative user scenarios, personas, and other artifacts typically produced when building a shared vision about a digital product or service. But this is different. Given the relations between design and community that would exist under a world that prioritizes conviviality and degrowth, it is unclear what kind of activity that today we understand to be "design" would even fall under the rubric of "design" as "necessary labor." As such, perhaps this would be less of a "design project" and more of an act—an act of love, an act of community, an act of service. It would maybe be something more akin to a "continual process of convivial reconstruction," that would enable "persons and collectivities to change and renew their lifestyles, their tools, their environments."[27] Nonetheless, the metaverse-free world that we can imagine should be informed by people and communities who do just this—who already understand that abundance is a social relation and is not predicated on a certain threshold of material wealth or technological advancement. Again, I implore readers to engage with the work of writers such as Arturo Escobar, theorists of degrowth such as Kallis et al., and, more importantly, to engage with the ideas of the communities that these theorists study and pay attention to their actions, the way they live out those ideas. I know that I still have much to learn.

A Luddite Design Education, Now

The project of addressing the systemic emergence and effects of the computable subjectivity is a much broader project of changing the very nature of design and the society within which it is done. Part of what the computable subjectivity does—one of the effects that we have studied in this book—is that it forecloses the possibility that things could be otherwise. To reopen those spaces of possibility and potential is part of the project of a new kind of design education that cultivates students' *imagination*, not just about design (in the limited disciplinary sense) but about how the world itself might be otherwise. Doing this *is in and of itself* a refusal to be bound by the computable subjectivity. A Luddite revolution *of design education itself* would require students to rethink and outright refuse the kind of political subjectivity they themselves have adopted, as well as the political subjectivity with which they imbue the technologies for which they design interfaces and which they thus encourage users to adopt.

A Luddite design education is not an education without technology. It is an education about the way technology and society intertwine, about the kind of people that are thus produced, and whether those are the kind of people we want to be. It is a design education not of negation but one of possibility. It is a design education that will cultivate an imagination of which those of us who teach design can barely conceive, because of the way our own imaginations have been stilted, stifled, and constrained. I hope you, dear reader, will join me in finding out what this Luddite design education looks like.

Notes

1   See, for example: the panel discussions held at the Society for the Social Study of Science (4S) in 2021, entitled "Using STS Methods in Design Education."

2   Aaron Bastani, *Fully Automated Luxury Communism: A Manifesto* (London; New York: Verso, 2019).

3   Aaron Benanav, *Automation and the Future of Work* (London; New York: Verso, 2020).

4   Adrian Lahoud, "Error Correction: Chilean Cybernetics and Chicago's Economists," in *Alleys of Your Mind: Augmented Intelligence and Its Traumas*, ed. Matteo Pasquinelli (Lüneburg: meson press, 2015), 37–51.

5   Ben Tarnoff, "To Decarbonize We Must Decomputerize: Why We Need a Luddite Revolution," *The Guardian*, September 18, 2019, sec. Technology, https://www.theguardian.com/technology/2019/sep/17/tech-climate-change-luddites-data.

6   Ivan Illich, *Tools for Conviviality*, Open Forum (London: Calder and Boyars, 1973).

7   Illich, *Tools for Conviviality*, 12.

8   Dourish, Paul, "User Experience as Legitimacy Trap," *Interactions* 26, no. 6 (October 30, 2019): 46–9, https://doi.org/10.1145/3358908.

9   Jorge Luis Borges, "On Exactitude in Science," in *Jorge Luis Borges: Collected Fictions*, trans. Andrew Hurley (New York: Penguin Books, 1999), 325.

10   Illich, *Tools for Conviviality*, 11.

11   Benanav, *Automation and the Future of Work,* 87.

12   Benanav, *Automation and the Future of Work.*

13   Arturo Escobar, *Designs for the Pluriverse: Radical Interdependence, Autonomy, and the Making of Worlds*, New Ecologies for the Twenty-First Century (Durham: Duke University Press, 2018): 9.

14   Benanav, *Automation and the Future of Work*, 89.

15   Illich, *Tools for Conviviality*, 20.

16   Giorgos Kallis et al., *The Case for Degrowth*, The Case for Series (Cambridge, UK; Medford, MA: Polity Press, 2020): 18.

17   Kallis et al., *The Case for Degrowth*, 19.

18   The famed Zapatista slogan.

19   Aubert, Danielle. *The Detroit Printing Co-Op: The Politics of the Joy of Printing* (Los Angeles, CA: Inventory Press, 2019).

20   See: https://techworkerscoalition.org/.

21   Gavin Mueller, *Breaking Things at Work: The Luddites Were Right about Why You Hate Your Job* (Brooklyn: Verso Books, 2021).

22   See: María Villarreal and Enara Echart Muñoz, "Extractivism and Resistance in Latin America and the Caribbean," *OpenDemocracy*, February 6, 2020, https://www.opendemocracy.net/en/democraciaabierta/luchas-resistencias-y-alternativas-al-extractivismo-en-am%C3%A9rica-latina-y-caribe-en/; and, Amazon Watch, "Indigenous Resistance Expels Oil Company GeoPark from Peruvian Amazon | Amazon Watch," July 17, 2020, https://amazonwatch.org/news/2020/0717-indigenous-resistance-expels-oil-company-geopark-from-peruvian-amazon.

23   https://designjustice.org/; see, also: Sasha Costanza-Chock, *Design Justice: Community-Led Practices to Build the Worlds We Need*, Information Policy (Cambridge, MA: The MIT Press, 2020).

24   https://detroitcommunitytech.org/.

25   Richard Stahler-Sholk, "Zapatistas and New Ways of Doing Politics," *Oxford Research Encyclopedia of Politics*, May 23, 2019, doi:10.1093/acrefore/9780190228637.013.1724.

26   See: Arturo Escobar, *Pluriversal Politics: The Real and the Possible*, Latin America in Translation (Durham: Duke University Press, 2020): 17; and, Anya Briy, "Zapatistas: Lessons in Community Self-Organisation in Mexico," *OpenDemocracy*, June 25, 2020, https://www.opendemocracy.net/en/democraciaabierta/zapatistas-lecciones-de-auto-organizaci%C3%B3n-comunitaria-en/.

27   Escobar, *Pluriversal Politics*, 10.

BIBLIOGRAPHY

"360 Smart Bed—Smart & Effortless Comfort—Sleep Number." Accessed October 15, 2017. https://www.sleepnumber.com/pages/360.

Academic Analytics. "Academic Analytics." Accessed December 14, 2018. https://web.archive.org/web/20181214002527/https://academicanalytics.com/.

"Accelerometer API." *FitBit Developer*. Accessed February 8, 2019. https://web.archive.org/web/20190208210247/https://dev.fitbit.com/build/reference/device-api/accelerometer/.

Accenture Research, and Serge Callet. "Channeling Growth: Accenture 2010 Global Survey on Multi-Channel Insurance Distribution," 2010. https://insuranceblog.accenture.com/wp-content/uploads/2013/07/Channeling_Growth-Accenture_2010_Global_Survey_on_Multichannel_Insurance_Distribution.pdf.

Adams, Rachel. "Michel Foucault: Biopolitics and Biopower." *Critical Legal Thinking*. Accessed October 8, 2017. https://criticallegalthinking.com/2017/05/10/michel-foucault-biopolitics-biopower/.

Affectiva. "SDK on the Spot: Emotion-Enabled App Hopes to Make People Happier—One Smile at a Time." Accessed August 3, 2017. https://blog.affectiva.com/sdk-on-the-spot-emotion-enabled-app-promotes-more-smiling.

Alper, Gerald. "The Theory of Games and Psychoanalysis." *Journal of Contemporary Psychotherapy* 23, no. 1 (1993): 47–60. doi:10.1007/BF00945922.

Amadae, S. M. *Prisoners of Reason: Game Theory and Neoliberal Political Economy*. New York, NY: Cambridge University Press, 2016.

Amadae, S. M. *Rationalizing Capitalist Democracy: The Cold War Origins of Rational Choice Liberalism*. Chicago: University of Chicago Press, 2003.

Amazon Developer Team. "Our Vision: Building a World of Ambient Computing Together." *Alexa-Blog*. Accessed July 12, 2021. https://developer.amazon.com/en-US/blogs/alexa/alexa-skills-kit/2021/07/building-a-world-of-ambient-computing-together.html.

"Amazon Halo Now Available for John Hancock Vitality Members." *John Hancock Insurance | News*. Accessed December 14, 2020. https://www.johnhancock.com/about-us/news/john-hancock-insurance/2020/12/amazon-halo-now-available-for-john-hancock-vitality-members.html.

ANS. "Are Chatbots the Future for Higher Education? | ANS." Blog. *ANS Blog*. Accessed April 12, 2021. https://www.ans.co.uk/are-chatbots-the-future-for-higher-education/.

Ansari, Ahmed, and Jabe Bloom. "Time and Transition." In *Proceedings of Relating Systems Thinking and Design (RSD5) 2016 Symposium*. OCAD University, Toronto, Ontario, 2016. https://rsdsymposium.org/time-transition/.

Anwar, Yasmin. "Scientists Use Brain Imaging to Reveal the Movies in Our Mind." *Berkeley News*. Accessed November 7, 2016. https://news.berkeley.edu/2011/09/22/brain-movies/.

Araujo, Saulo de Freitas, and Annette Mülberger. *Wundt and the Philosophical Foundations of Psychology: A Reappraisal*. Cham, Heidelberg, New York, Dordrecht, and London: Springer, 2016.

Aronowitz, Stanley. *Against Orthodoxy: Social Theory and Its Discontents*. 1st ed. Political Philosophy and Public Purpose. New York: Palgrave Macmillan, 2015.

Aronowitz, Stanley. "Henri Lefebvre: The Ignored Philosopher and Social Theorist." In *Against Orthodoxy*, edited by Stanley Aronowitz, 73–91. New York: Palgrave Macmillan US, 2015. doi:10.1057/9781137387189_5.

Aronowitz, Stanley and Robert Ausch. "A Critique of Methodological Reason." *The Sociological Quarterly* 41, no. 4 (2000): 699–719.

Aubert, Danielle. *The Detroit Printing Co-Op: The Politics of the Joy of Printing*. Los Angeles, CA: Inventory Press, 2019.

Banks, David. "Sherry Turkle's Chronic Digital Dualism Problem." *Cyborgology*. Accessed November 29, 2019. https://thesocietypages.org/cyborgology/2012/04/23/sherry-turkles-chronic-digital-dualism-problem/.

Barak, Erez. "How Azure Machine Learning Powers Suggested Replies in Outlook." *Microsoft Azure Blog*. Accessed March 23, 2020. https://azure.microsoft.com/en-us/blog/how-azure-machine-learning-service-powers-suggested-replies-in-outlook/.

Barlow, John Perry. "A Declaration of the Independence of Cyberspace." *Electronic Frontier Foundation*, 1996. Accessed January 20, 2016. https://www.eff.org/cyberspace-independence.

Barth, Brian J. "How a Band of Activists—and One Tech Billionaire—Beat Alphabet's 'Smart City.'" *OneZero*. Accessed August 13, 2020. https://onezero.medium.com/how-a-band-of-activists-and-one-tech-billionaire-beat-alphabets-smart-city-de19afb5d69e.

Barthes, Roland. *Mythologies*. Translated by Richard Howard and Annette Lavers. New York: Hill and Wang, 2013.

Bartlett, Tom. "Dead Man Teaching." *The Chronicle of Higher Education*. Accessed January 26, 2021. https://www-chronicle-com.proxy2.cl.msu.edu/article/dead-man-teaching.

Bauman, Zygmunt. *Modernity and the Holocaust*. Repr. Cambridge: Polity Press, 2008.

Beer, Stafford. *Designing Freedom*. London: Wiley, 1974.

Bennett, Jane. Review of *The Value of Convenience. A Genealogy of Technical Culture*, by Thomas F. Tierney. *Political Theory* 24, no. 2 (1996): 343–46.

Bennett, Jane. *Vibrant Matter: A Political Ecology of Things*. Durham: Duke University Press, 2010.

Bertsimas, Dimitris, Erik Brynjolfsson, Shachar Reichman, and John Silberholz. "OR Forum—Tenure Analytics: Models for Predicting Research Impact." *Operations Research* 63, no. 6 (December 2015): 1246–61. doi:10.1287/opre.2015.1447.

Bishop, Todd. "Microsoft Patents Tech to Score Meetings Using Body Language, Facial Expressions, Other Data." *GeekWire*. Accessed November 28, 2020. https://www.geekwire.com/2020/microsoft-patents-technology-score-meetings-using-body-language-facial-expressions-data/.

Blue Apron TV Commercial, "A Better Way to Cook," 2015. http://www.ispot.tv/ad/7F05/blue-apron-a-better-way-to-cook.

Bohn, Dieter. "Amazon Announces Halo, a Fitness Band and App That Scans Your Body and Voice." *The Verge*. Accessed February 28, 2021. https://www.theverge.com/2020/8/27/21402493/amazon-halo-band-health-fitness-body-scan-tone-emotion-activity-sleep.

Bohn, Dieter. "Amazon's Race to Create the Disappearing Computer." *The Verge*. Accessed September 28, 2021. https://www.theverge.com/22696187/amazon-alexa-ambient-disappearing-computer-limp-interview.

Bone, Daniel Kenneth, Chao Wang, and Viktor Rozgic. United States Patent: 10943604 - Emotion detection using speaker baseline. 10943604, issued March 9, 2021. http://patft.uspto.gov/netacgi/nph-Parser?Sect1=PTO2&Sect2=HITOFF&p=1&u=%2Fnetah tml%2FPTO%2Fsearch-bool.html&r=1&f=G&l=50&co1=AND&d=PTXT&s1=amaz on.ASNM.&s2=alexa&OS=AN/amazon+AND+alexa&RS=AN/amazon+AND+alexa.

Booth, Bruce. "Biotech Scientific Advisory Boards: What Works, What Doesn't." *Forbes*. Accessed October 13, 2021. https://www.forbes.com/sites/brucebooth/2012/09/10/biotech-scientific-advisory-boards-what-works-what-doesnt/.

Borges, Jorge Luis. "On Exactitude in Science." In *Jorge Luis Borges: Collected Fictions*, translated by Andrew Hurley, 325. New York: Penguin Books, 1999.

Bove, Arianna. "Notes on Americanism and Fordism." *Generation Online*. Accessed November 20, 2017. http://www.generation-online.org/p/fpgramsci.htm.

Bratton, Benjamin. "On Speculative Design." *DIS Magazine*, March 2016. https://web.archive.org/web/20170503110731/http://dismagazine.com/discussion/81971/on-speculative-design-benjamin-h-bratton/.

Bridgman, P. W. *The Logic of Modern Physics*. New York: MacMillan, 1927.

Brinton, Maurice. "The Bolsheviks and Workers' Control: The State and Counter-Revolution." *Solidarity*, 1970. https://www.marxists.org/archive/brinton/1970/workers-control/05.htm.

Brooks, Rodney. "An Inconvenient Truth about AI." *IEEE Spectrum*. Accessed September 29, 2021. https://spectrum.ieee.org/rodney-brooks-ai.

Brown, Clarence. "Translator's Introduction." In Yevgeny Zamyatin. *We*, translated by Clarence Brown. Penguin Twentieth-Century Classics. New York, NY: Penguin Books, 1993.

Brynjolfsson, Erik, and John Silberholz. "'Moneyball' for Professors?" *MIT Sloan Management Review*. Accessed January 10, 2018. https://sloanreview.mit.edu/article/moneyball-for-professors/.

Carlisle, Clare. "Creatures of Habit: The Problem and the Practice of Liberation." *Continental Philosophy Review* 38, nos. 1–2 (July 10, 2006): 19–39. doi:10.1007/s11007-005-9005-y.

Carey, Benedict. "California Tests a Digital 'Fire Alarm' for Mental Distress." *The New York Times*. Accessed October 19, 2021, sec. Health. https://www.nytimes.com/2019/06/17/health/mindstrong-mental-health-app.html.

Chang, Hasok. "Operationalism." In *The Stanford Encyclopedia of Philosophy*, edited by Edward N. Zalta, Fall 2021. Metaphysics Research Lab, Stanford University, 2021. https://plato.stanford.edu/archives/fall2021/entries/operationalism/.

Chapman, Adrian. "'Knots': Drawing Out Threads of the Literary Laing." *PsyArt: An Online Journal for the Psychological Study of the Arts*. Accessed November 1, 2021. https://psyartjournal.com/article/show/chapman-knots_drawing_out_threads_of_the_literar.

Chau, Stephen, Andrew Timothy Szybalski, Stephane Lafon, Andrea Lynn Frome, Jerry Howard Morrison, Derek King Prothro, and Huy Tuan Nguyen. Activity assistant. United States US10929486B1, filed October 23, 2017, and issued February 23, 2021. https://patents.google.com/patent/US10929486B1/en?oq=10%2c929%2c486.

Cheney-Lippold, John. "A New Algorithmic Identity: Soft Biopolitics and the Modulation of Control." *Theory, Culture & Society* 28, no. 6 (November 2011): 164–81. doi:10.1177/0263276411424420.

Cheney-Lippold, John. *We Are Data: Algorithms and the Making of Our Digital Selves*. New York: New York University Press, 2017.

Cronin, Blaise, and Cassidy R. Sugimoto, eds. *Scholarly Metrics under the Microscope: From Citation Analysis to Academic Auditing*. ASIST Monograph Series. Medford, NJ: Published on behalf of the Association for Information Science and Technology by Information Today, Inc, 2015.

Curry, Neil. "Review: Critique of Everyday Life, Volume 3: From Modernity to Modernism." *Capital & Class* 33, no. 98 (2009): 170–1.

Cuong, Dinh V., Dac H. Nguyen, Son Huynh, Phong Huynh, Cathal Gurrin, Minh-Son Dao, Duc-Tien Dang-Nguyen, and Binh T. Nguyen. "A Framework for Paper Submission Recommendation System." In *Proceedings of the 2020 International Conference on Multimedia Retrieval*, edited by Cathal Gurrin, Björn Þór Jónsson, and Noriko Kando, 393–96. ICMR '20. New York, NY: Association for Computing Machinery, 2020. doi:10.1145/3372278.3391929.

Davies, William. "Elite Power under Advanced Neoliberalism." *Theory, Culture & Society* 34, nos. 5–6 (September 2017): 227–50. doi:10.1177/0263276417715072.

Davis, Lennard J. "Introduction: Normality, Power, and Culture." In *The Disability Studies Reader*, edited by Lennard J. Davis. 4th ed., 1–14. New York: Routledge, 2013.

Davis, Martin. *Engines of Logic: Mathematicians and the Origin of the Computer*. New York, NY; London: Norton, 2001.

de Vries, Katja. "Identity, Profiling Algorithms and a World of Ambient Intelligence." *Ethics and Information Technology* 12, no. 1 (March 2010): 71–85. doi:10.1007/s10676-009-9215-9.

DeCook, Julia R. "A [White] Cyborg's Manifesto: The Overwhelmingly Western Ideology Driving Technofeminist Theory." *Media, Culture & Society* 43, no. 6 (September 2021): 1158–67. doi:10.1177/0163443720957891.

Deleuze, Gilles. "Postscript on the Societies of Control." *October* 59 (1992): 3–7.

Dilawar, Arvind. "The Very Human Labor That Powers Artificial Intelligence." Accessed October 27, 2020. https://www.thenation.com/article/society/amazon-mturk-artificial-intelligence/.

Dixon-Román, Ezekiel, T. Philip Nichols, and Ama Nyame-Mensah. "The Racializing Forces of/in AI Educational Technologies." *Learning, Media and Technology* 45, no. 3 (July 2, 2020): 236–50. doi:10.1080/17439884.2020.1667825.

Doody, Sarah. "Productized 19 Notes: Anticipatory Design & the Future of Experience." *Medium*. Accessed March 30, 2021. https://productized.medium.com/productized-19-notes-anticipatory-design-the-future-of-experience-sarah-doody-e239eb7e149f.

Dourish, Paul. "User Experience as Legitimacy Trap." *Interactions* 26, no. 6 (October 30, 2019): 46–49. https://doi.org/10.1145/3358908.

Drucker, Johanna. *Graphesis: Visual Forms of Knowledge Production*. MetaLABprojects. Cambridge, MA: Harvard University Press, 2014.

Dunne, Anthony, and Fiona Raby. *Speculative Everything: Design, Fiction, and Social Dreaming*. Cambridge, MA; London: The MIT Press, 2013.

Dyal-Chand, Rashmi. "Autocorrecting for Whiteness." In SSRN Scholarly Paper. Rochester, NY: Social Science Research Network. Accessed March 8, 2021. https://papers.ssrn.com/abstract=3800463.

Eastwood, Gary. "One Day Wearables Will Save Your Marriage | CIO." *CIO*. Accessed October 11, 2021. https://web.archive.org/web/20170802022444/http://www.cio.com/article/3195086/artificial-intelligence/one-day-wearables-will-save-your-marraige.html.

Edwards, Paul N. *The Closed World: Computers and the Politics of Discourse in Cold War America*. First MIT Pr. Paperb. ed. Inside Technology. London: MIT, 1997.

Escobar, Arturo. *Designs for the Pluriverse: Radical Interdependence, Autonomy, and the Making of Worlds*. New Ecologies for the Twenty-First Century. Durham: Duke University Press, 2018.

Escobar, Arturo. *Pluriversal Politics: The Real and the Possible*. Latin America in Translation. Durham: Duke University Press, 2020.

Etherington, Darrell. "Oura Ring Health and Sleep Tracker Review." *TechCrunch*. Accessed November 2, 2021. https://social.techcrunch.com/2020/08/12/the-oura-ring-is-the-personal-health-tracking-device-to-beat-in-2020/.

Finlayson, Alan. "E-Introduction & the Neoliberal University." Personal email communication.

Fisher, Mark. *Capitalist Realism: Is There No Alternative?* Winchester, UK: Zero Books, 2009.

Fisher, Mark. "Foreword." In *Economic Science Fictions*, edited by William Davies, xi–xv. London: Goldsmiths Press, 2018.

"FitBit Alta HR User Manual Version 1.4," 2017. https://staticcs.fitbit.com/content/assets/help/manuals/manual_alta_hr_en_US.pdf.

Flusser, Vilém. *Post-History*. Flusser Archive Collection. Minneapolis, MN: Univocal, 2013.

Flusser, Vilém. *Towards a Philosophy of Photography*. London: Reaktion, 2000.

Foucault, Michel. *The Birth of Biopolitics: Lectures at the Collège de France, 1978–79*. 1st pbk ed., [Repr.]. Lectures at the Collège de France. New York: Picador, 2010.

Foucault, Michel. *The History of Sexuality*. Vintage Books ed. New York: Vintage Books, 1990.

Friesen, Norm. "Doing with Icons Makes Symbols; or, Jailbreaking the Perfect User Interface." *CTheory*, April 17, 2012.

Fuller, Mark. "Review of Martin Davis, Engines of Logic." *The Review of Modern Logic* 9, nos. 3–4 (December 2003): 123–24.

Fuller, Matthew, and Andrew Goffey. *Evil Media*. Cambridge, MA: MIT Press, 2012.

Galison, Peter. "The Ontology of the Enemy: Norbert Wiener and the Cybernetic Vision." *Critical Inquiry* 21, no. 1 (1994): 228–66.

Galtung, Johan. "'The Limits to Growth' and Class Politics." *Journal of Peace Research* 10, nos. 1–2 (1973): 101–14.

Gervais, Estelle. "Emily Segal: How to Predict Hype." *PHI Antenna*. Accessed November 1, 2021. https://phi.ca/en/antenna/hyperstition-or-how-to-predict-hype/.

Gilliard, Chris. "Luxury Surveillance." *Real Life*. Accessed November 24, 2021. https://reallifemag.com/luxury-surveillance/.

Golumbia, David. *The Cultural Logic of Computation*. Cambridge, MA: Harvard University Press, 2009.

Golumbia, David. "Cyberlibertarianism: The Extremist Foundations of 'Digital Freedom.'" Clemson University. Accessed June 19, 2018. http://www.uncomputing.org/wp-content/uploads/2014/02/cyberlibertarianism-extremist-foundations-sep2013.pdf.

Graeber, David. *Bullshit Jobs*. New York: Simon & Schuster Paperbacks, 2019.

Gross, Jeremy. "Stafford Beer: Eudemony, Viability and Autonomy." *Red Wedge*. Accessed August 17, 2021. http://www.redwedgemagazine.com/online-issue/stafford-beer-eudemony.

Grosz, Elizabeth. "Habit Today: Ravaisson, Bergson, Deleuze and Us." Edited by Tony Bennett, Francis Dodsworth, Greg Noble, Mary Poovey, and Megan Watkins. *Body & Society* 19, nos. 2–3 (June 2013): 217–39. doi:10.1177/1357034X12472544.

Hacking, Ian. "How Should We Do the History of Statistics?" In *The Foucault Effect: Studies in Governmentality*, edited by Graham Burchell, Colin Gordon, and Peter Miller, 181–96. Chicago: University of Chicago Press, 1991.

Hacking, Ian. "Making Up People." *London Review of Books*, August 17, 2006.

Hacking, Ian. *The Taming of Chance*. Ideas in Context. Cambridge [England]; New York: Cambridge University Press, 1990.

Hall, Gary. *The Uberfication of the University*. Minneapolis: University of Minnesota Press, 2016.

Halpern, Orit. *Beautiful Data: A History of Vision and Reason since 1945*. Experimental Futures. Durham: Duke University Press, 2014.

Haraway, Donna Jeanne. *Simians, Cyborgs, and Women: The Reinvention of Nature*. New York: Routledge, 1991.

Hartnett, J. P. "Ontological Design Has Become Influential in Design Academia—But What Is It?" *Eye on Design*. Accessed October 11, 2021. https://eyeondesign.aiga.org/ontological-design-is-popular-in-design-academia-but-what-is-it/.

Hayek, Friedrich August. "The Use of Knowledge in Society." *The American Economic Review* 35, no. 4 (1945): 519–30.

Hayles, Katherine. *How We Became Posthuman: Virtual Bodies in Cybernetics, Literature, and Informatics*. Chicago, IL: University of Chicago Press, 1999.

Heater, Brian. "Wearable Growth Slowed—but Not Stopped—by Pandemic." *TechCrunch*. Accessed November 20, 2021. https://social.techcrunch.com/2020/06/03/wearable-growth-slowed-but-not-stopped-by-pandemic/.

Heaven, Will Douglas. "Gpt-3." In *MIT Technology Review*. Cambridge, United States: Technology Review, Inc., April 2021. Vol. 124, Issue 2, 34–35.

Helfand, Jessica, and William Drenttel. "Wonders Revealed: Design and Faux Science." *Émigré*, no. 64 (2003): 73–85.

"Help Article: How Does My Fitbit Device Calculate My Daily Activity?" Accessed February 1, 2018. https://web.archive.org/web/20180127030643/https://help.fitbit.com/articles/en_US/Help_article/1141.

Hern, Alex. "Microsoft Apologises for Feature Criticised as Workplace Surveillance." Magazine. *The Guardian*. Accessed November 4, 2021. https://www.theguardian.com/technology/2020/dec/02/microsoft-apologises-productivity-score-critics-derided-workplace-surveillance.

Hofweber, Thomas. "Logic and Ontology." In *The Stanford Encyclopedia of Philosophy*, edited by Edward N. Zalta, Spring 2021. Metaphysics Research Lab, Stanford University, 2021. https://plato.stanford.edu/archives/spr2021/entries/logic-ontology/.

Holton, Gerald. "Candor and Integrity in Science." *Synthese* 145, no. 2 (2005): 277–94.

Horning, Rob. "Sick of Myself." *Real Life*. Accessed November 9, 2018. https://reallifemag.com/sick-of-myself/.

"How Natural Language Processing Impacts Professions." *Wolters Kluwer | Expert Insights*. Accessed November 16, 2021. https://www.wolterskluwer.com/en/expert-insights/how-natural-language-processing-impacts-professions.

Humphreys, Paul. *Extending Ourselves: Computational Science, Empiricism, and Scientific Method*. New York: Oxford University Press, 2004.

IBM. *IBM TV Commercial, "Making the World Smarter Every Day,"* 2015. https://www.ispot.tv/ad/7mGT/ibm-making-the-world-smarter-every-day.

Illich, Ivan. *Tools for Conviviality*. Open Forum. London: Calder and Boyars, 1973.

"Introducing Amazon Halo and Amazon Halo Band—A New Service That Helps Customers Improve Their Health and Wellness." *Amazon.Com Press Center*. Accessed February 28, 2021. https://press.aboutamazon.com/news-releases/news-release-details/introducing-amazon-halo-and-amazon-halo-band-new-service-helps/.

Jakubowicz, Peter. "I'm a Lyft Driver. My Passengers Act Like I'm Part of the App." *Wired*. Accessed October 11, 2021. https://www.wired.com/story/im-a-lyft-driver-my-passengers-act-like-im-part-of-the-app/.

Kaiser, Zachary. "Creativity as Computation: Teaching Design in the Age of Automation." *Design and Culture* 11, no. 2 (May 4, 2019): 173–92. doi:10.1080/17547075.2019.1609279.

Kalman, Tibor, Abbot Miller, and Karrie Jacobs. "Retro-Spectives: Two Views of Deisgn-Er-Appropriation: Good History Bad History." *Print* 45, no. 2 (1991): 114–23.

Kamdar, Adi. "The Creepy Details of Facebook's New Graph Search." *Electronic Frontier Foundation.* Accessed November 2, 2021. https://www.eff.org/deeplinks/2013/01/facebooks-graph-search.

Kamola, Isaac. "Guest Blog: Where Does the Bizarre Hysteria about 'Critical Race Theory' Come From? Follow the Money!" *Inside Higher Ed.* Accessed November 21, 2021. https://www.insidehighered.com/blogs/just-visiting/guest-blog-where-does-bizarre-hysteria-about-%E2%80%98critical-race-theory%E2%80%99-come-follow.

Kim, Alan. "Wilhelm Maximilian Wundt." In *The Stanford Encyclopedia of Philosophy*, edited by Edward N. Zalta, Fall 2016. Metaphysics Research Lab. Stanford University, 2016. https://plato.stanford.edu/archives/fall2016/entries/wilhelm-wundt/.

Krause, Alexander G., Martin Winger, Tim D. Blasius, Qiang Lin, and Oskar Painter. "A High-Resolution Microchip Optomechanical Accelerometer." *Nature Photonics* 6 (October 14, 2012): 768.

Lahoud, Adrian. "Error Correction: Chilean Cybernetics and Chicago's Economists." In *Alleys of Your Mind: Augmented Intelligence and Its Traumas*, edited by Matteo Pasquinelli, 37–51. Lüneburg: meson press, 2015.

Lambert-Beatty, Carrie. "Make-Believe: Parafiction and Plausibility." *October* 129 (August 2009): 51–84. doi:10.1162/octo.2009.129.1.51.

LaPlante, Alex. "How Natural Language Processing Is Reshaping the World of Finance." *Global Risk Institute.* Accessed February 24, 2021. https://globalriskinstitute.org/publications/natural-language-processing-reshaping-world-finance/.

Lefebvre, Henri. *Critique of Everyday Life: The One-Volume Edition.* One-vol ed. London: Verso, 2014.

Leibniz, Gottfried Wilhelm, and George Henry Radcliffe Parkinson. *Philosophical Writings.* New rev. ed. Everyman's University Library. London: Dent, 1973.

Leonard, Allenna. "Stafford Beer and the Legacy of Cybersyn: Seeing around Corners." Edited by Dr Raul Espejo. *Kybernetes* 44, nos. 6–7 (June 1, 2015): 926–34. doi:10.1108/K-02-2015-0045.

"LIS2DH - 3-Axis MEMS Accelerometer, Ultra-Low-Power, ±2g/±4g/±8g/±16g Full Scale, High-Speed I2C/SPI Digital Output, Embedded FIFO, High-Performance Acceleration Sensor - STMicroelectronics." *ST Microelectronics.* Accessed October 3, 2018. https://web.archive.org/web/20180609091902/https://www.st.com/en/mems-and-sensors/lis2dh.html.

"Listen to Solar Storm Activity in New Sonification Video." *University of Michigan News.* Accessed March 23, 2017. https://news.umich.edu/listen-to-solar-storm-activity-in-new-sonification-video/.

Loveday, Vik. "The Neurotic Academic: How Anxiety Fuels Casualised Academic Work." *LSE Impact of Social Sciences.* Accessed December 3, 2021. https://blogs.lse.ac.uk/impactofsocialsciences/2018/04/17/the-neurotic-academic-how-anxiety-fuels-casualised-academic-work/.

Lunden, Ingrid. "Humane, a Stealthy Hardware and Software Startup Co-Founded by an Ex-Apple Designer and Engineer, Raises $100M." *TechCrunch.* Accessed October 12, 2021. https://social.techcrunch.com/2021/09/01/humane-a-stealthy-hardware-and-software-startup-co-founded-by-an-ex-apple-designer-and-engineer-raises-100m/.

Lupton, Deborah. *The Quantified Self: A Sociology of Self-Tracking.* Cambridge, UK: Polity, 2016.

Made by Google. *How Sleep Sensing Works on the Second-Gen Nest Hub from Google*, 2021. https://www.youtube.com/watch?v=oKRA6GhlthM.

Markie, Peter, and M. Folescu. "Rationalism vs. Empiricism." In *The Stanford Encyclopedia of Philosophy*, edited by Edward N. Zalta, Fall 2021. Metaphysics Research Lab. Stanford University, 2021. https://plato.stanford.edu/archives/fall2021/entries/rationalism-empiricism/.

Marcel, Gabriel. *The Philosophy of Existentialism*. New York: Citadel Press, 1995.

Martin, Dick, and Jonathan Rosenhead. "Stafford Beer." *The Guardian*. Accessed November 29, 2021, sec. Education. https://www.theguardian.com/news/2002/sep/04/guardianobituaries.obituaries.

Marx, Karl. *Grundrisse: Foundations of the Critique of Political Economy*. Translated by Martin Nicolaus. Penguin Classics. London: Penguin books, 1993.

Maurer, K., H. Biehl, C. Kühner, and W. Löffler. "On the Way to Expert Systems: Comparing DSM-III Computer Diagnoses with CATEGO (ICD) Diagnoses in Depressive and Schizophrenic Patients." *European Archives of Psychiatry and Neurological Sciences* 239, no. 2 (March 1989): 127–32. doi:10.1007/BF01759586.

Mayes, Rick, and Allan V. Horwitz. "DSM-III and the Revolution in the Classification of Mental Illness." *Journal of the History of the Behavioral Sciences* 41, no. 3 (2005): 249–67. doi:10.1002/jhbs.20103.

McCulloch, Sharon. "The Importance of Being REF-Able: Academic Writing under Pressure from a Culture of Counting." *Impact of Social Sciences*. Accessed December 4, 2021. https://blogs.lse.ac.uk/impactofsocialsciences/2017/02/09/the-importance-of-being-ref-able-academic-writing-under-pressure-from-a-culture-of-counting/.

Meadows, Donella H., and Club of Rome, eds. *The Limits to Growth: A Report for the Club of Rome's Project on the Predicament of Mankind*. New York: Universe Books, 1972.

Medina, Eden. *Cybernetic Revolutionaries: Technology and Politics in Allende's Chile*. Cambridge, MA: MIT Press, 2011.

Meggs, Philip B., and Alston W. Purvis. *Meggs' History of Graphic Design*. 6th ed. Hoboken, NJ: Wiley, 2016.

Mendel, Jake. "Building Your Startup Advisory Board | Silicon Valley Bank." Accessed November 24, 2021. https://www.svb.com/startup-insights/startup-strategy/building-startup-advisory-board.

Metz, Rachel. "The Smartphone App That Can Tell You're Depressed before You Know It Yourself." *MIT Technology Review*. Accessed December 1, 2019. https://www.technologyreview.com/2018/10/15/66443/the-smartphone-app-that-can-tell-youre-depressed-before-you-know-it-yourself/.

"Microsoft Productivity Score." *Microsoft Adoption*. Accessed November 28, 2021. https://adoption.microsoft.com/productivity-score/.

Mindstrong. "Science." *Mindstrong Health*. Accessed November 24, 2021. https://mindstrong.com/science/.

Mirowski, Philip. *Machine Dreams: Economics Becomes a Cyborg Science*. Cambridge and New York: Cambridge University Press, 2002.

Moore, George, Leo Galway, and Mark Donnelly. "Remember to Smile: Design of a Mobile Affective Technology to Help Promote Individual Happiness through Smiling." In *Proceedings of the 11th EAI International Conference on Pervasive Computing Technologies for Healthcare*, edited by Nuria Oliver and Mary Czerwinski. 348–54. Barcelona Spain: ACM, 2017. doi:10.1145/3154862.3154936.

Mor-Hagani, Shiri, and Dani Ben-Zvi. "Computer-Enhanced Dialogic Reflective Discourse." In *Learning and Becoming in Practice: The International Conference of the Learning Sciences (ICLS) 2014*, edited by Joseph Polman, Eleni Kyza, D. Kevin O'Neill, Iris Tabak, William Penuel, A. Susan Jurow, Kevin O'Connor, Tiffany Lee, and Laura D'Amico, 394–401. Colorado, CO: International Society of the Learning Sciences, 2014.

Morozov, Evgeny. "Google's Plan to Revolutionise Cities Is a Takeover in All but Name." *The Observer*. Accessed October 20, 2017, sec. Technology. http://www.theguardian.com/technology/2017/oct/21/google-urban-cities-planning-data.

Murphy, John W., and John T. Pardeck. "Technology and Language Use: Implications for Computer Mediated Therapy." *Journal of Humanistic Psychology* 28, no. 1 (January 1988): 120–34. doi:10.1177/0022167888281007.

Murphy, Mike. "Alphabet Wants to Build a Wearable Full of Needles." *Protocol—The People, Power and Politics of Tech*. Accessed March 14, 2021. https://www.protocol.com/alphabet-wearable-needles-injections.

Murphy, Mike. "Google Wants to Connect Everything You Own to the Internet." *Protocol — The People, Power and Politics of Tech*, February 7, 2021. https://www.protocol.com/google-patents-internet-everything.

Murphy, Mike. "Google Wants to Help You Get a Life." *Protocol—The People, Power and Politics of Tech*. Accessed February 28, 2021. https://www.protocol.com/google-personal-asistant-patents.

Nadesan, Majia Holmer. *Governmentality, Biopower, and Everyday Life*. Routledge Studies in Social and Political Thought 57. New York: Routledge, 2008.

O'Hagan, Sean. "Kingsley Hall: RD Laing's Experiment in Anti-Psychiatry." *The Observer*. Accessed November 24, 2021, sec. Books. https://www.theguardian.com/books/2012/sep/02/rd-laing-mental-health-sanity.

Osterloh, Rick. "Google Completes Fitbit Acquisition." *Google: The Keyword*. Accessed January 23, 2021. https://blog.google/products/devices-services/fitbit-acquisition/.

Pasquale, Frank. *The Black Box Society: The Secret Algorithms That Control Money and Information*. Cambridge: Harvard University Press, 2015.

Pasquinelli, Matteo. "Abnormal Encephalization in the Age of Machine Learning." *E-Flux Journal 75*, September 2016. https://www.e-flux.com/journal/75/67133/abnormal-encephalization-in-the-age-of-machine-learning/.

Perony, Nicolas. "How Amazon Could Improve Halo | OTO Systems." *OTO Blog*. Accessed November 28, 2021. https://www.oto.ai/blog/how-amazon-could-improve-halo.

Peters, Adele. "This Algorithm Can Tell if You're Depressed Just from Your Instagram Posts." *Fast Company*. Accessed December 1, 2019. https://www.fastcompany.com/40449192/this-algorithm-can-tell-if-youre-depressed-just-from-your-instagram-posts.

Plan, C. "We Are All Very Anxious." *We Are Plan C*. Accessed January 11, 2015. https://www.weareplanc.org/blog/we-are-all-very-anxious/.

Posner, Miriam. "The Software That Shapes Workers' Lives." *The New Yorker*. Accessed November 24, 2021. https://www.newyorker.com/science/elements/the-software-that-shapes-workers-lives.

Quart, Alissa. "Teachers Are Working for Uber Just to Keep a Foothold in the Middle Class." Accessed October 29, 2021. https://www.thenation.com/article/archive/teachers-are-working-for-uber-just-to-keep-a-foothold-in-the-middle-class/.

Randall, Natasha. "Translator's Introduction." In Yevgeny Zamyatin. *We*, translated by Natasha Randall. Modern Library paperback ed. New York: Modern Library, 2006.

Read, Jason. *The Politics of Transindividuality*. Historical Materialism Book Series 106. Leiden; Boston: Brill, 2016.

Reece, Andrew G., and Christopher M. Danforth. "Instagram Photos Reveal Predictive Markers of Depression." *ArXiv:1608.03282 [Physics]*. Accessed December 9, 2019. http://arxiv.org/abs/1608.03282.

Rey, P. J. "Social Media: You Can Log Off but You Can't Opt Out—Cyborgology." *Cyborgology*. Accessed June 10, 2015. https://thesocietypages.org/cyborgology/2012/05/10/social-media-you-can-log-off-but-you-cant-opt-out/.

Rochman, Davida. "Mic Basics: What Is Frequency Response?" *Shure: Louder*. Accessed November 28, 2021. https://web.archive.org/web/20210116003833/https://www.shure. com/en-US/performance-production/louder/mic-basics-frequency-response.

Roettgers, Janko. "Amazon Lights up Sidewalk, Its Wireless IoT Network." *Protocol—The People, Power and Politics of Tech*. Accessed July 28, 2021. https://www.protocol.com/ amazon-sidewalk-additions.

Roettgers, Janko. "The Big Story." *Protocol—The People, Power and Politics of Tech*. Accessed September 29, 2021. https://www.protocol.com/newsletters/sourcecode/ amazon-smart-home-ambitions?rebelltitem=1#rebelltitem1?rebelltitem=1.

Roettgers, Janko. "Google Built a Radar for Your Bedroom. It May Just Be the Company's First Step to Monetize Wellness." *Protocol—The People, Power and Politics of Tech*. Accessed March 16, 2021. https://www.protocol.com/nest-hub-sleep-tracking-radar.

Roettgers, Janko. "Plume Is Turning Wi-Fi into a Smart Home Intelligence Platform." *Protocol—The People, Power and Politics of Tech*. Accessed August 6, 2021. https://www. protocol.com/plume-wifi-data-intelligence.

Rosenwald, George C. "Why Operationism Doesn't Go away: Extrascientific Incentives of Social-Psychological Research." *Philosophy of the Social Sciences* 16, no. 3 (September 1986): 303–30. doi:10.1177/004839318601600302.

Rybak, Chuck. *UW Struggle When a State Attacks Its University*, 2017. https://search. ebscohost.com/login.aspx?direct=true&scope=site&db=nlebk&db=nlabk& AN=2458649.

Sacasas, L. M. "Superfluous People, the Ideology of Silicon Valley, and the Origins of Totalitarianism." *L.M. Sacasas*. Accessed January 3, 2018. https://thefrailestthing. com/2018/01/03/superfluous-people-the-ideology-of-silicon-valley-and-the-origins-of-totalitarianism/.

Salerno, Roger A. *Landscapes of Abandonment: Capitalism, Modernity, and Estrangement*. SUNY Series in the Sociology of Culture. Albany: State University of New York Press, 2003.

SAP. "Supply Chain Planning Software Systems." *SAP*. Accessed November 14, 2021. https://www.sap.com/products/supply-chain-management/supply-chain-planning. html.

SAP Ariba. *SAP Ariba Supply Chain Collaboration Demo NAMER/LATAM Session*, 2019. https://www.youtube.com/watch?v=Ad1iqMR5wHg.

SAP Ariba. "Supply Chain Collaboration." *SAP Ariba*. Accessed November 14, 2021. https://www.ariba.com/solutions/solutions-overview/supply-chain/supply-chain-collaboration.

Schaffzin, Gabriel. "Graphic Pain: A History of the Tools Mediating Pain Quantification." Doctoral Dissertation, University of California San Diego, 2020. https://escholarship. org/uc/item/4hj021v8.

Seven Dreamers. "Laundroid the World's 1st Laundry Folding Bot." Accessed April 5, 2017. https://web.archive.org/web/20170302174929/https://laundroid.sevendreamers. com/en/.

Shapiro, Aaron. "The Next Big Thing in Design? Less Choice." *Fast Company*. Accessed October 14, 2019. https://www.fastcompany.com/3045039/the-next-big-thing-in-design-fewer-choices.

Sidewalk Labs. "Sidewalk Labs Vision Section of RFP Submission," 2017. https:// storage.googleapis.com/sidewalk-labs-com-assets/Sidewalk_Labs_Vision_Sections_ of_RFP_Submission_7ad06759b5/Sidewalk_Labs_Vision_Sections_of_RFP_ Submission_7ad06759b5.pdf.

Silverman, Kaja. *The Subject of Semiotics*. 16. print. New York: Oxford University Press, 1984.

Simitive. "University Staff and Students." *Simitive*. Accessed November 10, 2021. https://www.simitive.com/university-staff-and-students.html.

Simonton, Dean Keith. "Creative Productivity: A Predictive and Explanatory Model of Career Trajectories and Landmarks." *Psychological Review* 104, no. 1 (January 1997): 66–89. doi:10.1037/0033-295X.104.1.66.

"SleepIQ Sleep Tracker—Sleep Number." Accessed November 24, 2021. https://www.sleepnumber.com/pages/sleepiq-sleep-tracker.

"SleepIQ® Technology in the Sleep Number 360™ Smart Bed." *Sleep Number Newsroom*. Accessed December 3, 2018. https://web.archive.org/web/20181203133247/http://newsroom.sleepnumber.com/phoenix.zhtml?c=254487&p=irol-product_siq.

Spataro, Jared, and Corporate Vice President for Microsoft 365. "Our Commitment to Privacy in Microsoft Productivity Score." *Microsoft 365 Blog*. Accessed February 20, 2021. https://www.microsoft.com/en-us/microsoft-365/blog/2020/12/01/our-commitment-to-privacy-in-microsoft-productivity-score/.

Spitzer, Robert. "Foreword." In *The Loss of Sadness: How Psychiatry Transformed Normal Sorrow into Depressive Disorder*, edited by Allan V. Horwitz, and Jerome C. Wakefield, vii–x. Oxford; New York: Oxford University Press, 2007.

Srnicek, Nick, and Laurent De Sutter. *Platform Capitalism*. Theory Redux. Cambridge, UK; Malden, MA: Polity, 2017.

Srnicek, Nick, and Alex Williams. *Inventing the Future: Postcapitalism and a World without Work*. London; New York: Verso, 2016.

SRT. "Blue Apron: Fixing the Food Delivery Supply Chain." *Harvard MBA Student Perspectives, Technology and Operations Management*. Accessed December 5, 2017. https://digital.hbs.edu/platform-rctom/submission/blue-apron-fixing-the-food-delivery-supply-chain/.

Strether, Lambert. "Neo-Liberalism Expressed as Simple Rules." *Naked Capitalism*. Accessed December 6, 2017. https://www.nakedcapitalism.com/2014/03/neo-liberalism-expressed-simple-rules.html.

Taulbee, Brenda. "Is the Future of UX Screenless? Savy Weighs in on UX Trends of 2021 and Beyond." *Branding, Web Design and Digital Marketing Agency*. Accessed November 20, 2021. https://savyagency.com/ux-trends-of-2021/.

Teschler, Leland. "Teardown: Inside the Fitbit Charge." *Microcontroller Tips*. Accessed November 11, 2018. https://www.microcontrollertips.com/inside-fitbit-charge/.

Tierney, Thomas F. *The Value of Convenience: A Genealogy of Technical Culture*. SUNY Series in Science, Technology, and Society. Albany: State University of New York Press, 1993.

Tiqqun. *The Cybernetic Hypothesis*, 2001. https://theanarchistlibrary.org/library/tiqqun-the-cybernetic-hypothesis.

Tonkinwise, Cameron. "What Things to Teach Designers in Post-Industrial Times?" *EPIC*. Accessed January 4, 2016. https://www.epicpeople.org/what-things-to-teach-designers-in-post-industrial-times/.

Treanor, Brian, and Brendan Sweetman. "Gabriel (-Honoré) Marcel." In *The Stanford Encyclopedia of Philosophy*, edited by Edward N. Zalta, Winter 2016. Metaphysics Research Lab. Stanford University, 2016. https://plato.stanford.edu/archives/win2016/entries/marcel/.

Tufte, Edward R. *Envisioning Information*. Fourteenth printing. Cheshire, CT: Graphics Press, 2013.

Tufte, Edward R. *The Visual Display of Quantitative Information*. 2nd ed. Cheshire, CT: Graphics Press, 2001.

Turner, Fred. *From Counterculture to Cyberculture: Stewart Brand, the Whole Earth Network, and the Rise of Digital Utopianism*. 1. paperback ed. Chicago, IL: University of Chicago Press, 2008.

Uber. *Meet Victor—Primary Teacher and Driver Partner*, 2016. https://www.youtube.com/watch?v=6WhC_w6uJRQ.

Uber. *Uber - Jenny Is a Full Time Math Teacher Who Drives with … | Facebook*, 2015. https://www.facebook.com/uber/videos/1018996768140608/.

"Upmood." *Upmood*. Accessed October 13, 2018. https://web.archive.org/web/20181013023538/http://www.upmood.com/.

van Bodegraven, Joël. "How Anticipatory Design Will Challenge Our Relationship with Technology." Technical Report. Association for the Advancement of Artificial Intelligence, April 2017. https://www.aaai.org/ocs/index.php/SSS/SSS17/paper/viewFile/15352/14582.

Vaughn, Liam. "'Most Americans Today Believe the Stock Market Is Rigged, and They're Right'." *Bloomberg.com*. Accessed September 29, 2021. https://www.bloomberg.com/news/features/2021-09-29/is-stock-market-rigged-insider-trading-by-executives-is-pervasive-critics-say.

Vogel, Matthew. United States Patent Application: 0200358627. US Patent & Trademark Office. Accessed November 28, 2021. https://appft.uspto.gov/netacgi/nph-Parser?Sect 1=PTO1&Sect2=HITOFF&d=PG01&p=1&u=%2Fnetahtml%2FPTO%2Fsrchnum.ht ml&r=1&f=G&l=50&s1=%2220200358627%22.PGNR.&OS=DN/20200358627&RS= DN/20200358627.

Von Neumann, John, and Oskar Morgenstern. *Theory of Games and Economic Behavior*. 60th anniversary ed. Princeton Classic Editions. Princeton, NJ; Woodstock: Princeton University Press, 2007.

Walsh, Amber. "Inquiries at the Intersection of Design and New Materialism." Conference Presentation presented at the Frontier: the AIGA Design Educators Conference, Montana State University, Bozeman, MT, October 9, 2016.

Wark, McKenzie. "The Sublime Language of My Century." *Public Seminar*. Accessed May 14, 2016. http://publicseminar.org.dream.website/2016/05/the-sublime-language-of-my-century/.

Wegerif, Rupert, and Louis Major. "Buber, Educational Technology, and the Expansion of Dialogic Space." *AI & SOCIETY* 34, no. 1 (March 2019): 109–19. doi:10.1007/s00146-018-0828-6.

Wiener, Norbert. *Cybernetics or Control and Communication in the Animal and the Machine*. 2nd ed., 14. print. Cambridge, MA: MIT Press, 2007.

Wiener, Norbert. *The Human Use of Human Beings: Cybernetics and Society*. The Da Capo Series in Science. New York, NY: Da Capo Press, 1988.

Wittes, Benjamin, and Jane Chong. "Our Cyborg Future: Law and Policy Implications." *Brookings*. Accessed November 24, 2021. https://www.brookings.edu/research/our-cyborg-future-law-and-policy-implications/.

Wojnowski, Konrad. "Telematic Freedom and Information Paradox." *Flusser Studies* 23 (June 2017). http://www.flusserstudies.net/sites/www.flusserstudies.net/files/media/attachments/wojnowski-konrad-telematic-freedom-and-information-paradox.pdf.

"World's First Emotion Sensor & Mental Health Advisor." *Myfeel.Co*. Accessed October 20, 2018. https://web.archive.org/web/20181020144036/https://www.myfeel.co/.

Wozniak, Robert H. *Classics in Psychology, 1855–1914: Historical Essays*. Bristol, UK; Tokyo: Thoemmes Press; Maruzen, 1999.

Wundt, Wilhelm. *Outlines of Psychology*. Translated by Charles Hubbard Judd. New York: Wilhelm Engleman, 1897. https://ia800207.us.archive.org/1/items/cu31924014474534/cu31924014474534.pdf.

Young, Virginia Alvino. "EduSense: Like a Fitbit for Your Teaching Skills—News—Carnegie Mellon University." Accessed November 14, 2019. http://www.cmu.edu/news/stories/archives/2019/november/edusense-fitbit-your-teaching-skills.html.

Zamyatin, Yevgeny. *We*. Translated by Clarence Brown. Penguin Twentieth-Century Classics. New York, NY: Penguin Books, 1993.

"The Zero Moment of Truth for Insurance Study." *Think with Google*, April 2011. https://www.thinkwithgoogle.com/consumer-insights/consumer-trends/zmot-insurance-study/.

INDEX

Facebook 4, 16–18, 31, 87, 127, 136
FastCompany 88
Feel® app 55–7
Fisher, Mark 135
Fit app (Google) 79–80
FitBits 8, 21, 41, 48–54, 60, 71, 73, 76, 78, 80, 83, 87, 100, 103, 111, 154
    3-axis implementation 49–50
    femtometer 50
Flusser, V. 88, 111
Foucault, M. 33
free-market capitalism 31–2

Gallant Lab 59
Game Theory 29, 38, 74, 88
Google 4, 16, 22, 27, 54. *See also specific apps*
Google Home 65
Google Maps 22, 70
Google's Nest Hub 78–81, 83, 85
governmentality 31–4, 44, 58, 69–70, 109, 128, 131, 145. *See also* neoliberalism
GPT-3 119
graphic design 6, 10–11, 43, 55
Graphic Design 1 (GD1) 138–9
grey media 52–3

habits 18, 20, 58–9, 77
Hacking, I. 100, 107
Halo app (Amazon) 121, 136
    body feature 103–4
    emotion-recognition system 105
    health and wellbeing 109
    promotional discourse 110
    superfluity 111, 113
    tone feature 104–5, 108
Hayek, F., market ideal 31
Helfand, J. 55
higher education 95–7, 127, 144, 155
Hodara, S. E. 39
HUGE (digital agency) 88

individualism 6, 31, 109, 112, 129, 161
individuality 112–13, 146
information-exchange
    cybernetic system 44–5
    optimal system 43–4
information processor 6, 25, 28, 43, 107. *See also* Game Theory; Rational Choice Theory
    market as 31–2

insurance platform 17–19, 22, 25–6, 30–1
interfaces
    algorithmic inference and recommendation 69
    manipulative capacities 70
    playfulness 58
    "smart" products and services 55
Internet of Things 23, 78, 111
interpersonal interaction 110
    instrumentalization 115–20
    moralized datafication 110–11
iOS interface 77

John Hancock Insurance 109

KnowledgeOne 114

Labor 70–74, 130, 156, 160–1
Logical Positivist movement 46
Luddism 162
Lupton, Deborah 109

machine learning (ML) 84, 87, 94–5, 103–4, 139
Marcel, G. 111–12
Marx, Karl 8, 71–2
meditation apps 55
Mel-frequency cepstral coefficients (MFCC) 106
MEMS-3 49–50, 52–3
mental health 56, 77, 85
    computational instruments 85
Microsoft 4, 8. *See also specific apps*
    365 workplace suite of software 115–16
    Excel 115–16
    Meeting Insight 116–17, 120
    MyAnalytics 4, 116–17
    Outlook 115–16, 119
    patent application 116–17
    productivity score 115–20
    Slack or Microsoft Teams 119
    value of convenience 118
    Word document 115–16, 119
Mindstrong platform 84–5
    interface designs 85
    patient-facing interface 86
mood-predicting smartphone app 84
mood-tracking products 57
morality 99, 109
muscle sensors 41

soft biopower 87–8
Soylent 22, 24
spectrogram 106
Spitzer, R. 101
Srnicek, N. 53, 145
    Platform Capitalism 53–4
ST Microelectronics 53
Strether, L. 32
superfluity 110–13, 120
    datafication 110–13
symbolism 43, 49

TechCrunch 80
temperature sensors 41, 78
Theory of Games and Economic Behavior
    (Neumann and Morgenstern) 29
Tierney, T. *The Value of Convenience: A*
    Genealogy of Technical Culture 23
Tonkinwise, C. 137
totalitarianism 112
Tufte, E. 54, 85
Turner, F. 24

TurnItIn (Microsoft) 119
typography 1, 43, 58

UI design 34, 58, 95
Upmood 56–7
user-experience(UX) design 16, 34, 43, 49
    anticipatory strategies 88
    convenience-enhancing features
        138–9
    examples 88
    ontological insecurity 69, 76–7

vocalizations, human 106–7

Wark, McKenzie 34
Watch OS 77
Whisper 65
    inference and recommendation
        algorithms 65–8
Wong-Baker scale 56

Zamyatin, Yevgeny 145–6